This book belongs to

P. Margaret Smith
26 · 4 · 94

BERLIOZ IN LONDON

Da Capo Press Music Reprint Series

Music Editor

BEA FRIEDLAND
Ph.D., City University of New York

BERLIOZ IN LONDON

BY

A. W. GANZ

DA CAPO PRESS · NEW YORK · 1981

Library of Congress Cataloging in Publication Data

Ganz, A. W.
    Berlioz in London.

    (Da Capo Press Music reprint series)
    Reprint. Originally published: London: Quality
Press, 1950.
    Includes index.
    1. Berlioz, Hector, 1803-1869. 2. Composers —
England — London — Biography. I. Title.
ML410.B5G24 1981   780'92'4 [B]   81-2074
ISBN 0-306-76092-4

Published by Da Capo Press, Inc.
A Subsidiary of Plenum Publishing Corporation
233 Spring Street, New York, N.Y. 10013

BERLIOZ IN LONDON

Hector Berlioz

BERLIOZ IN LONDON

BY

A. W. GANZ

Quality Press Ltd
Publishers

18 Adam Street
Adelphi London
W C 2

First published . . . 1950

TO THE MEMORY

of my father,

WILLIAM GANZ

My chief thought in publishing this book is to express my grateful thanks to M. Henri Chapot, as representing the heirs of Hector Berlioz, for his courtesy in permitting me to include in the book certain unpublished letters of Berlioz and of Mme. Henriette Berlioz-Smithson as well as portraits and documents. The librarian of the Paris Conservatoire kindly allowed me to photograph pages of full score as well as letters. Some of these letters now appear for the first time, and examination of the text of others has enabled me to add passages hitherto omitted in their published form. I must also record my thanks to Mr. Richard Northcott and Mr. Arthur Hill for kindly authorising me to include letters from their collections. Dr. William Wallace, a trustee of the Royal Philharmonic Society, permitted me to copy letters and minutes from the Society's records.

Berlioz in London

PREFACE BY SIR THOMAS BEECHAM, BART.

THE number of books on musical subjects written by amateurs is small. I am not sure that this has not been something of a misfortune for us having regard to the unreadability of most of the efforts turned out by so-called professionals. In very few of this latter sort can we discern any capacity for criticism or indeed little else but the expression of personal views which have no interest to the reader by reason of the comparative unimportance of their authors. Many of course are simply hack " jobs " undertaken to satisfy the demand of some publisher who has considered the time ripe for the commercial exploitation of a composer whose name happens to be well in the public eye. I see before me now on the shelves of my library dozens of volumes on Haydn, Mozart, Beethoven, Debussy, Delius, etc., etc., obviously written to order, and, for all they have to tell us of real consequence, almost wholly valueless. What is worst of all is the unmistakable evidence contained in them that their begetters have no real knowledge or understanding of the music of the men whom they are presuming to interpret to us.

It is a relief, therefore, to encounter a book of which one can say thankfully that its author writes both sympathetically and authoritatively, and, moreover, is a devout, though sane, admirer of the life and work of his subject. Mr. Ganz whom I had the pleasure of knowing for many years was not only a lover but a serious student of all that Berlioz had done, said or written. His acquaintance with the compositions of the great French master exceeded that of any professional musician I have known, and more than once did he draw my attention to some editorial ambiguity in a score that caused one to reconsider the significance of certain passages in it.

As a barrister Mr. Ganz was a member of a profession where exact thinking and cautious utterance are not only more necessary

7

but acknowledged to be more conspicuously present than in any other. Characteristically therefore he has limited the scope of his work to a chapter in the life of his hero about which (through his father mainly, whom some of us can well remember), he is able to tell a story, the accuracy of which may be accepted without hesitation.

Free from singularity, modest in dimensions, and inspired by a disinterested affection for a remarkable personality, this little book should appeal to those who, slightly weary of eccentric opinions and windy periods, may turn with relief to a plain narrative of events, always interesting and occasionally uncommon.

Author's Preface

To-day, when performances of his larger works attract such widespread attention, it is of interest to recall how Hector Berlioz and his music were received by our public in the middle of last century.

In framing this account of Berlioz' five visits to London, between 1847 and 1855, I have sought, as far as possible, to let him tell the story in his own words. His letters and other writings, vivid as they are, leave gaps in the narrative which I have endeavoured to fill in, and where explanations are necessary, I have supplied them. He was an observer who missed nothing; and he touches upon every aspect of London musical life in a style which affords a remarkable insight into his character. Moreover, he had a sense of humour of a kind attractive to English tastes, even though it appears to elude some of his own countrymen.

Before Berlioz came to London, his music was almost wholly unknown, or subject to misconceptions which a chance hearing of an overture, imperfectly rendered, did little to dispel. Conscious how much depended upon the conductor's capacity for interpretation, if his works were to be properly understood, he had withheld publication of the principal symphonies, until he could himself introduce them to a wider audience. As he had said to Schumann:—

> I am afraid I should lose the esteem of musical people for ever, if, by premature publication, I exposed my symphonies as yet too young to travel without me, to the risk of being mutilated still more cruelly than my old overture (the *Francs Juges*).

European tours undertaken with the object of presenting his music himself had yielded brilliant results. Wherever he appeared, his concerts stirred musicians to enthusiasm, while an occasional undercurrent of opposition merely tended to cement the ranks of his adherents. Inability to achieve popular recognition for his works in France provided a further reason for seeking it abroad. Only a few months before his first visit to England, Berlioz had suddenly decided upon a journey to St. Petersburg and Moscow as the only means of repairing the ruin caused by the expense of bringing forward his *Damnation of Faust* in Paris. With the active support of the Imperial Family and the Russian nobility, immense audiences were collected, and his shattered fortunes promptly retrieved. Echoes of his recent experiences recur in the following pages.

I have been greatly assisted in my task by the kindness of those who have enabled me to include several of his unpublished letters. An examination of the text of others disclosed suppressed passages, which I have reinserted, and I have incorporated throughout a large amount of uncollected material, the result of my researches. Throughout I have endeavoured, as far as possible, to verify all facts and dates by reference to letters, contemporary newspapers and periodicals. On examining the many works touching on Berlioz's life, I found errors in facts and dates too numerous for description. I accordingly decided not to burden this book with a succession of foot-notes, which would only be a source of irritation to the reader. In some instances, however, where a writer has blundered into rash conjectures, I have had to deal with the matter in some particularity.

Contents

Illustrations

MARCHE HONGROISE

HENRIETTE SMITHSON

Chapter One

HECTOR BERLIOZ paid his first visit to England on November 4, 1847. The valiant attempt of M. Jullien, a Frenchman, to establish English opera on a firm basis provided Berlioz with the opportunity for which he had waited so long. He arrived in this country with a six-year contract to conduct opera, and an engagement to give orchestral concerts of his own works.

An earlier tentative proposal by the Philharmonic Society had come to nothing. Writing to his sister in June, 1843, just after returning to Paris from a tour in Germany, he says:

> Henriette[1] is beginning to fret again because I have had two invitations from the London Philharmonic Society to go there and conduct a concert; nothing is yet decided, I have had no answer to the letter in which I told them what I wanted in musical matters and what my fee would be.

In fairness to the Philharmonic Society it should be said that the minutes of the directors' meetings show that, in spite of the mixed reception his *Benvenuto Cellini* overture had had the year before, the directors decided (December 11, 1842) to ask Berlioz whether he would accept an engagement during the season to "superintend" the performance of his *Symphonie Funèbre et Triomphale*. The inquiry was repeated later; but owing to his absence on an extended tour in Germany, Berlioz did not know of the proposal until his return home. He had hastened to communicate with the directors, who by then could only express their regret that owing to his not having replied sooner they were "not enabled to enter into any agreement with him." Their last letter must have reached him only a few days after he had written to his sister. As will be seen it proved a source

---

[1] His wife, Harriet Constance Smithson, the Shakespearean actress. As Berlioz called her Henriette, it has seemed as well to follow him in this book.

of keen disappointment to him that, although his presence in London was well known, he failed to obtain any further recognition by our leading orchestral society until his fourth visit to this country. He had to look elsewhere in London.

Although the possibility of a visit to England had long been in his thoughts, Berlioz was under no delusions in regard to conditions prevailing here, or the difficulties that stood in the way of his work gaining appreciation. Looking back, he recalled how, as early as February, 1834, his *Francs Juges* overture had been incontinently rejected, after a trial at rehearsal by the Philharmonic Society. In his own humorous description of the occasion given to Robert Schumann, he related how he had been told that the conductor took the *adagio* at double the proper pace, and slowed down the *allegro* to a *tempo* "*confortabile*," how the trombones came in ten bars too soon, the drummer lost his head on the rhythm changing to triple time, and a " delightful hubbub " resulted. Contemporary taste may, indeed, be gauged by what Moscheles, the conductor at this rehearsal, wrote to Mendelssohn about it. He complained bitterly of the furious sounds emitted by the brass, the " shocking, nay wicked scoring," and of the " screeching harmonics " as not fit for human ears. Time, however, was bringing its revenges. Rumours had reached this country of the deep impression made in Paris by the great *Requiem*. Then, the publication of some orchestral scores enabled Henry Forbes (March 30, 1840) to give a successful first public performance in England of the same *Francs Juges* overture, at a concert of the Societa Harmonica, in the hall adjoining Her Majesty's Theatre. But when in 1841 another work, the *Benvenuto Cellini* overture, was given a hearing at a Philharmonic concert under Charles Lucas, the audience hissed. Well might Berlioz have despaired of winning his way here, but he did not give up hope.

The early years of Queen Victoria's reign saw the beginning of a new phase of public interest in orchestral music with the introduction of promenade concerts on a French model, that rapidly gained popularity. In the winter of 1840-41 as many as three series were running at the same time, at Drury Lane under Musard, Eliason and Jullien, at the Lyceum under Negri, and at the Princess's Theatre under J. T. Willy. The odd mixture of light and frivolous music combined with serious works made a strong appeal to the general taste. The amazing M. Jullien. a master of every device that could arouse curiosity and excite enthusiasm, became a popular hero, and crowds flocked nightly to his concerts. But he happened also to be an artist. It was his proud boast that he first taught the masses to appreciate what was best in music, by offering elaborate dance numbers as an inducement to listen to serious works. In truth they came to watch *him*, but certainly did stay to hear the symphonies. When it suited his humour, if Jullien's patrons were not as orderly during a performance of classical music as he thought decorous and expedient, he would chide them like children.

For his first concert in January, 1841, Jullien selected the last movement of Beethoven's Choral Symphony and a quadrille based on the *Huguenots*, with chorus of assassins and a conflagration to represent the Massacre of St. Bartholomew. Maroons were actually fired, and the promenade illuminated with red flames! The *Atlas*, while it approved the policy of gently coaxing the public to the endurance of small doses of Beethoven's music, thought it possible to run the principle to extremes. "The sanctity of music was violated to an extent no musician can endure," when " Beethoven's most extraordinary and least understood composition was triumphed over by ultra-abominations of M. Jullien "!

When Berlioz, in Paris, read desciptions of these entertainments, he concluded that a promenade concert was no place for him, nor was he pleased to learn that his *Francs Juges* and *King Lear* overtures had been heard there. Accordingly, when approached by a manager of such a concern for his personal participation, he had no hesitation in stating terms which he knew would not be accepted. An unpublished letter to a correspondent in London (whose name is unknown) gives his point of view.

Paris, January 1841

Sir,

I have read with much interest the article in the " Atlas" which you have been good enough to send me. If a few like it were inserted in the Press, the taste for musical trivialities might perhaps be less general and less bare-faced.

It is, indeed, to avoid being mixed up with such executions that I am on my guard, as far as possible, against all proposals coming from England; and, so that I may not be executed in spite of myself, I have resolutely refused up to now to let my symphonies be published. I even regret, at the present moment, that the printing of some of my overtures has put them into circulation.

The vulgarity of people who speculate on satisfying the coarse appetites of a certain public is the meanest and most odious thing I know in our artistic world, and as far as possible I endeavour not to be its victim.

No doubt Mr. Hollcroft[1] has realised, as Mr. Eliason did some weeks ago, that my " pretensions " admit of no answer. I am none the less grateful for the interest you have been good enough to take in the matter, and I beg of you to accept my best thanks. I have the honour to be, sir,

Your obedient servant,

H. BERLIOZ.

P.S.   If you have occasion to mention me in your correspondence, kindly do so in the sense I have just indicated; that is, present me to the English as an artist who relies too much on the appreciation of the intelligent public not to insist upon every guarantee for the proper performance of his works and the absolute certainty that he will have nothing to do with the musical ethics which the critic of the " Atlas " has just stigmatised so energetically.

Close on seven years had passed since this letter was written. Michael Costa, now regular conductor of the Philharmonic concerts, had raised their standard of performance considerably, though the repertoire still remained rigidly conservative in character. Jullien had pursued his policy of educating the musical public in his own fashion, while he had collected a magnificent body of English and foreign players to form his orchestra. Then, on a sudden determination to establish English opera in London, he turned to Berlioz, who had achieved a great reputation as a conductor on his foreign tours.

Jullien's proposal that he should come over to conduct the London Winter Season at Drury Lane came at a dramatic moment. The Pillet régime at the Paris Opera had come to an inglorious end, and been succeeded by the dual directorship of Nestor Roqueplan and Duponchel. These worthies had made

---

[1] W. Allcroft, music seller and opera agent in New Bond Street.

use of Berlioz to assist them in getting the position, in recognition of which he had fondly hoped to gain artistic control of the whole enterprise, and conduct the orchestra; but once installed, they did their best to put him off with an offer of the post of chorus master. Naturally Berlioz jumped at Jullien's bid.

Joseph d'Ortigue, the musical critic, a close friend and active supporter of his, was at once informed of the turn of events.

> *I have just accepted an engagement in London infinitely better than the grudging offer made me here. So I have told the directors of the Opera they can keep their precious job, and I have accepted Jullien's offer to be conductor of the English Grand Opera at Drury Lane Theatre. I am to get ten thousand francs, and another ten thousand francs for a performance of my own works at four concerts. Further I have undertaken to write a three-act opera for the second year. I shall only be wanted in London for four months of the year. You see there was no room for hesitation—I had no option but to renounce la Belle France for perfide Albion.*
>
>

August 26, 1847.

Before leaving Paris on his journey to London, Berlioz sent a parting word to Humbert Ferrand, his " Horatio."

November 1, 1847.

My Dear Friend,

> *I am leaving for London the day after tomorrow. I have a very good engagement there as conductor of the English Grand Opera and four concerts. Heaven only knows when we shall see each other again, my engagement being for six years, and for the four months of the year when there might have been a chance of our occasionally meeting in Paris.*
>
> *You have heard of the excellent results of my Russian tour; they gave me an imperial reception. Big successes, big receipts, big performances, etc., etc.*
>
> *Now for England. France is sinking to the lowest depths of stupidity in music; and the more I see of foreign countries the less I love my own.[1] Pardon the blasphemy! . . But art, in France, is dead—rotting in fact . . . One must go to places where it is still alive. It seems that ten years ago a remarkable revolution took place in England in the musical taste of the nation. We shall see, however.*

---

[1] An inversion of P. L. Buriette de Belloy's saying: *plus je vis d'Etrangers, plus j'aimai ma patrie.*

Berlioz clearly refers to the influence of Queen Victoria and Prince Albert, who were both fond of music. The interest they took in all new enterprises provided the stimulus that was needed, and so helped to mould public taste.

The first Sunday after his arrival in London Berlioz wrote a letter to his father Dr. Berlioz at La Côte-Saint-André, where he had been on a visit with his son Louis, then a lad of thirteen, a short while before—this was the last time Berlioz saw his father.

London, November 7, 1847.

Dear Father,

I am writing you a few lines, in rather a hurry, to let you know that I have now settled down in London, and to give you my address. I am staying at M. Jullien's (a French artist who is married to an Englishwoman), manager of Drury Lane Theatre of which he has appointed me conductor. I have known him a long time, so I feel quite at home here.

The crossing was delightful, the sea calm and the boat might have been on a lake.

I travelled with an English literary man, Mr. Gruneisen, who, as soon as we got into Folkestone, hurried off the boat in front of me in order to greet me with outstretched hand, and say: " Welcome to British soil! " It was one of those good ideas that the English have, prompted by national pride—which would never occur to a continental.

The vastness of London appals me. It takes three quarters of an hour to get from Jullien's to Drury Lane, and they call it " a few steps."

All the rest of this month and some days of the next will be spent rehearsing, as the English Grand Opera is not to open till about December 10. I have already seen my orchestra at work, and a finer I could not have wished for; I found a number of French and German artists that I knew, who were delighted to see me and gave me a hearty reception.

I rather think the business of my department will go all right. I am now engaged in writing a piece on " God Save the Queen" for the opening night. I had not thought of it, but Jullien, who never misses anything, would like me to repeat the Buda-Pesth business in London, by striking the same chord in the national lyre of England. Besides, it is customary for this famous tune to be used at all functions of this kind.

My concerts will not begin before the middle of January; by
then the English translator will have had time to finish his task,
I shall know the performers better, and we shall have settled down;
so the respite suits me, and makes for safety. I am quite surprised at
my knowledge of English; I can say almost all I want to without
much accent, but I do not understand half of what is said. There
is a lot of hard work to be done. Good-bye, dear Father, affectionate
greetings. Do let me hear from you as soon as possible.

H. BERLIOZ
c/o Mr. Jullien, 76 Harley Street.[1]

Charles Lewis Gruneisen, whose gesture of welcome appealed
so strongly to Berlioz as typically English, was indeed a Londoner
by birth. He had had an adventurous career as special correspondent in the Carlist wars, and had narrowly escaped being
shot as a spy. Later he turned his attention to the less perilous
business of musical critic, and was now acting in that capacity
on three London papers, the *Britannia*, the *Morning Chronicle* and
the *Illustrated London News*. The journey from Paris to London
in those days was a matter of sixteen hours. The two had left
Paris together the night before (November 3), travelling to
Abbeville by the newly opened railway, and thence by the
diligence of the Messageries Royales et Laffitte to Boulogne,
which they reached in the small hours. The steam-packet
crossed to Folkestone in the morning. On his arrival in London
Gruneisen hurried to the offices of the *Illustrated London News*
to inform his readers of Berlioz' movements.

It may be recalled that when Berlioz was leaving Vienna for
Buda-Pesth, a musical amateur suggested to him that the most
direct appeal to the hearts of the Hungarians was by way of their
national airs, and handed him a book from which to make a
selection. Berlioz' choice fell upon the *Rakoczy* march, and the
task of arrangement was completed during the night before he
started. On reaching Buda-Pesth he had the orchestral parts
copied. On examining them, Horváth, a journalist, said " I feel
horribly nervous about it all. You begin *piano*, and we are
accustomed to have the tune played *fortissimo*." "Don't be
afraid," retorted Berlioz. " You'll hear the forte of your life! "
The concert was at the National Theatre. As the moment
approached Berlioz says he felt rather anxious. The people

---

[1] Later No. 27, and since rebuilt.

listened to the quiet phrases of the opening with unruffled calm. But when the *crescendo* began, with snatches of the tune punctuated by the sound of distant cannon, strange murmurs were heard in the house. At the *fortissimo* the audience went mad with excitement; they drowned the end with wild shouts and cries. Berlioz turned and glanced inquiringly at the box in which Horváth was behaving like one possessed. " What about your *forte* now ? " Upon consideration, Berlioz decided that *God Save the Queen* was not adaptable for a similar purpose.

Berlioz next bethought him of the cellist Tajan-Rogé,[1] whom he had left at St. Petersburg the previous Spring, lamenting his lot and, like a true Frenchman, sighing to get back to Paris. Berlioz, as will be seen, was ever ready to correspond with anyone who understood his point of view; moreover, he had a confidence to impart.

London, November 10, 1847.

My dear Rogé,

I should feel very guilty for not having answered your kind letter before, but I have the excuse that I have been beset by a thousand and one worries since I got back to Paris. You can have no idea of my existence in that infernal city which claims to be the centre of the arts. At last I have got away. Here I am in England in an independent position (financially speaking) such as I could not have dared to hope for. I am entrusted with the conductorship of the orchestra of the English Grand Opera which is to open at Drury Lane in a month; further, I am engaged for four concerts for my works exclusively, and in the third place to write an Opera in three acts for the season of 1848. *The English Opera will only last three months this year and the list of singers will be very incomplete owing to the haste with which everything has been arranged at the last moment, and a fatal mischance which will deprive us this year of the services of Pischek (a wonderful German artist on whom we were counting). The manager is ready to make every sacrifice, and is really looking to next year for results. As a set-off, the chorus and the orchestra are splendid. My concerts will not come on till January; I think they will go all right. Jullien (the manager) is a bold clever fellow who knows London and the English better than anybody. He has already made his own fortune and he has got an idea he will make mine. I'll let him go ahead as what he does is always artistic*

---

[1]Tajan-Rogé was in London in 1852, and played in the New Philharmonic Orchestra.

and in good taste. But I lack faith . . . I had the pleasure of seeing Mme Rogé in Paris once; no doubt she is now back home. I introduced your friend to Alfred de Vigny,[1] *who has requested him to look him up from time to time and to avail himself of his assistance in any literary business in which he could be of service.*

You ask for notes for your pamphlet; but I really know nothing more than I have told you. Our artists are growing more and more unhappy, because the direction of artistic matters is becoming worse. Anyhow, here is an anecdote which might do for your work. During the latter part of the Pillet régime, the final rehearsals of new works became more and more numerous without regard to the necessities of the case. As the musicians complained, Habeneck[2] *and Tulou, who knew the reason for this increased work, at last replied: " Ah! Why don't you applaud Mme. X . . . ? Can't you see that she is furious at your keeping quiet, and as long as she has not had a success at rehearsals, a success with the orchestra, she'll make you sweat like galley slaves!" So the orchestra, who wished to have done with it, decided the next day to give her a rousing reception. This satisfied the Diva, who found that the work went all right and the first performance could be announced. What do you think of this system of extracting enthusiasm? . . Now the Opera has lost Mme. X . . . , but God knows if it will go any better for that. Everybody thinks it will be exactly the same as under Pillet. Duponchel and Roqueplan are just as ignorant as he is and detest any musical purpose much more. It is easy to foresee what will happen . . .*

I shall have five or six months free every year, I am engaged here for six years. My only publications during my stay in London this Winter will be the continuation of my letters on my musical excursions . . .

I have come to London alone; you can guess the reason. Moreover I was badly in need of the liberty which I have never had till now. It required not one coup d'État, but a succession of coups d'État to be able to regain it. However, as long as we have not begun our big rehearsals, the isolation in which I live the great part of my time will appear strange.

As I am in the confidential vein, would you believe that I let myself in for a love affair at Petersburg as genuine as it was absurd with one of your chorus girls? (Here you may laugh, full orchestra,

---

[1]The poet had helped with the libretto of Berlioz' opera *Benvenuto Cellini*.
[2]This famous conductor was the first to perform Beethoven's symphonies in Paris.

and in the major key! . . . Go on! Go on! Don't mind me . . .)
I continue my story—a poetical love affair, frightful and absolutely
innocent with a young (not too young) girl who said to me, " I will
write to you " and who, in speaking of her mother's obsession about
her marrying added: " What a bore! " What a number of walks
we took together in the outlying parts of Petersburg and into the
country, from nine to eleven at night! . . . What bitter tears I
shed when she told me like Marguerite in " Faust ": " My God, I
cannot understand what you can see in me . . . I am only a poor
girl far beneath you . . . it is impossible you could love me so
much, etc., etc." Yet it is so possible that it is true, and that I
thought I should die of despair as I passed by the Grand Theatre
when leaving Petersburg in the mail coach. Further, I was really ill
at Berlin at not finding a letter there from her. She had promised so
faithfully that she would write! . . . No doubt she's married now.
Her fiancé, who left the evening of my first concert, must certainly
be back by this time.

O God! I can still see the scene on the banks of the Neva one
evening at sunset . . . What a torrent of passion! I crushed her
arm against my chest; I sang her the phrase from the Adagio of
" Romeo and Juliet."

I promised her, I offered her all I could promise and offer . . . Yet
not a line since I left. I cannot even be sure it was she who waved me
adieu from the distance at the moment I was getting into the
coach! . . . Adieu, adieu. You, at least will write to me, you will.

" Mme X." must be Rosine Stoltz, a singer at the Opera who
throughout the Pillet régime was given the principal rôles. In
the general management her word was law. Alizard, a real
artist with a fine bass voice, could not obtain an engagement;
" Mme. Stoltz was not at all pleased with Alizard." In his
articles in the *Débats* Berlioz did not mince matters. " I have had
a nice row with Pillet and the Stoltz lady. I gave them both a
jolly good shake-up." At the end of her reign at the Opera she
left Paris. She then married in rapid succession a baron, a duke
and a prince.

When Berlioz left his wife, Henriette Smithson, some years
before, to start on his tour in Germany, he took the singer Marie
Martin-Recio[1] with him as travelling companion, and she had
been living with him off and on ever since. She was a tall

[1]Her father was a Commandant of the Grande Armée, her mother a Spaniard.

hard-faced brunette of uncertain temper, and life with her was not easy. Of her musical ability Berlioz was critical. " She sings like a cat," he said, " but that does not matter much; the trouble is she insists on appearing at all my concerts." " The bare idea of another prima donna infuriates her." And the letter to Tajan-Rogé indicates that he was not sorry to be separated. But, she did not fail to join him here a month later; and when his friend J. W. Davison brought her over from Paris (they were both sick crossing the Channel), Berlioz was waiting at the station for the train to arrive. She was just in time for the opening night at Drury Lane.

His next letter from London was written to Auguste Morel[1] an intimate friend.

> *London, November* 31, (1847), 76 *Harley Street.*
> *My dear Morel,*
>
> *Jullien has asked me to write you confidentially to know the truth about the success of Verdi's Opera (" I Lombardi "). Never mind the merits of the work, what does the management say about it?*
>
> *We shall not open the season for a week; I feel that " The Bride of Lammermoor" Lucia with Mme. Dorus-Gras and Sims Reeves cannot fail to go well. Reeves has a sweet natural voice and he sings as well as anyone can in such an awful language as English.*
>
> *The baritone Whitworth is not so good; we are expecting Staudigl every day. In the meantime we are putting on Balfe's opera.[2] The orchestra is splendid, and, apart from some imperfections in the wind instruments, one couldn't find a better. We have a chorus of* 120 *who also sing well. Everybody gave me a very warm reception the day that Jullien included the " Invitation à la Valse " at one of his concerts. The orchestra gave me an ovation and the public encored the piece by . . . Weber! And then there are several French, German and Italian artists—old acquaintances who are devoted to me, such as Tolbecque, Rousselot, Sainton, Piatti, Eisenbaum, Baumann, etc. I shan't begin my concerts till January.*
>
> *Now would you be so good as to go and see Théophile Gautier, Villa Beaujon, No.* 14 *Avenue Byron (excuse the running about), and ask him for an answer to the letter I wrote him more than a*

---

[1] Auguste Morel, the composer, afterwards became head of the Marseilles Conservatoire.
[2] Balfe's opera, which had been written for and was produced during this season, was *The Maid of Honour.*

fortnight ago; it was about a ballet which Jullien wants from him immediately for Mlle. Fuoco[1] which is to be produced by Coralli senior. Jullien must know at once if Gautier is willing to do it, and on what terms, and if he can deliver the manuscript by the 15th of December—I beg of you to do this job.

I am terribly bored in the pretty rooms which Jullien has given me. However, I have received a number of invitations since my arrival, and your friend M. Grimblot has been good enough to come often and see me. He has had me made an honorary member of his Club; but God alone knows what fun one can get out of an English Club!

Macready a week ago gave a magnificent dinner in my honour; he is a charming fellow and not really at all stuck-up. He is a terror at rehearsals, and quite right too. I saw him the other day in a new tragedy, " Philip van Artevelde "; he was superb. And he has mounted the piece in a really extraordinary manner; no one here understands as he does the art of handling stage crowds. It is admirable.

In the letter to his friend Théophile Gautier, Berlioz had asked for one of those " pretty, graceful, brilliant and anti-philistine " ballets, of which he had the secret. His own orchestral concerts at Drury Lane were postponed till the middle of January, as the Court and Society were not expected to be in London till then. " Jullien wants them to be a flaming success." Gautier had early shown a true appreciation of Berlioz' work, and helped him by his advocacy in *la Presse*. " With Victor Hugo and Eugène Delacroix, Hector Berlioz appears to us to form the Trinity of Romantic Art." The exquisite setting of the *Nuits d'Été* was Berlioz' tribute to the poet's genius.

Henry Taylor's *Philip van Artevelde* was given during Macready's season at the Princess's Theatre[2] in Oxford Street. Berlioz would pass by there, when walking as he did, from Harley Street to Drury Lane for his own rehearsals. At the dinner party given by Macready, Berlioz had met, amongst others, Thackeray and his physician Dr. John Elliotson (the mesmerist), Julius Benedict who composed the " Lily of Killarney," Tom Taylor the playwright and Philip Hardwick the architect; and the company was joined, during the evening, by " Barry Cornwall " the poet, and his daughter Adelaide Procter who wrote the words of " The

[1]Mlle. Fuoco appeared in February in a *pas de deux* with Zavystowski. So there were Russian Dancers in those days.
[2]The site, facing the top of Poland Street, is now occupied by a Woolworth store.

Lost Chord," Mrs. Charles Dickens and Georgina Hogarth, and Tom Cooke, who had arranged incidental music for some of Macready's productions. In paying this compliment to a distinguished Frenchman, Macready no doubt wished to mark his sense of the cordial nature of his own reception by Victor Hugo, Alexandre Dumas, George Sand and the artistic world, when he appeared in Paris three years previously. Berlioz might well have spoken of a still earlier time when Macready, associated with Henriette Smithson, then the idol of Paris, had acted in Knowles's tragedy *Virginius*, and been hailed as another Talma.

A series of letters written at this time to M. Scribe show that Berlioz had been commissioned by Jullien to write an opera on the Faust legend, for the second winter season at Drury Lane. Scribe was invited to collaborate by preparing a libretto which, with slight additions, should incorporate all the scenes from the *Damnation of Faust* which already existed in musical form; and Berlioz assured him " the scene of the horses at the end does not frighten the London stage carpenters; they can be trusted to carry it out in a very ingenious and dramatic way." To avoid comparison with other settings, the opera was to be called *Mephistopheles*. The project fell through, and Berlioz abandoned all idea of adapting his work for the stage. He determined, however, to give the first two acts in concert form at Drury Lane. These letters did not see the light until they were published by the *Revue bleue* in 1917, and the staging of the work at Monte Carlo in the nineties provoked considerable criticism, based on the alleged disregard of the composer's intentions. The Carl Rosa Opera Company, at the suggestion of the present writer's father, William Ganz, who at that time was a director of the company, followed suit soon afterwards, and gave the *Damnation of Faust* at Liverpool, black horses and all, on February 3, 1894. London had to wait until the year 1933, when Sir Thomas Beecham, recalling his early impressions as a boy at Liverpool and his experiences abroad, decided to produce the work at Covent Garden.

Apropos of Scribe, Berlioz later wrote to a friend:

I am sending you a divine quatrain by Scribe; I discovered it in an album which has been brought to me. Please admire the latinity of this pupil of Sainte-Barbe! He thinks that you can say Vobis-cum to a single person. The quatrain is addressed to Mlle. David, owner of the album.

> *Angelus Vobis cum*
> *Enfant pleine de grace*
> *Et que l'amitié fasse*
> *Prospérer votre album.*

This is the pendant to the heraldic device on his carriage " Fortuna et libertas." He also thinks that Fortuna in Latin means Wealth; and his compliment to Mme. Rossi (Sontag)!

> *Car de tout temps Rossi*
> *Fut la moitié de Rossigno!*

What a fellow!

The opera season at Drury Lane having started, Berlioz' chief concern was to ensure the success of his first orchestral concert by beginning rehearsals well ahead.

London, December 8. (1847).

My dear Morel,

Still more commissions! . . . Will you be so good as to go on receipt of this letter to my engraver, Parent, 43 Rue Rochechouart, and tell him to send me on at once by diligence, the parts of " Harold " in duplicate. Further, if he cannot send me some sort of proof of the full score will he send back the manuscript. I am anxious that you should make quite certain that it will reach me safely as you can understand I should not like to lose a full score.

Now I must tell you that the opening night of our Grand Opera was an immense success; the English press is unanimous in its praise. Mme. Gras and Reeves, the tenor (in " Lucia "), were frantically applauded and had four or five calls. And they thoroughly deserved it. Reeves is a priceless discovery for Jullien; he has a charming voice, of an essentially distinguished and sympathetic quality, he is a very good musician, his face is very expressive and he acts with the attractive fervour of an Irishman. When I appeared in the orchestra, the house gave me a splendid reception. We began with Beethoven's beautiful " Leonora " Overture No. 1—splendid performance. The big sextet in D flat in " Lucia " which begins the finale of the second act was encored, and this evening, at the second performance, the chorus in E flat in the third act was also encored.

The English are astounded at hearing in an English opera-house this massed chorus of one hundred and twenty voices and this fine orchestra and at having such a remarkable tenor and such a prima donna. The ballet is poor, but we shall have something better presently.

I shall begin rehearsing my symphonies six weeks ahead, as soon as the orchestral parts and the " Harold " score arrive.

A thousand pardons for making you run about in this matter but I have not anybody else I can trust.

Sims Reeves says, " I was born at Shooter's Hill in Kent, of English parents. Why Hector Berlioz insisted on regarding me as an Irishman I never could make out. It may be that the French, unwilling as a rule to admit that anything good may come out of England, are more tolerant in regard to Ireland and Scotland."

On Monday, December 6, the opening night of the Season, *God Save the Queen*, in its customary form, was sung after the opera. The critic of the *Morning Herald* records that " the eccentric Berlioz was scarcely recognised when he entered the orchestra; but his subsequent official deportment denoted a conductor of promptitude, decision and intelligence." The absence of an overture to *The Bride of Lammermoor* had suggested the inclusion of the *Leonora*, " admirably adapted " as was observed " for the display of the orchestral force."

When speaking of *Leonora* Overture No. 1, Berlioz is referring to the one first composed, now known as *Leonora* No. 2. He preferred it to the more famous No. 3, and conducted it on several evenings before the opera. The evening concluded with a new *ballet divertissement* entitled *le Génie du Globe*. There was a ballet after the opera nightly, except during the Christmas season, when a pantomime was substituted.

Jullien had had the house freshly done up. In the words of the press: " The new drop scene, painted to imitate white satin, surmounted by blue hangings, well accords with the general light effect of the beautifully decorated *salle*."

On the Saturday of that week, Berlioz' forty-fourth birthday, there was no Opera, not that it would make any difference to him. He had his own views on the subject, as he told Richard Wagner. " You Germans take particular notice of birthdays, as they afford you a welcome chance of showing family affection, if you've got a family, or friendship, if you've got friends. Now you see the sort of fellow I am; I have a family, I possess valued friends, but I might keep thirty birthdays a year, and it would never occur to anybody to notice one of them, as it is well known how I dislike this sort of thing . . . Please do not laugh, I am so ill . . ." As will be seen in a later chapter, it was in London that they met on the most cordial terms.

Chapter Two

THE success which attended the opening of the Season was only short-lived. *The Bride of Lammermoor* drew crowded houses, but Balfe's *Maid of Honour* produced a fortnight later failed to take with the public. Sims Reeves did however manage to make a hit with the song " In this Old Chair my Father Sat." Thackeray, who was present at the first performance (which was conducted by Balfe) said that this ballad drew tears from his heart as well as his eyes. Balfe conducted his opera till the end of the year, and Berlioz did not take his place till New Year's Day, so he appears to have had a short respite from his labours. Jullien's fortunes were already impaired when he embarked upon his operatic venture, and he was looking to it to rehabilitate him. But he soon found that the receipts scarcely covered the daily outlay, not to speak of the lavish expenditure he had made on the production. So he decided to start on a tour in the provinces, where he was sure of making money with promenade concerts, and left the opera to take care of itself.

Just before he went away the subject of finding an opera which should be a draw had been under discussion. Jullien seriously proposed to give a performance in six days' time of *Robert the Devil*, though he had no copies, no English translation, no costumes, no scenery, and his singers did not know a note of it. In this connexion Berlioz tells a highly coloured story which he describes as " typical of the man accustomed to appeal always to the childish instincts of the crowd and to succeed by the most stupid methods."

Jullien, at the end of his resources, seeing that Balfe's opera was not bringing in money, and dimly realising the impossibility of putting on " Robert the Devil " in six days, even resting on the seventh, collected his executive committee to ask their advice. This committee consisted of Sir Henry Bishop, Sir George Smart, Mr.

Planché (author of the book of Weber's " Oberon ") Mr. Gye (the manager at Drury Lane), the chorus master Mr. Maretzek and myself. He explained his difficulties and spoke of different operas (as usual not translated and not copied) which he wanted to put on. You should have heard the ideas and opinions of these gentlemen, on the masterpieces trotted out! . . . I listened in amazement. At last they came to " Iphigenia in Tauris " which Jullien, following the custom of London managers who announce the work every year but never give it[1], had promised to the public in his prospectus. The members of the committee not knowing a note of it, did not know what to say. Jullien, losing patience at my silence, turned sharply to me and asked: " Hang it all. Can't you say something, you must know the thing! "

" Oh yes, I know ' the thing,' but what is the question? What do you want to know? Tell me and I will answer."

" I want to know how many acts there are in ' Iphigenia in Tauris,' who are the characters, what kind of voices, and most of all, the kind of scenery and costumes."

" Well take a sheet of paper and a pen; I will dictate, and you can write it down. ' Iphigenia in Tauris,' an opera by Gluck (you know that of course), is in four acts. It comprises three men's parts: Orestes (baritone); Pylades (tenor); Thoas (bass with very high notes); a big woman's part, Iphigenia (soprano); another a small part, Diana (mezzo soprano) and several small part choristers. The costumes, unhappily, will not appeal to you; the Scythians and their King Thoas are ragged savages on the shores of the Black Sea. Orestes and Pylades appear in the simple garb of two ship-wrecked Greeks. Pylades alone has two costumes; he comes back in the fourth act with a helmet on his head . . ."

" He wears a helmet! " cried Jullien, interrupting me enthusias-tically. " We are saved! I'll write to Paris at once to order a gilt helmet with a crown of pearls and a plume of ostrich feathers, as long as my arm; and we shall have forty performances."

I have forgotten how this amazing sitting ended, but I'll remember to my dying day Jullien's wild gestures and his eyes blazing with enthusiasm at the news that Pylades wore a helmet, and his sublime idea of ordering this helmet in Paris, no English workman being

---

[1]Not invariably. On July 9, 1840, during a season of German Opera at the Prince's Theatre, King Street (later the St. James's), Gluck's *Iphigenia in Tauris* was given for the first time in England in its entirety. The production was a great success, and a week later was honoured by the presence of Queen Victoria and Prince Albert. It was conducted by Adolphe Ganz.

capable, according to his notion, of creating one dazzling enough, and his hope of getting Gluck's masterpiece to run for forty nights on the strength of the crown of pearls, the gilt and the length of the plumes on Pylades' helmet.

Prodigious! as good old Dominie Sampson said, pro-di-gious!

I need not add that " Iphigenia " was never put into rehearsal. Jullien left London a few days after this conclave of wiseacres, leaving his theatre to go hang. Besides, the singers and the chorus-master had quite rightly declared against this old score, and the godlike tenor (Reeves) had laughed heartily when he was offered the part of Pylades.

Sims Reeves in his book *My Jubilee* says: " Berlioz somehow conceived the idea that I objected to the production of *Iphigenia in Tauris* or at least that I was unwilling to sing it. As a matter of fact I was not only willing, but eager to appear in Gluck's great work. When the question of presenting the opera was discussed in solemn conclave, the conclusion arrived at was that it would never pay. Accordingly it was never put into rehearsal. Berlioz was undoubtedly a good conductor, but like all conductors I have met in England, except Costa, Balfe and Alfred Mellon, he thought too much of his orchestra and too little of his singers. I met him frequently in private, and although he was always lively in general conversation, he gave me the idea of being a disappointed man . . . Every Sunday afternoon I used to meet Berlioz at Jullien's house, where we heard portions of the *Damnation of Faust* and other works of his; though it was his *Faust* music that left upon me the deepest impression."

Donizetti's *Linda of Chamouny* (as it was called) first given at Drury Lane on January 12, did not help to mend matters.

A letter to Morel shows the hopeless pass to which things had come at Drury Lane:

London, January 14, 1848

My dear Morel,

Many thanks for your letter which gave me great pleasure . . . I am on a treadmill here rehearsing every day from mid-day to four and conducting the opera every evening from seven to ten. Rehearsals finished the day before yesterday and I am beginning to get over a chill which worried me, and did not yield to treatment by fatigue and the cold draughts in the theatre. No doubt you already *know something about the awful mess which Jullien has got himself and us into. However, as far as possible so as not to ruin his credit in Paris, don't mention to anyone what I am going to tell you. It is not the Drury Lane venture which has been his undoing; he was a ruined man before the opening, and he had doubtless counted on absurdly big receipts to recover himself. Jullien is still the madman you already know; he hasn't the least idea of what is wanted in an opera-house, nor even of what is most obviously necessary to obtain a good musical result. He opened his theatre without having a single full score of his own, and with the exception of Balfe's opera of which of course he had to get copies made, we have been relying up to the present on the good will of Lumley's agents who lend us the orchestral parts of the Italian operas we produce. Jullien is now on tour in the provinces, making a lot of money out of his promenade concerts. The receipts of the theatre here are very good and the net result is that after agreeing to a $33\frac{1}{3}$ per cent. reduction in our salaries, we are not being paid at all. Every week it is only the chorus, the orchestra and the stage hands that are paid to keep the show going. Meanwhile a fortnight ago Jullien sold his music shop in Regent Street for nearly two hundred thousand francs . . . and I cannot get paid, and the principal singers, the scene-painter, the chorus and the ballet masters and the stage manager, all of them are in the same boat . . . What do you think of that, I ask you?*

However, he protests that we shall lose nothing; and we go on, and the public asks nothing better than to come along. But Jullien's credit in London is entirely gone . . . My concert is still announced for February 7. I did not want to start the rehearsals for it during the last few days. Anyhow I shall resume them next Thursday. We have now some hope that the theatre will not close, thanks to a loan which a music publisher has been able to arrange for Mr. Gye, who represents Jullien in his absence.

If Jullien on his return does not pay up, I shall try and come to terms with Lumley to give concerts at Her Majesty's Theatre. For there is a fine position ready for me here now that poor Mendelssohn is dead. Everybody keeps telling me so from morning till night, the press and the profession are very friendly. The two rehearsals which I have had of " Harold " and the " Carnaval Romain," and of two parts of " Faust," have made them open their eyes wide and their ears still wider; I have every reason to think that here I could have an established position. As for France, I no longer think of it; and God preserve me from yielding to temptations such as you offered me in your last letter, when you suggested my coming to give a concert in Paris in April. If ever I have enough money to GIVE concerts for my friends in Paris, I shall do so; but don't any longer think me so simple-minded as to count on the public to cover the cost. I shall not make fresh appeals to its attention in order merely to be met by indifference, and to lose the money which I earn with so much trouble on my travels. I shall be deeply grieved, for the sympathy of my French friends is still my dearest possession. But the evidence is too clear: when I consider the reception my music has had from all the different audiences of Europe that have heard it, I am forced to the conclusion that the Parisian public understand it least. Have I ever seen in Paris, at my concerts, society people, men and women, so stirred as I have seen them in Germany and Russia? Have I seen royal personages so interested in my compositions as to get up at eight in the morning to come into a cold hall to hear them rehearsed, as the Princess of Prussia did at Berlin? Have I ever been asked to take the least part in the Court concerts? . . .

Felix Mendelssohn, the unspoilt darling of Music, died on the day of Berlioz' arrival in England. Soon after, shrewd people began to detect in him the Man of Destiny, a natural successor to their idol. They did not realise that the influence of the composer who had gone, so far from being arrested by his premature death, was to increase its hold in England and persist for many years after. Berlioz' music, though much talked about in London during his visits, was forgotten directly he left. It was a long time before interest in it revived. Berlioz was well able to see what the English love for Mendelssohn's music meant. He had been to Exeter Hall for the Memorial Concert. " I lately had a great emotional experience on hearing Mendelssohn's *Elijah*. It is wonderfully great and beautiful. We have all felt the loss of this eminent artist very keenly; death has dealt our art a heavy blow."

When they met at Leipzig some years earlier they had exchanged bâtons, a pleasant custom of the time among conductors.

To Chief Mendelssohn!
  Great Chief! We promised to exchange tomahawks. Here is mine, it is rude, and yours is plain! Only Squaws and Pale-faces like gaudy weapons. Be my brother! And when the Great spirit

sends us to the happy hunting grounds, may our warriors hang up
our tomahawks together at the Council door.

In spite of the disquieting position of affairs at Drury Lane,
Berlioz resolved to press on with the plans for his orchestral
concert. He knew that he could rely upon J. W. Davison, the
musical critic of *The Times*, to do all he could for him. The
consistent support he gave Berlioz was based not only on an
admiration for his work, but on strong feelings of personal
regard[1]. The opinions of both were virile and outspoken.

My dear Davison,

 Please do not put the name of Miss Birch in my programme; I
have nothing for her to sing; and after having seen her name in the
advertisements, she might perhaps be upset if she did not appear
at the concert.

 We are to have a full rehearsal of the two parts of " Faust "
next Tuesday; if you can, do come to Drury Lane at half-past
twelve. I am having a good deal of trouble with the chorus; they
have been spoilt by the habit of singing those damnable Italian
rhapsodies in two parts, and even in unison.

 In time we shall manage it.

 Only I want your help, you might transfer to me a little of the
interest you took in Mendelssohn.

         Friday, January 21, 0000.

Miss Charlotte Birch had sung in *The Maid of Honour*. She
was an energetic figure in the musical world. Finding that the
Royal Society of British Musicians had made no provision in
their rules for the admission of women to membership, after the
accession of Queen Victoria she decided with Mrs. Anderson,
Miss Dolby and Miss Mounsey to form The Royal Society of
Female Musicians. The two Societies were subsequently merged
in happy union.

As the Christmas season at Drury Lane was still in progress,
Berlioz had to conduct an opera on every night of the week
(before the pantomime). The strain of it all proved too much
for him: he broke down and took to his bed. In turning to a
Russian friend he found ready scope for his characteristic
humour:

[1]In Davison's Memoirs, published many years after his death, several letters
from Berlioz are included.

London, January 29, 1848.

My dear General (Lwow),

It is a sick man who is writing to you; so don't scold him too much for having been so long in answering. I am sorry that you thought I was put out by the publication of my letter on " Undine." It contained nothing which I particularly wished to keep secret; whether it be my feelings of friendship for you, my high opinion of your talents, or my remarks on the unwholesome lot of tenors with which we are generally afflicted, all of us, that is, who unhappily look for a mind behind the voice. My jokes at their expense will have made me a few dozen more intimate enemies; they amuse me like a comic opera about which I haven't got to write a notice. Really I am very glad; I like being detested by idiots, it's my licence for giving them tit for tat. Talking of idiots, if you only knew into what a den of idiots I have fallen here! . . . But God knows who manages the manager of this unhappy theatre! . . .

Just imagine it, it's called Royal Academy of Music,[1] English Grand Opera, and since the opening, that is for two months, I have only conducted Donizetti's " Lucia " and " Linda di Chamounix " and Balfe's Maid of Honour. We had a splendid orchestra; the manager took away the best of them with him on his tour in the provinces, where he gives popular concerts, and we have to be content with his leavings, and get along somehow.

I hear arguments on music, on the public, on the artists, which would make your four fiddle strings snap with rage if they could hear them; I put up with English women singers who would make the hairs of your bow curl . . .

I am also engaged for four concerts; I shall give the first in a week's time on the 7th February. We have not yet once been able to have a complete orchestra for the rehearsals. These gentlemen come when they please and go away on their business, some in the middle, others a quarter of the way through the rehearsals. The first day, I hadn't any horns at all; the second I had three; the third, I had two who left after the fourth piece. That's how discipline is understood in this country. The chorus alone are almost as devoted to me as those of St. Petersburg . . . Oh, for Russia! with its hearty hospitality, its literary and artistic life, and its music and drama run on strict clear principles without which, in music as in many other

---

[1]In adopting this style, Jullien had in mind the Paris Opera, which was called *Académie royale de musique et de danse.*

*things nothing good or beautiful can be done. Who will give me
these? Why are you so far away? . . .*

*Think of it, General, I have been ill for five days, in bed with
violent bronchitis; it is due simply to anger, disgust and grief.
However, there is much to be done here, because of the public, which
is attentive, intelligent and really loves serious works. I have heard
poor Mendelssohn's last oratorio (" Elijah "). It is magnificent,
its harmony indescribably gorgeous . . .*

*To-night at Drury Lane they are doing " Linda di Chamounix,"
I am lucky to be ill, and not conducting. I shall try to sleep soundly
as one sleeps in a room with the windows tight shut and the rain
pouring in torrents outside.*

General Alexis Lwow, Chamberlain to the Czar, was a
violinist and wrote operas. He earned immortality as the
composer of the Russian National Anthem, which Tschaikowsky
used in his overture " 1812." In a previous letter to the General
on the subject of his opera *Undine*, Berlioz had said, whilst
referring disconsolately to prevailing conditions of performance,

*And I do not know if the Englishman who in one of our big Parisian
restaurants asked for a tenor or a melon for dessert was right in
leaving the choice to the waiter; in my case I should always ask for
the melon; there is a much greater chance of avoiding gripes;
vegetables are a good deal more harmless than animal food.*

Chapter Three

THE most important event of his stay in London had now come, the orchestral concert upon which he had set so much store. The announcement, no doubt drafted by Jullien in the language of the day, reads:—

THEATRE ROYAL, DRURY LANE — Under the especial Patronage of His Royal Highness Prince Albert — M. BERLIOZ'S GRAND CONCERT — M. Hector Berlioz begs most respectfully to inform the nobility and gentry, and the public, that his FIRST GRAND VOCAL AND INSTRUMENTAL CONCERT in this country will take place at the above Theatre this evening (Monday) February 7, on which occasion he will have the honour of presenting to an English audience several of those compositions which, during the last few years, have received the most distinguished approbation of His Majesty Louis Philippe, His Majesty the Emperor of Russia, His Majesty the King of Prussia, His Majesty the Emperor of Austria &c.

Principal Vocal Performers:— Mr. Sims Reeves, Mr. Weiss, Mr. Gregg, Miss Miran, and Madame Dorus-Gras.

The Orchestra and Chorus will consist of 250 performers.

The Orchestra will be conducted by M. BERLIOZ, the Chorus directed by M. Maretzek.

The whole of the Music is the Composition of M. Berlioz.

PROGRAMME

PART I

Overture to the *Carnival of Rome*.

Romance, *The Young Shepherd* (words by M. de Vere) sung by Miss Miran.

Harold in Italy. Symphony in four parts, with Solo on the Tenor, performed by Mr. Hill.[1]

1. Harold in the Mountains—Scenes expressive of Melancholy, Happiness and Joy.
2. March of Pilgrims, singing their Evening Prayer.
3. Serenade, The Mountaineer of the Abruzzi to his Mistress.
4. Souvenirs of the foregoing scenes. Revels of Brigands.

PART II

First and Second Acts of the lyrical drama of *Faust.* Pastoral, the Recitative sung by Mr. S. Reeves. Dance of Peasants with Chorus. Hungarian March. Faust's Soliloquy in his Study. Easter Hymn. Recitative from the scene in the Tavern of Leipsic. Drinking Song. Song of the Student, sung by Mr. Gregg. Song Mephistopheles, sung by Mr. Weiss. Aerial Flight of Faust and Mephistopheles. The Scene laid on the Banks of the Elbe. Air Mephistopheles sung by Mr. Weiss. Chorus and Dance of Sylphs. Finale, Grand Double Chorus of Students and Soldiers.

PART III

Cavatina from the opera *Benvenuto Cellini* sung by Madame Dorus-Gras.

Chorus of Souls in Purgatory taken from the *Requiem* of M. Berlioz.

Funeral Oration and Apotheosis, being the Finale of the Triumphal Symphony composed for double orchestra and chorus expressly by order of the French Government, on the Removal of the Remains of the Victims of July, and on the Inauguration of the Column of the Bastille. The solo part performed by Herr Koenig on the Alto Trombone.

[1]Henry Hill, a distinguished viola player, brother of William E. Hill, violin maker of Wardour Street. The firm is now William Hill & Sons of New Bond Street.

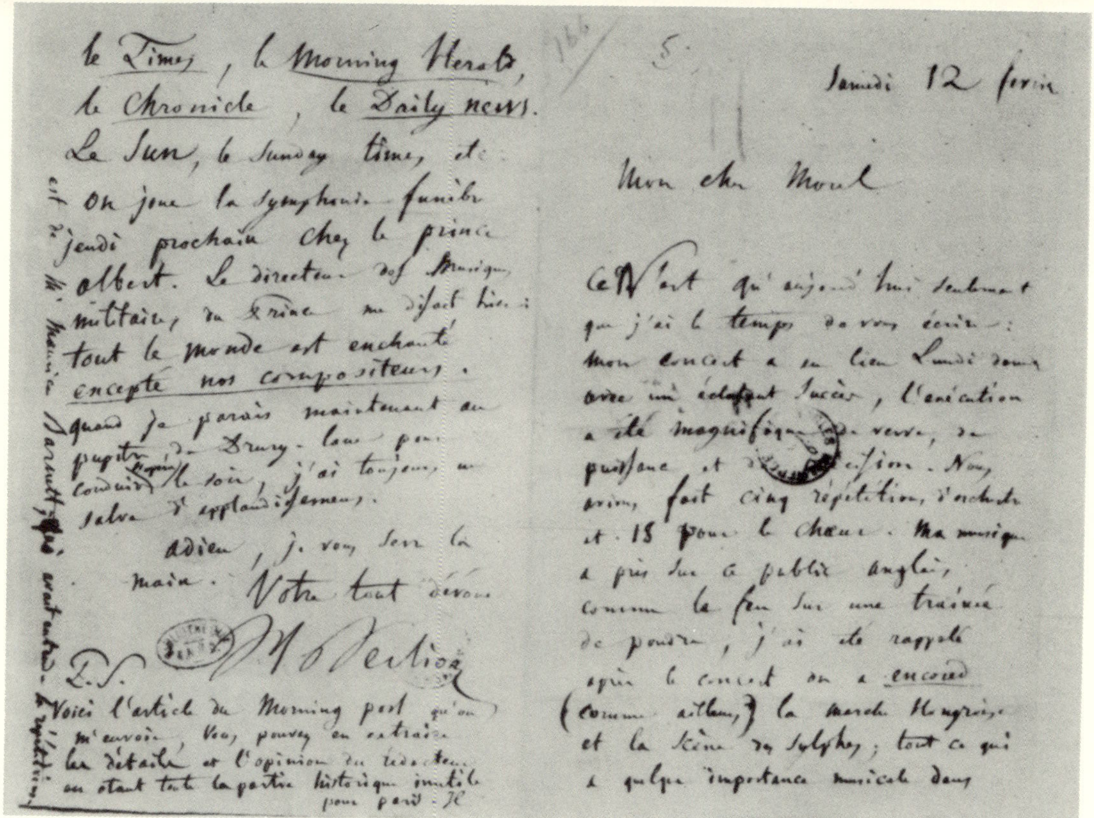

Samedi 12 février

Mon cher Morel

Ce n'est qu'aujourd'hui seulement que j'ai le temps de vous écrire: mon concert a eu lieu Lundi dernier avec un éclatant succès, l'exécution a été magnifique de verve, de puissance et de précision. Nous avons fait cinq répétitions d'orchestre et 15 pour le chœur. Ma musique a pris sur le public anglais, comme le feu sur une traînée de poudre, j'ai été rappelé après le concert on a encored (comme ils disent) la Marche Hongroise et la Scène des Sylphes; tout ce qui a quelque importance musicale dans

le Times, le Morning Herald, le Chronicle, le Daily news. Le Sun, le Sunday times, etc. On joue la Symphonie funèbre jeudi prochain chez le prince Albert. Le directeur des Musiques militaires du Prince me l'a dit hier; tout le monde est enchanté excepté nos compositeurs. Quand je parais maintenant au pupitre de Drury-Lane pour conduire le soir, j'ai toujours une salve d'applaudissemens.

Adieu, je vous serre la main. Votre tout dévoué

H Berlioz

P.S. Voici l'article du Morning post qu'on m'envoie. Vous pouvez en extraire les détails et l'opinion du rédacteur en ôtant toute la partie historique inutile pour Paris. H

c'est Mr Maurice Barnett, qui avait entendu les répétitions.

LETTER OF BERLIOZ

Londres, était à Drury lane ce
soir là, et la plupart des artistes
de quelque valeur sont venus après
le concert au théâtre me féliciter.
Ils ne s'attendaient à rien de
pareil; ils croyaient à une musique
diabolique, incompréhensible, dure,
sans charme .... il faut voir
comment ils arrangent maintenant
nos critiques de Paris. Davison
lui même a fait un article dans
le Times dont on lui a, faute
de place, ôté la moitié; ce qui
en est resté a produit son effet
néanmoins. Mais je ne sais ce
qu'il pense au fond; avec des
opinions comme les siennes il
faut s'attendre à _tout_. Le vieux
Hogarth du _Daily-news_ était
dans une agitation des plus comiques
« J'ai _tout mon sang en feu_,

m'a-t-il dit, jamais de
ma vie je n'ai été _excité_
de la sorte par la musique. »

Maintenant je cherche comment
~~je pourrai~~ donner mon second concert.
Jullien ne payant plus les
musiciens ni les choristes, je n'ose
m'exposer au danger de les voir
me manquer au dernier moment.
Hier soir après Figaro, la
défection a commencé! Les cors
m'ont averti qu'ils ne viendraient
plus. Et mes appointements courent
les champs.. Dieu sait si je
les attraperai jamais.

Mille choses à Desmarest et à
Lecieux. Tachez de faire quelque
chose sur le concert dans vos journaux,
voyez les feuilles anglaises du 8
chez Galignani et celles de demain
dimanche 13. Ce sont le _Morning post_

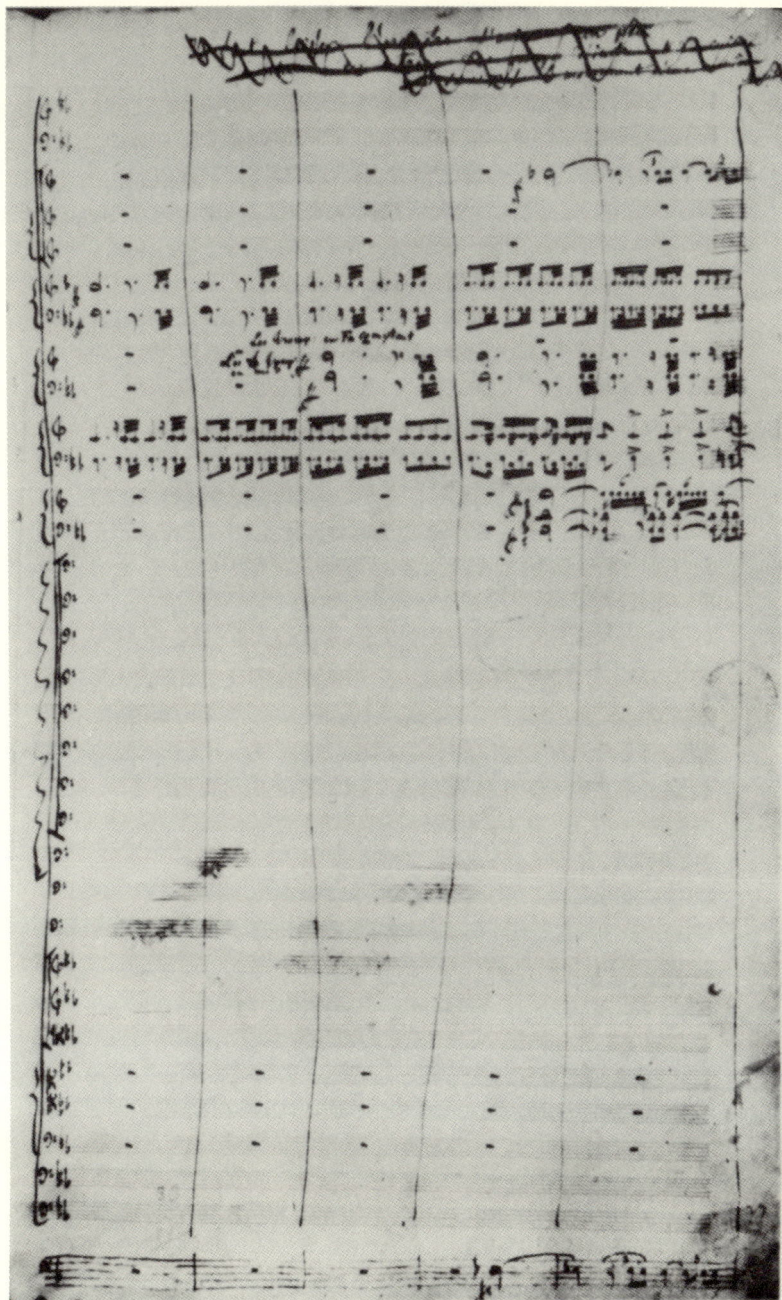

TUBA MIRUM (autographed score)

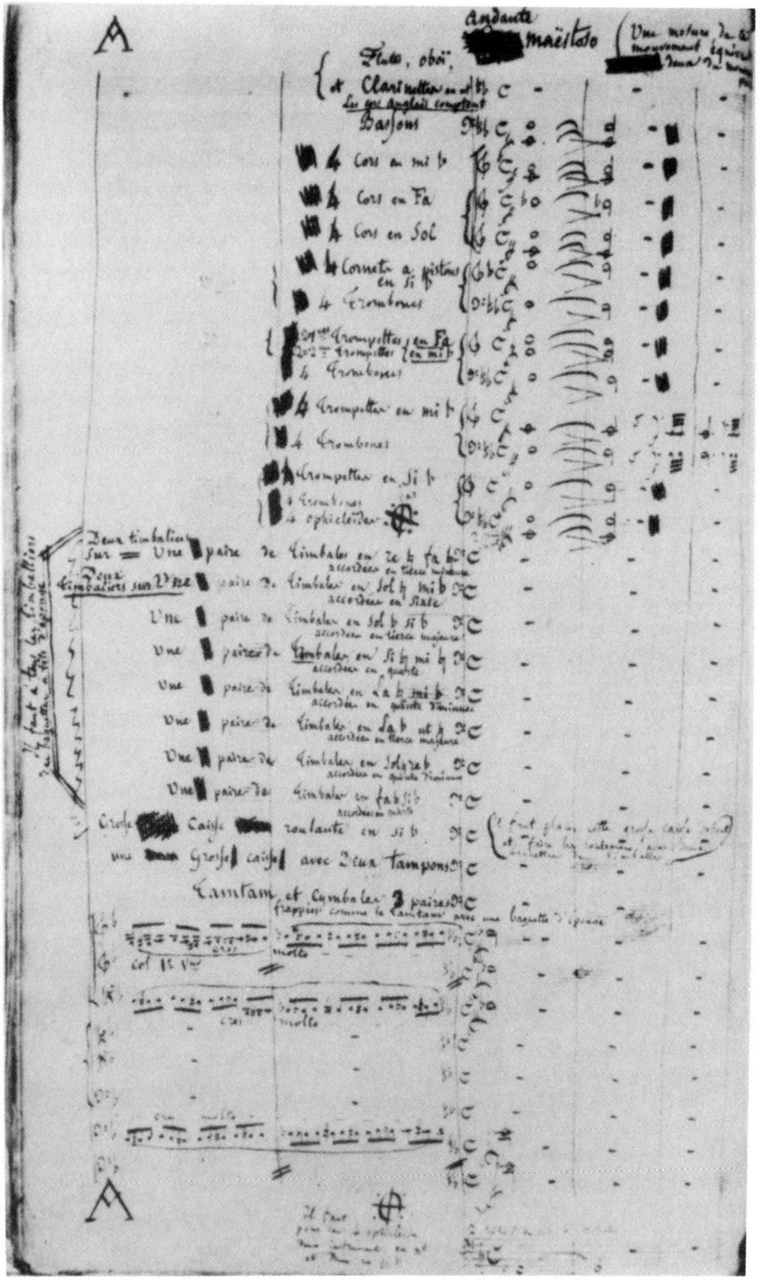
Andante
maëstoso
Bassons
4 Cors en mi b
4 Cors en Fa
4 Cors en Sol
4 Cornets à pistons en Si b
4 Trombones
4 Trompettes en mi b
4 Trombones
Trompettes en Si b
4 ophicléides
Une paire de timbales en Sol b Si b
Une paire de timbales en Si b mi b
Une paire de timbales en La b ut b
Une paire de timbales en Sol et La b
Une paire de timbales en fa b Si b
Grosse caisse roulante en Si b
une Grosse caisse avec Deux tampons
Tamtam et Cymbales 3 paires
molto

The concert and the programme, consisting of works *all new* to London, had aroused considerable interest in the musical world, and Drury Lane Theatre was well filled, though many had secured " orders". The orchestral players, with the chorus below them, occupied tiers of seats erected on the stage. Berlioz on entering was received with general applause, and threw himself into his task with energy and complete command of the situation. The spirited character of the *Carnaval Romain* overture with its impetuous rhythm and novel effects of instrumentation excited evident surprise. The *Harold* Symphony, magnificently played, was listened to with close attention, though it appeared to leave the audience somewhat cold; they applauded with discretion. But when the second part started, all was changed. The dramatic effect of the *Faust* music electrified the house. The peasants' dance and the stirring *Hungarian March* brought thunders of applause, and an encore. Curiously enough the soloists did not do much with their parts. The *Song of the Flea* sung by Willoughby Weiss[1] failed to take the fancy of the audience. The *Dance of the Sylphs* was encored, and after the chorus of soldiers and students the house rang with cheers.

As a contrast to this came the *Offertorium* from the *Requiem*, in which the voices are heard repeating one plaintive phrase through the moving harmonies of the orchestra. It made a deep impression. In conclusion the *Finale* from the *Triumphal* Symphony produced a scene of indescribable enthusiasm, Berlioz being called out again and again.

Morel was his first thought.

Saturday, February 12. (1848).

My dear Morel,

 Only to-day have I had time to write to you. My concert took place last Monday with startling success; the performance was magnificent in verve, in power and precision. We had five orchestral rehearsals and eighteen for the chorus. My music caught on with the English public like wild-fire; I was called at the end of the concert. As elsewhere the " Hungarian March " and the " Scène des Sylphes" were encored. All musical London of importance was at Drury Lane that night, and the greater part of the artists worth anything came after the concert to congratulate me. They had expected nothing like it; they thought it would be diabolic,

[1] He composed the *Village Blacksmith.*

incomprehensible, harsh music without charm . . . you should see what they now have got to say about our Parisian critics. Davison himself wrote an article in the " Times," half of which was cut out for want of space; what was left produced its effect, nevertheless. But I don't know what he really thinks; with opinions like his, one must expect anything. Old Hogarth[1] of the " Daily News " was in a most comic state of agitation: " All my blood is on fire," he said to me, " never in my life have I been so excited by music." Now I am looking out how I can give my second concert. Jullien no longer paying either his musicians or his chorus, I daren't expose myself to the danger of seeing them fail me at the last moment. Last night, after " Figaro," the defection began. The horns warned me they would not come again. And my fees go hang . . . God knows if I shall ever get them.

A thousand greetings to Desmarest and Lireux. Try and get something into your papers about the concert, look at the English papers of the 8th at Galignani's and at those of to-morrow, Sunday the 13th—" The Morning Post," " The Times," " The Morning Herald," " The Chronicle," " The Daily News," " The Sun," " The Sunday Times," etc.

The " Symphonie Funèbre " is to be played next Thursday at Prince Albert's. The Prince's military band-master told me yesterday: " everybody is delighted excepting our composers." Now when I appear at the conductor's desk at Drury Lane to conduct the Opera in the evening, I am always met by a burst of applause.

P.S. Here is " The Morning Post " article which has been sent me. You can extract the details and the opinion of the writer, leaving out all the historical part which is of no use in Paris. It is by Mr. Morris Barnett; he had heard four rehearsals.

The band-master mentioned was Charles Godfrey of the Coldstream Guards, Musician-in-Ordinary to the Queen. The Court Circular shews that he was in attendance with his band at *Buckingham Palace* the following Friday, and included Berlioz' *Grande Marche Triomphale* in the programme.

Charles Godfrey knew Berlioz' work, for he had been one of the first to give the *Francs Juges* overture, with his band of sixty wind instruments, at the Surrey Gardens. Sir Dan Godfrey,

---

[1]George Hogarth, father-in-law of Charles Dickens. In the *Daily News* next day he wrote: " In England Berlioz' music cannot be said till now to have come before the public at all."

formerly conductor of the Bournemouth Symphony Concerts, so well known for his broad outlook in musical matters, was his grandson. He, too, inherited a love of Berlioz' works. Morris Barnett, who spent the early part of his life in Paris, was brought up as a musician. He, however, decided to go on the stage, and obtained celebrity as a delineator of French characters; he also wrote successful plays. For a time he was on the staff of *The Morning Post* and *The Era* as musical critic.

His masterly critique of the concert contained a remarkable appreciation of Berlioz' music:—

" The programme consisted of portions of his greatest works; and we will here state at once that so perfect an execution we have seldom, if ever, heard. Each individual seemed determined to prove to Hector Berlioz that the fullest justice should be awarded to him . . . The whole of the music was from his pen, and, perhaps no greater test could be afforded of the variety of his genius, than the circumstance that no sign of weariness was expressed by look or word during the entire performance. The triumph was complete— those who had come to blame remained to praise—those who had heard that the music of Berlioz was characterised by its want of intention, as well as by its lack of science, were astonished to find new effects, learned combinations, and poetical feeling—in a word, all the attributes necessary to constitute the great musical writer. The music of Hector Berlioz must not be judged by models past or present. It is *sui generis* . . . His symphonies are neither in form nor structure those of the received symphonies of those composers whom we delight to honour . . . Is it forgotten that Words- worth was condemned, Shelley despised ? . . . The daring to cast aside the tinsel trammels of the French School—the courage to resist the tune-spinning of the Opéra Comique—the moral endurance to withstand the scornings of the contra- puntists and the gibes and sneers of the pseudo-classicists, have arrayed against him the rout and rabble of the stereotyped musical incapables. But Berlioz has pursued his onward path, supported by the strength of his intellect, the full consciousness that music was something better than a mere sensuous art; that it is worthy to be the natural exponent of the loftiest aspirations and the deepest passions of the poet . . .
With Hector Berlioz the poetical sense invariably prompts the melodic passage, but the melody is suggestive, the orchestration objective . . . Want of continuity has been urged as being the ruling sin of his works, but the composer's design once grasped, each passage illustrates the passing thought, and each instrument forms a link in the poetical chain.

It is a singular fact that Berlioz does not play upon any instrument, with the exception of the guitar. Every other composer has been a pianist, and has necessarily been enabled to form some idea of the wished for effects; and, therefore, marvellous is it that Berlioz, without any external aid, has produced works so extraordinary . . . The secret is, that the orchestra is his sole instrument—through this he lives, breathes, and has his being . . ."

All the works performed are then discussed in detail.

Charles Gruneisen, who had returned from Paris for the concert, gave an account of it in *The Illustrated London News*, and inserted a biographical sketch of his friend, adorned with a woodcut after Prinzhofer's portrait. Berlioz was surprised to read that on seeing Henriette Smithson play Juliet in Paris he exclaimed to his neighbour in the pit " ' that actress shall be my wife, and that play shall suggest to me the subject of a grand musical work.' Both prophecies were fulfilled." He agrees that both things eventually happened but demurs to having said anything of the kind. " My biographer attributed to me an extravagant ambition."

Lively scenes marked the Sims Reeves' benefit two nights later. Immense applause had greeted the *Carnaval Romain* overture; then came a prolonged wait. The opera *The Bride of Lammermoor* shewed no signs of starting, and the audience grew restive, stamped on the floor, and called loudly for Jullien. A serious row was imminent, when Berlioz walked into the orchestra, and " turned the tide from exasperation to commendation." After the short instrumental introduction there was a pause, and a gentleman in sombre garb stepped forward from the wings to announce that Madame Dorus-Gras refused to appear. " Madam Dorus-Gras," says *The Times*, " was ready dressed for her part in her room "; it would seem she was waiting for Jullien to settle the matter of her fees. The house broke into an uproar, then began cheering for Miss Miran; the young contralto had gallantly offered to read the music from a vocal score. At the end of the first act she was relieved by Miss Messent who had just reached the theatre, knew the part and sang it with extraordinary success. " She reaped a harvest of wreaths, probably never intended to grace her brows, but she deserved them." The chief interest of the concert after the opera was a fine rendering of the Pilgrims' March from the *Harold* Symphony.

The Marriage of Figaro, the last opera chosen for production, was first given on February 11, before a crowded and enthusiastic house. An opportunity having come for carrying out his own cherished ideas, Berlioz saw to it that the work was presented exactly as it was written, without omissions or alterations. The hint to established institutions, however, passed unheeded, as Berlioz observed at his next visit.

The historian Taine gives us Berlioz' account of an incident at a rehearsal of this opera: " I was conducting the orchestra at Drury Lane, when a lady sang *Voi che sapete* with *fioriture* etc. I stopped everything and said, " Mademoiselle, is it your music master who has pencilled in these embellishments for your song ? "—" Yes, Sir," she replied. " Well, tell him from me that he's a fool. You will sing the song as it is, or we shall not accompany you." The performance enabled everybody who heard it to realise that no one conducted Mozart's music with greater sympathy or a finer appreciation of its beauties. As a writer remarked, " Hector Berlioz has seized the very inner spirit of the scene."

The next week there was a Command Performance of Balfe's new opera *The Maid of Honour*. Queen Victoria and Prince Albert and the Duke and Duchess of Saxe Coburg, with their suites, entered the crowded house a little before half-past seven. The royal box had been decorated for the occasion. Jullien saw to that. It was lined with rose and white gauze and stripes of gold; festoons of flowers clustered on the borders and cornices. The Royal party followed the opera with evident interest, and at the close were seen to their carriages by Jullien in his most gorgeous attire. Berliox conducted the performance. The season ended on February 25, a benefit night for the entrepreneur.

An incident, which has been the means of tracing out many of the details of Berlioz' life in London, occurred at this time.

The writer's father, William Ganz, then a little boy of fourteen, came over to London with his father, Adolphe Ganz,[1] who was for twenty-five years conductor of the opera at Mayence, and arrived at Brydges Street, Drury Lane, on Sunday, February 20. William Ganz had started writing a diary in a little book while on the journey here, and in the first extract appears the name

---

[1] Father and son settled in London, and were both naturalized.

of Berlioz: " The next day, Monday, went to see Balfe at 123, Regent Street, who received us in a very friendly way. We had a look at the town. I cannot describe the impression it made upon me; so many beautiful shops, and so many carriages that we could not walk in the road, but had to keep to the pavement. In the evening went across to the Opera at Drury Lane Theatre. M. Berlioz was conducting *Figaro*." One wonders what that little boy would have thought had he foreseen that in later years he was to play under Berlioz' bâton and himself conduct the first performance in London of the *Symphonie Fantastique*.

Berlioz was now able to assure Brandus, his Paris publisher, that he was making a position for himself in London:

76, *Harley Street, Thursday, (February* 24).

My dear Brandus,

    I have just read the " Gazette Musicale " and thank you for the article on my concert. I amuse myself every day making a collection of the English papers[1] *which are increasing in number and enthusiasm. It is only the two articles in " The Athenaeum," actually written by one of my friends, Chorley*[2]*, who did the English translation of " Faust," which are ambiguous, colourless and cold. It is often like that. If you could get in the " Atlas " article which I sent to Mademoiselle Recio, it would have a great effect. I have found out the name of the writer: it is Mr. Holmes, one of the leading musical critics in London, whom up to this moment, I have never seen. He came, I am told, with most hostile ideas. I have had to write an incredible number of letters to newspaper publishers to thank their staff on my behalf, as their articles are never signed.*

    I have an offer from Beale[3] *for the publication of some piano arrangements of " Faust "; so far we have not quite come to terms, but if it comes off, will you on your side do something for the work in France? Write me your ideas on the subject. At Covent Garden they are busy preparing the " Musical Shakespeare Night," of which you spoke in the "Gazette Musicale." Indeed, I shall be giving there " Romeo " (in English), " King Lear," " The*

---

[1] The cuttings from 16 English papers are now in the library of the Paris
Conservatoire.

[2] *N.B.* It is fair to recall that the eminent critic Mr. Chorley attributed the
obscurity of Berlioz' works to " a too partial delight in the last compositions of
Beethoven "!

[3] Frederick Beale of Cramer & Beale, music publishers in Regent Street.

*Tempest " (in Italian) and the Ballad on the " Death of Ophelia "
(for female choir with orchestra). The question now is can they
give me fifteen choral rehearsals and five orchestral. Otherwise I
won't do it.*

*I have just been to the annual banquet of the Society of English
Musicians, presided over by the Duke of Cambridge.[1] This
Society has existed for 110 years; it is wealthy and very influential.
I was invited shortly after my arrival in London. After dinner there
was a concert at which old Braham sang, as well as Miss Dolby,
Miss Lyon and Reeves; we had a large number of Glees or
Madrigals by Old English Masters. At dessert, the president
proposed my health, although this was, so I was told, a breach of
the rules of the Society; a toast received with cheers and the applause
of the 600 guests and the ladies accommodated in a special gallery.
I had to respond in a speech (in French of course) and contrary
to my usual habit, I found myself so much at my ease that I was
able to speak all right and to thank both the public for their
reception on the day of the concert, the artists for their admirable
performance of my music and the writers of the press for the good
fellowship with which they had supported me. The effect was
admirable. And I think you could easily make a piece of news of
all this for the "Gazette". But don't mention the Covent Garden
proposal. The concert of the 24th at Drury Lane has collapsed
amid the complications of Jullien's business affairs. Beale has
suggested my giving a huge one at his own risk at Exeter Hall.*

This, the one-hundredth-and-tenth anniversary festival of the
Royal Society of Musicians was held at the Freemasons' Tavern,
Great Queen Street, on February 22. Being disabled by an
attack of gout, the Duke of Cambridge, always a great patron
of music and musicians, was unable to be present. Berlioz no
doubt mistook Robert Palmer, M.P., who took his place, for
the Duke. The glees and madrigals, which included Wilbye's
Flora gave me Fairest Flowers, were sung by eight young gentlemen
from Westminster Abbey and eight experienced glee-singers.
After Sims Reeves had given *In this Old Chair my Father sat* with
telling effect, the veteran Braham sat down to the piano and
sang *Stand to your Guns, my Hearts of Oak!* with an energy that
belied his years.

With startling suddenness news came of the outbreak of the

[1]Grandfather of Queen Mary.

February revolution in Paris, the political upheaval and the flight of Louis Philippe. Berlioz feared for the safety of his friends; no word from them reached him. Writing urgently to Morel, he says:

> *What has become of you? Why don't you let me have a line? What is really happening about music? I asked Desmarest[1] a week ago, and of course he has not replied. Paris is certainly an agreeable spot, and above all the place to cry out, like someone or other of old: " Oh, my friends! I have no friends any more[2] "*
>
> *I have written to Brandus suggesting his publishing three pieces from " Faust " which Beale is going to publish here as piano duets: the " March," the " Ballet des Sylphes " and the " Ballet des Follets "; I have not had an answer. At the moment I am arranging the " Apotheosis " for voice and chorus (in E flat) with piano accompaniment. Beale is going to publish it with the " Marseillaise," the " Chant du Départ " and the geniune " Mourons pour la Patrie " of Rouget de Lisle, which I am likewise writing for him. Brandus would certainly sell a lot of copies of the " Apotheosis " reduced in this way and singable. I will send it to him. But please go and see him and talk to him about it. I cannot imagine that people with whom one has for so long been on intimate terms could forget so soon and so completely . . . When shall I stop thinking of what's brewing in Paris! . . . I hope there are to be no more subsidies for our stupid opera-houses, I hope the managers of those " sinks " will depart as they came, and in double-quick time, I hope the censorship of songs will be abolished, in short I hope we shall be free to enjoy freedom, if we have not to put up with some fresh piece of humbug.*
>
> *What has become of M. Bertin? They say here that he is in hiding . . . What has become of all our precious enemies— " precious villains,"[3] as Shakespeare says?*
>
> *Do please write to me. I am giving a concert at Exeter Hall in a few weeks' time.[4] Good-bye, good-bye.*
>
> *March 6, (1848).*

[1] Violoncellist at the Opera, since his youth a friend of Berlioz.
[2] A saying of the Greek sage Chilon.
[3] He quotes in English.
[4] It did not take place.

Armand Bertin, then editor of the *Journal des Débats*, which had upheld the fallen monarchy, was the son of the great Bertin, founder of the paper, whose superb portrait by Ingres is in the Louvre. The family had consistently supported Berlioz' cause ever since his acceptance of the post of musical critic on the *Débats* in 1835. He was naturally disturbed as to the fortunes of the house, and the danger he was in of losing the income derived from his articles. Bertin was told how things were going in London:

> *I rather think I shall remain here another two months, as I have nothing to do in Paris. In London, on the contrary, there are various opportunities for earning money, and I expect the approach of the big musical season may bring me still better openings.*
>
> *I am happily well supported by the press and the artists, and public interest in me is getting keener and keener.*

Buoyed up by his recent success at Drury Lane, Berlioz tells d'Ortigue of what seemed his brilliant prospects here, so different from his tragic lot in Paris:

> *76 Harley Street, London.*
> *March 15.*
>
> My dear d'Ortigue,
> *I have been wanting to write to you for a long time but until to-day I have not had the time. Life in London is even more absorbing than in Paris; everything is in scale with the vastness of the city. I get up at mid-day; at one o'clock come the visitors, friends, new acquaintances, artists with introductions. Whether I like it or not I lose three good hours in this way. From four to six I work; if I have not got an invitation, I go out then to dine a good way off; I read the papers, after which it is time to go to the opera or a concert; I go on listening to music, such as it is, till half-past eleven. Finally three or four of us artists go off to supper at some tavern and smoke till two in the morning. That is my outward and visible life . . . You have heard, more or less, of the sudden and startling success of my concert at Drury Lane. It disconcerted in a few hours all favourable or hostile anticipations and upset the whole structure of theories which people had built up here on the subject of my music based on the academic criticism of the Continent. Thank God! The whole English Press has expressed its opinion in terms of*

extraordinary warmth, and, apart from Davison and Gruneisen, I didn't know one of the writers. It is different now; the principal ones have come to see me, have written to me, and we often meet in a friendly way. It is a long while since I felt so lively a satisfaction as when I read the article in the " Atlas " which I sent to Brandus and which he has not had translated. It is by Mr. Holmes, author of a " Life of Mozart " which is much admired here.

Mr. Holmes had come convinced that he was going to hear harshness, madness and nonsense, etc.

I can assure you this great victory would have made you happy. Now to follow up the enemy and not go to sleep at Capua. Jullien as you know has not paid me. His opera-house is now a circus. The two Italian opera-houses are disputing as to which gives the better performance of the Italian masterpieces. Last night they played Verdi's "Attila " at Her Majesty's Theatre . . . After " Attila " hola.[1] The managers of Covent Garden want to put on my Shakespearean Concert, consisting of " Romeo," " King Lear," the " Ballad on the death of Ophelia" and " The Tempest." The day before yesterday we had a conference on the subject, and I told them that not at any price would I consent to organise this performance unless they could guarantee me a fortnight's rehearsals for the vocal parts and four orchestral rehearsals. They are now considering the matter with Costa, but I am sure that he will say the thing is impossible. My stay here is strangely annoying to him. Balfe, on the other hand, is a good fellow and I am particularly pleased with him; we meet very often and in the friendliest way.

The day before yesterday the Philharmonic Society conducted by Costa began its season. They performed a symphony by Hesse (organist at Breslau) quite well-made, quite cold, and quite futile stuff; another in A by Mendelssohn, admirable, magnificent, much superior as I think to the one, also in A, which is given in Paris.[2] The orchestra is very good; with the exception of certain wind instruments, there is nothing to cavil at, and Costa is an admirable conductor. No one would believe, that evening, that the Society had not yet asked for anything of mine for their concerts; yet it is true. It is said they will be forced to do so by the newspapers and by

---

[1] Berlioz here alludes to Boileau's famous quatrain on a play of Corneille:

> *Après l' Agésilas,*
> *Hélas!*
> *Mais après l'Attila,*
> *Holà!*

[2] He preferred the *Italian* symphony to the *Scotch*.

their committee. But I shall be pretty cautious about handing myself over to the velvet paws of Costa, Anderson and all the obstinate old men who direct that institution. It is a repetition of the " pretty ways " of the Conservatoire at Paris . . . I shall remain here as long as possible, for it needs time to find a place here and establish myself. Happily the circumstances are favourable, sooner or later I shall gain this position and it will be a sure one, they tell me. I can no longer think of any country for my musical career except England or Russia. I had long ago done with France; the last revolution has only made me more decided. I had to contend under the old government with the hatred aroused by my articles, the ineptitude of operatic managers and public indifference; there would now be besides, the crowd of great composers just hatched out by the Republic, popular, philantrophic, national and economic music. The arts in France are dead, and music, in particular is already beginning to rot; bury it quickly! I can smell the fumes . . . I don't know if they have condescended to keep my place in the Conservatoire Library open for me, it brought me in 118 francs a month. I have written about it to the Minister of the Interior, who of course has not replied . . .

While he was away in England, a proposal was actually made to suppress Berlioz' post of sub-librarian at the Conservatoire, on the ground of his frequent and lengthy absences abroad; but it was not persisted in. For this he had principally to thank Victor Hugo, who " notwithstanding his genius, just then enjoyed a certain amount of authority in the Chamber, as a popular representative," and intervened on his behalf. Two years later Berlioz succeeded to the post of librarian, at the same salary, and held it till his death.

Edward Holmes, a school-fellow and friend of John Keats, was in his day the most accomplished musical critic in this country. His enlightened views, and rooted belief in Berlioz' music found expression in articles which he wrote for the *Atlas* and for *Fraser's Magazine*. At a later date he penned the following impressions of Berlioz:—" Immersed in the arduous duties of the day, he showed before the audience the most simple and unaffected demeanour . . . Personally, his easy, gentlemanly address, and great promptitude, admirably adapt him for a position at the head of the orchestra. Not less so does his admirable temper. We have seen him on occasions that would,

in one of the irritable race, have almost justified a fit of anger—
mild, considerate, and good-humoured. This is a trait which
characterises the habitual repose of lofty powers." Again: " He
has the art of conciliating musicians, and of engaging their best
efforts in his behalf, perhaps beyond any composer of our time ;
his demeanour being perfectly simple, free from airs of
superiority, or any assumption of the great man."

Chapter Four

THE startling events in Paris accompanying the fall of Louis Philippe and the declaration of a republic had filled the musicians there with consternation. The possibility of earning their livelihood for the time was gone, and England seemed the only haven of refuge. Charles Hallé, a close friend of Berlioz, was one of the first to appear. Rumours had reached him in Paris of the fiasco of Jullien's operatic schemes and the straits in which Berlioz now found himself. Directly he arrived at his lodgings at 28 Maddox Street and had unpacked a few things he hurried round to Harley Street to find Berlioz. He was out, but later that evening Hallé found a note waiting for him:

> *My dear Hallé,*
>
> *I am very "sorry" to have the pleasure of seeing you, thank you all the same for having come round to my place directly after your shipwreck on the coast of England. If you are at home this evening, we will weep together over a cigar. I shall look you up again about 10 o'clock.*
>
> Yours ever,
HECTOR BERLIOZ.

Berlioz called Hallé " the model pianist, the musician *sans peur et sans reproche* " and this is how Hallé describes Berlioz: " And what a picture he was at the head of his orchestra, with his eagle face, his bushy hair, his air of command, and glowing with enthusiasm. He was the most perfect conductor I ever set eyes upon, one who held absolute sway over his troops, and played upon them as a pianist upon the keyboard."

The veracity of Hector Berlioz' Memoirs has been so persistently impugned, that it is pleasant to be able to cite Charles Hallé as a witness to the truth of one remarkable incident upon which doubt has been cast. Berlioz in his

Memoirs gives a dramatic account of what happened at the first performance of his great *Requiem* in 1837. Commissioned by the Minister of Interior for the July celebrations, Berlioz had the mortification of finding that it was not to be given a hearing. Then, with the death of Marshal Damrémont, came the order to prepare for its performance at the Invalides in December. Intrigues were rife to prevent it. They failed, but Habeneck who, Berlioz says, for some unexplained reason had not spoken to him for three years past, was to conduct. It was a momentous occasion, when success would mean everything to Berlioz, and failure irretrievable disaster.

For the trumpets of the Last Judgment Berlioz had devised a novel and startling effect by means of four groups of brass instruments placed at the four angles of the massed orchestra. The *Tuba mirum* followed the *Dies Irae* without a break, and it was of vital importance that at this point the conductor should be on the alert.

> *At the critical bar when action on the part of the conductor is absolutely indispensable, Habeneck laid down his bâton, quietly pulled out his snuff-box and started taking a pinch of snuff. I had kept my eye on him all the time; instantly I swung round on my heel and darted in front of him, stretched out my arm and beat the four big beats of the next movement. The orchestra followed me, everything started off right, I conducted the piece to its end, and the effect I had dreamed was produced. When, at the last words of the chorus, Habeneck saw that the " Tuba mirum " was saved: " I was all in a cold sweat," said he, " but for you we were done! " " I know that very well," said I, looking him straight in the face. Not another word did I utter . . . Did he do it on purpose? . . . Could he in concert with M. XX . . ., who hated me, and Cherubini's friends, have dared to think out and attempt so vile an action? . . . I can't bear the thought of it . . . But I don't doubt it. I ask God's pardon if I do him a wrong.*

Doubts have been cast by a succession of Berlioz' biographers upon the whole incident. First stated with a certain amount of tactful discretion, the process of repetition has at last reached a point where scornful derision is freely indulged in. Berlioz is accused of having deliberately invented the whole story of the snuff-box, and waited till Habeneck's death to tell it. It seems a pity that the writer's investigations should have been so restricted. Happily for Berlioz' memory, his friend Charles Hallé described the incident in detail in a book published in 1896. Hallé was present at the Invalides, and saw the whole incident of the snuff-box and Berlioz' prompt action to save the situation. He confirms Berlioz' account in every particular, and says that " Habeneck after the performance thanked Berlioz profusely for his timely aid, and admitted that his own thoughtlessness might have caused a break-down, but Berlioz remained persuaded that there had been no thoughtlessness but that the break-down was intended." Hallé himself was disposed to exonerate the conductor from having such an intention. Due weight must also be given to what Berlioz wrote to Humbert Ferrand in 1859, where he speaks of the incident in a manner inconsistent with his having invented it. He would scarcely seek to impose upon his greatest friend.

The two pages of the autograph full score in the illustration show the lay-out of the instruments for the *Tuba mirum*.

" M. XX " was Cavé, director of the department of fine arts; it was he who admitted to Berlioz that Beethoven *was not without talent*.

On December 8, 1837, three days after the ceremony, *The Morning Post*, always distinguished for its interest in artistic matters, printed a long description from the Paris *Galignani*. Speaking of Berlioz' *Requiem* it said, " the effect of this noble composition was prodigious . . . we can unhesitatingly affirm that, as a whole, it is one of the highest efforts of modern musical genius." It was the first account of a work of Berlioz in an English newspaper.

It is not difficult to realise how dreary a Sunday in London at this time must have seemed to foreign musicians. It was therefore a great thing for them to know that they could always count on a warm welcome on Sunday evenings at Mme. Dulcken's house in Harley Street.[1] She lived four doors off where Berlioz was staying. A fine pianist, a lively hostess, it was her delight to see them all together in her drawing-room. William Ganz, a boy of fourteen, was often there with his father. His diary says :— " Sunday March 19. After tea went to Mme. Dulcken, where I accompanied Steglich (the famous horn

---

[1] No. 80 Harley Street, afterwards re-numbered No. 19. Sir Morell Mackenzie the great throat specialist, who never charged an artist a fee, lived here in later years.

player) on the piano. Molique and Berlioz were there. She lives in a fine house; there is a good piano in every room."

Ganz says that he frequently saw Berlioz there. He was struck by his " fine big head, eagle nose, high forehead and piercing eyes." The lady with him whom Ganz took to be Mme. Berlioz, the famous Shakespearean actress Henriette Smithson, in fact was Mlle. Recio. There Berlioz met his friends from Paris, the pianists Charles Hallé and Émile Prudent. Molique the violinist he had known at Stuttgart. The handsome old beau Kalkbrenner, another refugee from over the water, cut a fine figure in a blue dress-coat with gilt buttons. Walking away one evening from Mme. Dulcken's with William Kuhe, the pianist, the conversation turned upon the revolution in France, and Berlioz said, " It is a curious thing; I have noticed that the street bands in London always play a phrase in the *Marseillaise* in the minor instead of the major key."

The D flat should be D natural. A similar variation occurs in Richard Wagner's version of the *Marseillaise*, used as a conclusion to his song *The Two Grenadiers*. They may have been German bands, up to the end of the century a feature of London streets.

When, later, on June 16 Mme. Dulcken gave her annual concert at Covent Garden, she made a point of asking Berlioz to take part. The orchestra, under his direction, did the *Hungarian March*, then the rage in London as a piano duet, with superb élan. Of course he was delighted when she offered to play at his own concert at Hanover Square Rooms. Mme. Dulcken was the sister of Ferdinand David, the violinist, whom Berlioz had met at Leipzig. Introduced by Mendelssohn as " his *fidus Achates*," David had helped to arrange his concert, and given a brilliant rendering of Berlioz' violin piece *Rêverie et Caprice*.

Julius Benedict was living in the immediate neighbourhood, and Berlioz used to go round to No. 2 Manchester Square to talk over musical matters. His great friend J. W. Davison, critic of *The Times* and the best of fellows, was another of Benedict's circle. Davison's friend G. A. Macfarren, the composer, Berlioz did not meet this time, as he was in America. But later on when the ill-starred Paris Philharmonic Society was formed Berlioz was anxious that Macfarren should become an honorary member.

Macfarren subsequently wrote a sketch of the main incidents of Berlioz' life for the Imperial Dictionary of Universal Biography, which is chiefly remarkable for its non-committal attitude to his music. " The most contradictory judgments have been passed on the music of Hector Berlioz. We therefore leave his position as a composer to be decided by the future."

A musician of very different type was William Vincent Wallace, the Irish composer, whom Berlioz saw frequently when he was in London. While confessing that he did not know Wallace's opera *Maritana,* of which therefore, unhappily, we hear nothing, he found great delight in his company. Berlioz describes him as " an excellent, eccentric man, phlegmatic in appearance like many Englishmen, bold and impetuous by nature like an American." Wallace had been for a tour in the Antipodes. " We were often together in London for half the night over a bowl of punch, he relating his strange adventures and I an eager listener. Carrying off women, fighting several duels which proved unlucky for his adversaries, he lived a savage life—yes savage or more or less so— for six months on end."

The Musical Union, founded by John Ella for the cultivation of chamber music, was then at the height of its influence. With Prince Albert as Patron, the Duke of Cambridge as President and the Earl of Westmorland as Vice-President, it included among its members a large number of " noblemen and gentlemen " to whom music appealed. John Ella made a practice of inviting all the distinguished foreigners staying in London to attend the matinées, held at Willis's Rooms[1] in King Street, St. James's. The opening meeting was noteworthy for the first performance in England of Schumann's Quartet for pianoforte and strings. As a matter of course Ella invited Berlioz, Molique, Émile Prudent and others to be present, and placed them in prominent seats for his patrons to see.

At the next meeting he was there again with Charles Hallé and his great friend G. A. Osborne, the composer, and heard Sterndale Bennett and Piatti play a Mendelssohn duet.

In the notes to his analytical programmes, a new feature at London concerts introduced by him, Ella always told his patrons of the chief musical events of the day, and he did not fail to draw especial attention to Berlioz' next orchestral concert in June. Ella's advocacy of Berlioz' music was vigorously maintained during all his visits to London.

[1] Now used as auction rooms.

The new Amateur Musical Society with its many titled performers, including an honourable as bassoonist, a baron as trumpeter and a duke as double-bass, felt honoured when Berlioz consented to come on April 7 and conduct the *Hungarian March* at one of their concerts. He was enthusiastically received and the March encored.

The Musical World published an appeal to the Philharmonic Society in the name of Charles Rosenberg the journalist, backed by a vigorous editorial, asking them to give Berlioz' music a hearing. To ignore his presence in London was nothing short of a scandal. It fell on deaf ears. In his difficult position, he turned to Davison:

March 17, 1848.

My dear Davison,

I am obliged to try and get along here as best I can, now that all art is dead and buried in France. Consequently, while waiting till I can do something in the musical way, perhaps, with your help I may succeed in using my pen to some purpose. So will you find out from the editor of " The Times," what possibility there is of printing some unpublished articles of mine in that paper to be translated by you into English, and what we should both of us get out of it[1] . . .

I looked for you the other night at Exeter Hall but it was like looking for a needle in a haystack. I wanted to tell you, a thing you know as well as I do, that the Mendelssohn Symphony is a masterpiece created like a gold medal by a single stroke of the die. Nothing could be fresher, livelier, nobler or more accomplished in its free inspiration. The Paris Conservatoire does not even suspect the existence of this magnificent work, it will discover it ten years hence.

The small amount of concert work was not enough to occupy his restless spirit. During his stay in London he conceived the idea of collecting together his various writings and preparing his Memoirs for publication.

The preface is headed:—" London, 21 March, 1848." It contains the remark " England since I have been here has offered me a noble and cordial hospitality." The grave troubles which beset him were cast aside for a while, in tracing the story of his boyhood. " A ray of Spring sunshine " lit up his room, as

---

[1] This came to nothing. He used to chaff Davison: " Of course, in your case *The Times* is money! "

he recalled his youthful passion for the fair Estelle, and the poems of Florian which embodied his thoughts. Then he broke off his narrative to speak of the stirring events in the political world; they produced these interesting comments:—

> *To-day (10th April) the Meeting of the two hundred thousand English Chartists is to take place. In a few hours perhaps England will be convulsed like the rest of Europe, and even this asylum will no longer be left me. The question will soon be decided.*
>
> *(8 o'clock at night) Come now, the Chartists are muffs at revolution. Everything passed off well. The cannon, those powerful speakers, those great logicians whose irresistible arguments penetrate so deeply into the minds of the masses were in the tribune. They were not even obliged to speak, the sight of them was enough to drive into the heads of all the conviction that a revolution was ill-timed, and the Chartists dispersed in good order. Worthy fellows! You know nearly as much about insurrections as the Italians do about writing symphonies. It's the same very probably with the Irish, and O'Connell was right in always saying: " Agitate, Agitate! But do not budge! "*

The great meeting on Kennington Common was a complete fiasco; only some twenty thousand persons attended, and the demonstration ended in a petition discreetly driven to the House in a four-wheeler. Special constables to the number of two hundred thousand had been sworn in for duty. They included Prince Louis Napoleon and Mr. Gladstone; in his diary the latter records: " On duty from 2 to 3¾ p.m." Prince Louis, after escaping from the Castle at Ham, disguised as " Badinguet," was nursing his ambitions for the future in the fashionable world of London. His habitat at No. 1c King Street, St. James's is recorded by a plaque. Berlioz had been presented to him by Count d'Orsay when attending one of Lady Blessington's brilliant receptions at Gore House, in Kensington. That autumn in Paris he often saw him visiting an aunt, who lived close by. " I met him (*the Prince*) yesterday as he was going in; no doubt he did not recognise the person who spoke with him last winter in London and called him *Monsieur* straight out. Who knows, perhaps he would be an excellent Emperor." It is curious that Berlioz' opinion of him, which appears in the foot-note to page 130 of the first, is suppressed in the later editions of the Memoirs:

" He is to-day President of the French Republic, and performs his sad function with self-sacrifice, good sense and energy." Any hopes he later formed of support by the Emperor were to be disappointed.

Monday, April 24, 1848.

Many thanks, my dear Morel, for the trouble you have taken on my behalf and for your very kind letter. It is lucky at a time like this if one can get a reply from any of one's friends in Paris . . . It is true, as the saying is, it takes all sorts to make a world . . . Marie has now moved (in Paris), and I am expecting her here to-day. Don't write till you have received a second letter from me; I do not yet know where I am going to stay.

I had to leave Jullien's house four days ago, another execution having been levied there, in the name of the Queen, for the " Queen's Taxes " which he had not paid.

The day before yesterday the London newspapers announced Jullien's bankruptcy, and at this moment he is said to be in prison. So I have nothing more to hope for from him.

The newspapers here are still full of me and my doings; but the resistance of the committee of the Philharmonic Society is an odd business. They are all English Composers, and Costa is at the head of them. Well, they have engaged Mr. Moliqne and they are giving the new symphonies of Mr. Hesse and others; but it seems that they are in holy terror of me. Beale, Davison, Rosenberg and some others have an idea of forcing them to engage me. I am doing nothing about it. We must wait and see. I have got to knock down an old wall. The public and the press are waiting for me all right on the other side.

Beale is just publishing a song which I have written for voice and choir on the theme of the " Apotheosis."[1] *It might take in Paris if it were made known, and Brandus would make a mistake in not printing it. It has a piano accompaniment, and is very simple and effective. Benedict is busy arranging the " Scène des Sylphes " and the " Ballet des Follets " as piano duets. To-day the " Hungarian March " is on every piano in London—shocking affair that our halfpenny press might allude to without making fun of it.*

Paris seems to be settling down a bit. God grant it . . .

Apropos of the *Hungarian March* Berlioz wrote to Brandus, " it is a piece which, properly puffed, and played this winter by

---

[1] A unique copy is preserved in the Boston Public Library, U.S.A.

a few pianists in an arrangement for four, eight or sixteen hands, and even for two, should have a fine sale . . . It is easy to play."

When telling his friend Ferdinand Hiller about the levy made in Harley Street for the Queen's Taxes, he said, " one morning, while I was still asleep they seized the whole of my worldly possessions. I was living with Jullien, so we were in the same boat."

It was at this juncture that Marie Recio came back to join him in London. She had returned to Paris some time before. On her arrival they moved to a more modest address, No. 26 Osnaburgh Street,[1] near Albany Street, Regent's Park. During the depressing moments he spent in his new quarters Berlioz was able to continue the study he had begun in Germany of the harmonic resonance of church clocks. At Mannheim, where he was horribly bored and it rained without ceasing, he noted that a neighbouring clock had a resonance of a minor third. Observations in other German towns convinced him of the inaccurate conclusions propounded by learned theorists. He now had the melancholy satisfaction of finding a new interval in the clock of Holy Trinity Church round the corner. It was a major third.

[1] Now demolished. It is strange that at this very house the poet Heine, in exile from Germany in 1827, had visited Kitty Clairmont, the girl who inspired the *Kitty Cycle*, which was to be set to music by Berlioz' friend Ferdinand Hiller. The artistic world was indeed small in those days.

Chapter Five

BERLIOZ was now beginning to be seriously worried by financial embarrassments. From Paris he heard that, in his absence, a bill had been presented for payment at his address, although it was not even due. Escudiers, the music publishers, who owed him 500 francs, had been made bankrupt. They acted as his agents in arranging the terms of the Jullien engagement, and he had agreed to pay them a ten per cent. commission on his fees while in London. He appears to have been called upon to pay up the percentage on the first month's salary, all he ever got, without being able to set off the debt they owed him. Morel undertook the duty of negotiating for the renewal of the bills falling due.

> *Masset asks me if there is anything to hope for from Jullien who owes him three thousand francs; tell him from me that nobody will get anything (from Jullien). So the Escudiers cannot be forced to pay me what they owe me, and I am obliged to pay what I don't owe them.*

In another letter he says:

> *My dear Morel,*
> *. . . I cannot say how touched I am by your solicitude about me and your insistence on trying to get me back to Paris. Unfortunately, bitterness apart, I am bound to admit that the true reason which makes me stay on is money. I have still to get from Beale the price of two pieces which are not yet finished, and a concert has been arranged at small cost for June 29. If I can earn some £50 thereby it will be a great help. Whereas in Paris I am sure to earn nothing at all, and by going there at present I should lose what little I can get here. Besides my expenses in London are very small. As soon as I am certain that there is nothing more to do here I shall go back*

to Paris, hoping against hope that you are not mistaken about my chances of finding some musical work to do there . . . Once I am at the end of my resources, there will be nothing for me to do but to go and sit in the gutter and die of hunger like a lost dog, or blow out my brains . . . But one may as well do it in Paris as here . . .

May, 16, 1848.

To Shakespeare, the divinity he worshipped, " the expounder of life's mysteries," he was wont to " confide the secret torments of his soul." Just then a chance performance of *Hamlet* rekindled his old enthusiasm for the poet. It inspired a profound criticism of that play, which he wrote to a friend, and moved Berlioz to revise the plaintive *Ballad on the Death of Ophelia* and the majestic music of his *Funeral March for the last scene of Hamlet.* The one he headed: " London, July 4, 1848," the other: " Paris, September 22, 1848," and added the lines spoken by Fortinbras:

> " *Let four captains*
> *Bear Hamlet, like a soldier, to the stage;*
> *For he was likely, had he been put on,*
> *To have prov'd most royally: and, for his passage,*
> *The soldier's music, and the rites of war,*
> *Speak loudly for him.*
> *Take up the bodies: such a sight as this*
> *Becomes the field, but here shows much amiss.*
> *Go, bid the soldiers shoot.*"

On the title page he inscribed a motto from Ovid:

> *qui viderit illas*
> *de lacrymis factas sentiet esse meis*

Those of us who heard Sir Hamilton Harty's moving interpretation of the March[1] could only marvel that such a work had so long remained almost unknown to the concert room.

Berlioz died without ever having heard it.

May 26, (1848).

My dear Duc,[2]

Our piece (the " Apotheosis ") has just come out at last. They thought it advisable to mutilate the title. I had written: " Composed

---

[1] December 4th, 1933.

[2] Joseph Louis Duc, the brilliant architect, had been one of Berlioz' companions, as a student at the Villa Medici, Rome. He designed the modern extensions of the *Palais de justice* in Paris.

for the inauguration of the Column of the Bastille,"—and further on " Dedicated to M.Duc, Architect of the Column of the Bastille " which showed what the Column had to do with it and the relevance of the dedication. But since the last Chartists' movement the London citizen has a profound horror of anything relating however distantly to revolutions, consequently my publisher did not want to have any reference in the title of the piece to the monument or to those for whom it was put up . . .

I saw " Hamlet " a few days ago; Marie and I came out literally in a state of collapse, trembling all over and carried away with admiration and the pity of it. The new actor Brooke is sublime and much finer than Macready and Kemble. He is the man, he is Hamlet. Besides he is a very handsome and distinguished looking fellow. Three other parts were very well filled, the ghost, Polonius, and the first grave-digger. What a world appears in this masterpiece! What a shattering effect on the mind and the feelings! Shakespeare wanted to depict the emptiness of life, the vanity of human plans, the despotism of chance, the indifference of fate or of God to what is called virtue, crime, beauty, ugliness, love, hate, genius, stupidity. And he is cruelly successful. They deigned on that night to give us Hamlet such as it really is, almost in its entirety, a rare thing to do in this country where there are so many people who are superior to Shakespeare that the greater number of his plays are " corrected " or " augmented " by Cibbers, Drydens and other rogues, who ought to be publicly whipped. Moreover the same thing is done with music: Costa has " orchestrated " and " corrected " Rossini's " Barber," Mozart's " Don Juan " and " Figaro " for Covent Garden. There is lots of the big drum now . . . Let us to the Capitol and return thanks to the gods. The two Italian opera-houses are fighting it out by pitting the singers against each other, Lumley puts up Jenny Lind, Delafield replies with Viardot-Garcia; " Sonnambula " is played at the two houses, and concerts are given consisting of 37 Italian pieces, flanked for form's sake by a " Euryanthe overture " or a Beethoven concerto. And the public swallows it all with the same patience, sorry nevertheless that it cannot hear anything better. For the London public is very attentive and very serious in its love of music, and I have not failed to recognise its excellent qualities.

I may tell you, to end my rigmarole, that I am getting up a concert at Hanover Square Rooms, and that the artists hearing of the bankruptcy of that beast Jullien and all the loss it has been to me, wish to take part without any pay. So I shall probably have a splendid orchestra, consisting of the élite of the musicians of Her Majesty's and Covent Garden. My expenses will still amount to sixty pounds (1,500 francs). It is on June 29. That is all my news . . .

The poignancy of Berlioz' feelings as he sat in the theatre was increased as his thoughts returned to the night at the Odéon in Paris, when he first saw a company of Shakespearean actors in *Hamlet*. Overwhelmed by the revelation of the poet's genius, and carried away by Henriette Smithson's personality in the part of Ophelia, he had begun a passionate courtship ending in their marriage, when she could no longer charm the fickle public, and was lame and crushed by debt. To-day she was lying ill and alone in Paris. Their boy Louis was at school at Rouen, where Berlioz had taken him in October, a month before starting for London.

Berlioz had finally separated from his wife four years previously, but he did not cease to visit her, and never failed to provide for her.

The Irish actor Gustavus Vaughan Brooke was playing at the Royal Olympic Theatre, Wych Street (where Aldwych now is), and appeared as Hamlet on four nights during May of this year. Others in the cast were G. Bennett (the Ghost), H. Mellon (Claudius) and Miss Day (Ophelia). Sir Squire Bancroft, when a young man, acted with Brooke in Dublin; he compared him for nobility of voice and dignity of bearing with Salvini. On the voyage to Australia, where Brooke was going on a farewell tour, the ship *London* foundered in the Bay of Biscay. He refused to leave his sister who lay ill below; and as the boats rowed away they saw him leaning quietly over the bulwark, waiting for the end.

Edward Delafield was the hero of a sensational bankruptcy. A brewer with a passion for music, he took over Covent Garden Opera at the age of twenty-three. Within two years he had lost £81,355 in the venture!

In the rivalry between the two opera-houses, Lumley held the trump card with Jenny Lind, who was drawing all London. Berlioz would go of an evening and watch the crowds waiting at the stage-door of Her Majesty's for their divinity to appear, and an invitation to his box by Morris Barnett gave him the chance of applauding her consummate talent, "a talent of gold without alloy." Especially did he note her skill as an actress in *Lucia di Lammermoor*, the only *Lucia* indeed who foreshadowed the final mad scene, by her agony at the moment when her brother impresses on her the faithlessness of her lover.

A year later, when writing confidentially to Barnett from Paris, Berlioz had something to say of operatic impresarios in London.

> *Jullien has made me many fine promises of paying what he owes, but I have received nothing in the shape of cash. "Words!! Words! . . . If you see him, touch a little this question "*[1] *. . . After the article I did for Mr. Lumley in the "Débats" two years ago, and took so much trouble to get inserted, I had a right to expect a certain amount of civility on the part of that sublime impresario. When I went to London, he sent me a ticket for Her Majesty's Theatre every evening when it was empty, so I was of use in adorning the house, and as soon as Mlle. Lind began her performances I could not gain admittance. But for you, Barnett, giving me a seat in your box I could not have heard Mlle. Lind. If Mr. Lumley thinks that such behaviour is proper, he is strangely mistaken. I am quite ready at times to be a good fellow to money grubbers, people who speculate on artists' talents, but I will never let them forget that they count for nothing, that artists are and will always remain their superiors everywhere, and that they had better not treat writers so contemptuously, especially those they may have need of, for they know perfectly well how to put them in their place one of these days.*
>
> *This, my dear Barnett, is strictly between ourselves. I don't want to complain or let it even be suspected that I pay the least attention to these managers and their little ways.*

The concert at Hanover Square Rooms was to prove another triumph for Berlioz. The magnificent band which took part showed the high esteem in which he was held by the English profession. His courteous manners and general kindness, when at Drury Lane, had won the affections of all. Leading members of the orchestra from both Her Majesty's and Covent Garden joined in fraternal rivalry to do him honour. One and all declined to hear of any pay. Among those who came forward to

---

[1] Berlioz here drops into English.

help were Henry Hill and Adolphe Ganz, both of whom played the viola. Hill was at Covent Garden and Ganz at Her Majesty's. Berlioz asked Hill to play the viola solo in the *Harold* Symphony, as he had done at the first concert at Drury Lane, and sent him a letter to be read to the members of the Covent Garden orchestra; it was in English:

> *Mr. H. Berlioz has the intention to give at Hanovre Square room a concert, Wednesday the 28 Juin at half past two, there will be a rehearsal the 27 at ten o'clock. Mr. Berlioz will be most happy to excite as much interest to the Gentlemen whose names follow, as to receive their assistance at this occasion, and he takes the liberty to ask them for it.*

Then follow the names of thirty-six artists.

> *26, Osnaburgh Street,*
> *Regent's Park.*
>
> *My dear Mr. Hill,*
> *I do not know how to thank you and the other gentlemen, who have all been so good to me. While I am expecting later to be able to do so personally, would you be so kind as to tell them how very grateful I am. The Concert is not on the 28th but on the 29th (Thursday). I chose that day, a day when the opera is on, so as to run less risk of a rehearsal at Covent Garden or Majesty's Theatre. My rehearsal remains fixed for the 27th at 10 o'clock in the morning (also an opera day). I shall have the honour of writing to each of the gentlemen to let them know.*

The lithograph notification sent to Adolphe Ganz, with his name in Berlioz' own handwriting, is in the present author's possession.

> *Mr. Ganz.*
>
> *M(ajesty's) Th(eatre)*
> *Saturday, June 24, 1848.*
> *Sir,*
> *I have the honour to inform you that the rehearsal for my concert, at the performance of which you have been so good as to promise to take part, will take place at Hanover Square Rooms on Tuesday June 27 at 10 o'clock in the morning. Will you be so good as to be present and believe that I am very grateful for your extreme kindness.*
> *Yours truly,*
> *HECTOR BERLIOZ.*

QUEEN'S

. . . .

CONCERT   . . . .   ROOMS

. . . .

HANOVER SQUARE

Programme[1]

of

M. HECTOR BERLIOZ'

Grand Morning Concert

on Thursday June 29th 1848

to commence at Half past Two o'clock

PART I

Overture   " Carnaval de Rome "   *H. Berlioz*

Ballade   " Le Chasseur Danois " M. Bouché   *H. Berlioz*

Symphony   " Harold " the three principal

Movements with Viola obligato,

Mr. Hill,   *H. Berlioz*

1st movement " Harold in the Mountains,"

" melancholy," " happiness " and " joy "

2nd movement " Pilgrims' March singing the

evening hymn "

3rd movement " The Abruzzian Mountain-

eer's Serenade "

Bolero—" Zaïde "   ⎫ Made. Sabatier

Romance Francaise   ⎭   *H. Berlioz*

Adagio et Rondo. Piano-forte from Concerto   *Mendelssohn*

Made. Dulcken

La Jota, Serenada de los Estudiantes

Madame Pauline Viardot Garcia

and Mdlle. Molina de Mendi

Choeur et Ballet des Sylphes—fragment from⎫

" Faust "   ⎬ *H. Berlioz*

" Mephistophele's Song," M. Bouché   ⎭

[2] A copy of this programme is in the Berlioz Museum at La Côte-Saint-
André. This is now installed in his father's house, which was acquired in
1935 by the Society known as " Les Amis de Berlioz."

PART II

Marche Hongroise (Faust)		*H. Berlioz*
Air	M. Massol	
Rêverie " La Captive " Madame Pauline		
Viardot Garcia		*H. Berlioz*
Aria " Ah non giunge " (Sonnambula)[1]		*Bellini*
Solo Violin	M. Molique	
" Invitation à la Valse," Rondeau de Weber		
arranged for full Orchestra		*H. Berlioz*

The Orchestra and Chorus
will comprise the most eminent artistes of
Her Majesty's Theatre and the Royal Italian Opera.
Amounting to upwards of
One Hundred performers

Conductor: M. Hector Berlioz
Principal Violins: M. Sainton and M. Tolbecque
Director of the Chorus: M. Maretzek

Inspired by Berlioz' example—he was in great form—the
artists one and all gave of their best.

The *Carnaval Romain* overture, the *Pilgrims' March* (Harold)
and the *Hungarian March* were encored with enthusiasm, although
the last piece was shorn of some of its effect. Before starting it
Berlioz came forward on the platform to say a few words—
" Ladies and Gentlemen, I wish to make an apology for my
work and to offer an explanation. The effect of the March will,
I regret to say, be somewhat marred by the absence of the
drums and cymbals. They are in the room, but their use is
prohibited by the proprietors of the concert hall." Situated at
the corner of Hanover Street, it may be that the distinguished
residents of Hanover Square did not regard the Hall as an
addition to its amenities.

[1] Mme. Viardot Garcia had sung the soprano role in *Sonnambula* at Covent
Garden.

It is noteworthy that the song *la Captive*, sung by Mme. Viardot Garcia with rare pathos and depth of expression, was given for the first time in Berlioz' new version with its rich orchestral accompaniment. Paris as yet did not know it.

Berlioz in his Memoirs tells an amusing story about this melody. As holder of the Rome scholarship he was staying at the Villa Medici; and Horace Vernet, the famous painter, was head of the French School.

" When you go to the mountains again," Vernet said, " I hope you will not bring back any more songs; your *Captive* is beginning to make life in the villa unbearable; one can't move a step in the palace, in the garden or the wood, on the terrace or in the corridors, without hearing sung, hummed or growled *Along the shady wall . . . The sword of the Spahis . . . I am not a Tartar . . . The Black Eunuch*, etc. It is enough to drive one mad. I am sending one of my servants away to-morrow; I shall not engage a new one, except on the express condition that he will not sing *la Captive*." Later I developed the melody and scored it for orchestra, and it is, I think, one of the most highly coloured things that I have done.'

The poem is by Victor Hugo.

At the end of the Concert, Berlioz had a great ovation. Musical London in all its aspects was represented; the audience included Michael William Balfe, John Parry the entertainer, Henry Smart the organist and William Vincent Wallace.

When back in Paris, Berlioz gave Franz Liszt a succinct account of his first visit to London.

Sunday, July 23, 1848.

My dear Liszt,

. . . I am just back from London, where I spent nine months; the manager of Drury Lane, Jullien, a Frenchman, an idiot of a man, made bankrupt and I lost nearly everything. He did not even hand over the receipts at my first concert. When his bankruptcy was declared, I recovered my freedom of action and gave another concert on my own account at Hanover Square Rooms, this was as recently as June 29, *what time they were shooting each other in Paris. I made scarcely anything, panic had long since made the English tie up their purse strings, and the French refugees in London had too much of the national spirit not to stop resolutely at home. Nevertheless, these two hearings have thoroughly established my position in England; the entire press lauded me to the skies, with the sole*

*exception I think, of a silly old fellow in the " Morning Herald,"
who asserts that I do not know counterpoint.*[1] *I have left behind
me in London a number of supporters, a few friends, and a good
many people with mouths agape, whom the sight of novelties only
makes more stupid. They watch men in the movement going by, with
the eye of a postilion at the side of the railway track reflecting on
the passing of a locomotive. Indeed I miss London very much,
especially since I am back here . . .*

This was one of many letters that marked the long and
intimate friendship between Franz Liszt and Berlioz, a friendship the *Symphonic Fantastique* had greatly helped to bring about.
They only met the night before the first performance.[2] At that
concert Liszt's enthusiasm was unbounded, and when it was
over he literally dragged off his new friend to dinner in a
transport of admiration. By his transcription of the Symphony,[3]
a model of its kind, which he published at great expense to
himself and popularised by playing it at concerts, Liszt laid the
train for a wider recognition of Berlioz' work. An immediate
result was Robert Schumann's famous analysis of the Symphony,
based on this transcription. Liszt had attended at the British
Embassy in Paris when Berlioz married Henriette Smithson, and
signed the register as a witness.[4]

[1] A quotation or two from the "Morning Herald" of February 8th, 1848, to which
Berlioz refers, may be of interest. The critic begins guardedly:—" the cool and
unprejudiced English listener of last night probably came to the conclusion, as
far as a single performance of such matter would admit of decision, that he had
been overrated by his adherents and underrated by his detractors." But he had
obviously decided against Berlioz:—" He is evidently more ambitious than accomplished, although his astonishing knowledge of the resources of the orchestra
enable him to conceal what cannot be overlooked in the structure and development
of his works,—a disregard altogether of the principles of design and a want of
contrapuntal skill (or a disdain of it, to be more charitable) which must ever
expose him to the censure of scientific musicians " It is conceded that " his
originality is however his great distinction. He has never courted popular favour
by descending to frivolity or by writing *under* the lofty standard he has set for
himself."

[2] Paris, December 5, 1830.

[3] Christian Wessel of Frith Street, Soho, with rare enterprise, had published the
Marche au Supplice in 1840, when Liszt was giving recitals in London. Two of
Berlioz' songs also appeared, the *Strophes* from *Romeo and Juliet* and *la Belle Voyageuse*.

[4] When in Paris the author found that his register had been transferred to
Somerset House, where it may now be seen. The signature of Berlioz' other witness
is usually regarded as illegible, but it appears to be that of the composer Jacques
Strunz, to whom Balzac dedicated *Massimilla Doni*, in recognition of his help in
describing the music of Rossini's *Moses in Egypt*, a leading element in the story.

Writing to Count Wielhorski, a Russian friend, Berlioz said:

I gave two concerts in London (it is a wonder I could do so much) and the English welcomed me as if I had been a " national talent "
. . . Would you believe it, the English are now a really musical people; they like fine things, and despise trivialities.

On the eve of his departure Berlioz called upon Henry Hill, but did not find him at home. He left a note for him.

Mr. H. Berlioz being on the point of leaving for Paris came to bid Mr. Hill good-bye, and to beg him convey his thanks and his compliments to the gentlemen of the orchestra and the chorus of Covent Garden.

He started on July 13th, after sending out a farewell letter which appeared in the different newspapers.

To the Editor of " The Morning Post."

London, July 10, 1848

Sir,
Permit me to avail myself of your newspaper that I may express in a few words the feelings naturally aroused by my reception in London. I am going away, back to the country which is still called France, and which after all is my own. I am going to see in what manner an artist can live or how long he takes to die in the midst of the ruins under which art lies crushed and buried. But whatever be the term of the ordeal in store for me, I shall retain to the end the most grateful remembrance of your excellent and skilful artists, of your intelligent and attentive public, and of my colleagues on the Press for their ungrudging and constant support. I am doubly happy to have been able to admire in them the fine qualities of good feeling, talent, intelligent attention, combined with honest criticism; these afford clear evidence of a real love of art and an assurance to all the friends of music for its future; inasmuch as they have the certainty that you will not let it perish. The personal question here is only secondary; for believe me I love music much more than MY music, and I only wish that I had had more opportunities of showing it.
Yes, our Muse, frightened by all the horrible clamour which resounds from one end of the continent to the other seems to me assured of an asylum in England; and the hospitality will be the more splendid the oftener the host remembers that one of her sons

is the greatest of poets, that music is only one of the different forms of poetry, and that on the same liberty which Shakespeare used in his immortal conceptions depends the entire development of the music of the future.[1]

Good-bye, all you who have treated me so kindly, I am heart-broken at leaving you, and I repeat involuntarily the sad solemn words of Hamlet's father: "Farewell! farewell! remember me!"

HECTOR BERLIOZ.

---

[1] When this phrase was subsequently adopted by others to designate a new tendency in music, Berlioz declined to enrol himself under their banner.

Chapter Five (Sequel)

A NOTEWORTHY estimate of Hector Berlioz' place in the music of the time was published in *Fraser's Magazine* in the Autumn of the year 1848. The article was unsigned, but there can be no question, judging by internal evidence, that it was the work of Edward Holmes, for he refers to his school-fellow John Keats and quotes a letter of Mozart, whose biography he had written.

The generally high standard of musical criticism of the day, of which Edward Holmes was the acknowledged leader, provides a refreshing contrast to the present time, when a small coterie, itself incapable of appreciating the genius of Berlioz, has vainly endeavoured, until confronted with judgements of the past,[1] to arrest the growing public enthusiasm for his works.

Berlioz' impressions of his recent visit to Russia were communicated to Holmes in the course of the many friendly talks they had together. This article therefore anticipates the full account, which later was included in the *Memoirs*.

HECTOR BERLIOZ.

The most disastrous contingent of the failure of Jullien in his late operatic scheme at Drury Lane, was the disappointment which it involved to the distinguished composer Berlioz. What can make amends to the aspiring author of orchestral symphonies, overtures, etc., the mortification of success just within the grasp—a success which only wanted time to confirm, and repetition to popularise it. Let it suffice to Berlioz that he

---

[1] The present writer has in recent years supplied several such passages for insertion in the programmes of our orchestral concerts and observed with amusement the effect they have had on the critics of certain London journals,

has left a profound impression in England—that he has by the united voice of criticism been recognised as the composer who best responds to the general desire for novelty in the instrumental art, in an age where it is not composition but invention which sleeps. Nature has given him genius—the freshness, the vigour, the lion port of the great composer are his; but with these gifts on the one hand, he has received from her on the other no slight share of personal suffering and disappointment in which every distinguished master fulfils his career. It is an old story, in the main, this life of genius, in advance of its age, disdaining the lucrative path of the conventional and all its well paid toils, and devoting itself to receive the homage of posterity. But though his music may be what Keats called his own poetry— " a secretion," composed because he cannot help himself when the fit is on, we should none the less owe him our sympathy. Indeed it is the presence of simple native power in the music of Berlioz, together with the originality of his style, which mark him out as destined to resolve the problem of progress in music, by showing that everything is permitted to a composer who will dare to be personally responsible for his innovations.

The annals of music combine no more extraordinary series of facts than those which form the history of Berlioz. The laureate student in 1830, in the contest for the prize of counter-point at the Institute of the Fine Arts in Paris, he became a master of that science chiefly, it would seem, for the purpose of breaking through its rules. Considering the long time which academies have subsisted, and the very meagre fruits of genius they have produced, the conclusion that something is wanted for a composer beyond the received laws of composition was natural enough, and may have occurred to others who lacked boldness and self-reliance to act upon it. The pressure of rules forbidding this or that progression or resolution of harmony in opposition to taste and feeling, has long been an incubus on the imagination. Even Mozart himself seems to have felt it, for in a passage in one of his letters he has these words— " Rules which we composers, when *we knew nothing better*, so slavishly adhered to." This is to appreciate at its true value the doctrine of the schools, in restraining the rash and supporting the timid; yet it is plain, that if the past is to be the everlasting type of the future there can be no progress. Nor, in admitting the composer to be himself his own law, is there any fear that

the foundations of the art will become unsettled. Mere extrava-
gance is a monster, not a model; it begins and ends in itself,
with no influence to stir a stronger feeling than transient
curiosity. But whatever moves the heart of man in music, be
its form or style as strange and original as it may, will always
be found to possess some secret analogy with those principles
of art, whose truth we recognise in the permanent and the
classical. Whoever in his music transports us by emotion of
grandeur, tenderness, or grace, is certainly a great composer.
He may be a bad model for royal academies, and the horror of
professors of thorough bass but, *nascitur non fit*, he is a musician
of the true Parnassus breed.

We include in this category the youthful scape-grace Berlioz.
At 28 years of age he formed certain theories, which were
admirably adapted to his genius, because based upon a most
judicious estimate of his own powers. The academies had armed
him to encounter themselves with their own weapons, and he
possessed the advantage of transgressing in counterpoint with
a perfect knowledge of what he was doing. Having passed the
usual time in Italy, enjoined by the rules of the academy for
the completion of a laureate's education, he returned to Paris
to pursue composition on a system of his own. The academy
disowned him, and he disowned the academy; the professors
wrote and uttered severe criticisms on his productions, and he
retorted with witty ridicule. The spirit of youth turns everything
to geniality, and Berlioz was only the more confirmed and
fortified by opposition in the course which he had taken.

In the compositions which have subsequently made his fame
European—the four great symphonies, *The Requiem* the lyric
dramas, *Faust, Benvenuto Cellini*, etc., we admire the course of
a consistent and vigorous originality. No works of art struggle
with such difficulty into their true place in public estimation
as orchestral compositions of a high order. Repetition alone
affects the mass, whose eyes are always slowly opened to read
merit. How slow Beethoven's symphonies were to make their way,
and in the midst of what calumny and pre-judgment they
struggled on, is well known. In multiplying hearers of all sorts,
ignorance retains its preponderance, and the path of the heroic
composer is just as arduous as it ever was. The successor of
Beethoven must be animated by a fortitude equal to his genius.

If we consider the prosperous musicians of the day, Meyerbeer and Mendelssohn, we shall find their good fortune greatly favoured by circumstances and position in society. Both members of opulent and distinguished families, in which the art was cherished and cultivated from their infancy—introduced by degrees from the admiration of the private circle to that of the public, they naturally assumed positions of importance at the head of orchestras. But when a young man, unknown to fame, destitute of family influence, and not ushered into public with the favourable prepossessions of a coterie—not even playing any instrument, arrives by his own exertions at the same eminence, it excites wonderment and interest. Berlioz, the son of a physician at Grenoble, was sent to Paris to study medicine; accident, however, seems to have determined his bias towards music. He was probably too old to apply himself to the pianoforte, through which composers generally make their first researches in harmony; or he was disinclined to it, as too mechanical an agent for one in pursuit of purely mental music. The guitar, indeed, which in masterly hands is a splendid vehicle of modulation, we know that Berlioz touches. But the possession of this modest practical acquirement in no degree detracts from his honour in penetrating into the profoundest recesses of counterpoint and combination by the invisible steps of a purely mental process. " Who trusts to his fingers " exclaims Weber,[1] alluding to those who compose by the aid of the pianoforte, " is the child of poverty." However, the young man who assayed to take up the pen of Beethoven was a composer, and nothing more—he was no phenomenon of practical skill, and was destined to arrest public attention solely by high compositions produced at intervals, and brought into public with great expense, risk, and difficulty.

To succeed Beethoven, it was necessary to do more than Beethoven; and the readiest means to this end offered by opening a new form in the symphony. No works of art become landmarks, in which the author has not escaped the trammels of custom; and we can scarcely be said to know Beethoven in his true, vigorous originality, until he shows himself in his third symphony, the *Eroica*. Berlioz, in his *first* work, the *Sinfonie Fantastique*, developed a new style of composition, introducing new movements, an original orchestration, and a programme. From the outset he disclaimed the authority of the past, adopted

[1] Professor Max Muller tells us that Weber at times would compose with a guitar.

a design which enabled him to express vividly what he felt strongly. Music has various routes to the same goal. In listening to the symphonies of Mozart and Beethoven, we feel the power of great but vague emotions; but the invention of Berlioz seems to require the stimulus of a scene or a situation. We do not expect of music, the inarticulate art, that it shall describe with the precision of painting or poetry; but if a composer, borrowing a sentiment or situation from life, translates it into the language of sound, and so addresses the imagination, the inspiration is legitimate. So rare a thing is it to meet a true composer, that we must be prepared to take him by the hand, let him come upon us in what guise he may.

The consistency and perseverance with which Berlioz has continued in the route which he at first opened, and his success in all that he has yet attempted in music, denote that accurate estimate of his own genius which is a sign of greatness. He knows his own individuality, and has not weakened it by imperfect attempts at universal command in his art. As soon as we become reconciled to the novelty of form in his symphonies, the poetical design of the composer begins to make its true impression. The *obbligato viola* running through *Harold*, which at first appeared so eccentric a conception, embodies an idea which is at once natural and the source of peculiar beauties of effect. In like manner, the chorus introduced into the symphony *Romeo and Juliet* heightens the instrumental painting, and the work closes with a fine situation expressive of the remorse of the contending factions when too late. To know what is wanting for a composition, and to introduce it, is masterly; in most composers this is the result of habit and experiment, but in Berlioz it is a kind of intuition. Where he acquired his unheard melodies—his new rhythm—those effects of harmonising and instrumentation which hold the hearer in the utmost suspense and interest to know what he will do next—is inconceivable. No one ever exercised in music a more complete independence.

. . . .

(After describing the *Messe des Morts* he continues)

This *Requiem* seems to have settled the vexed question of the genius of Berlioz; it extorted the unanimous praise of the journals, its fame rapidly extended to Germany and Russia, and there, and, indeed, wherever else it has been heard, either in fragments or entire, it has excited general admiration.

In every art peculiar difficulties beset the progress to fame, but none are so formidable as those encountered by the composer who does not pander to the base appetite of the vulgar, but lives with fidelity to a lofty ideal. He must depend upon the zeal and ability of many people for the true expressions of his ideas, which, the newer they are, require the stricter propriety in the deliverance. How is he to gain the money or the influence necessary to put a great scheme in operation? How to prove in performances casually got up, and at long intervals, the truth of conceptions never before experimented? The progress of a composer, without post or pension, depending absolutely on his own speculations, is always curious and interesting. Had Berlioz merely possessed musical genius it might have been crushed under the difficulties of giving it utterance, but something within him rose against opposition. Success in the great departments of music, pre-supposes in the composer many distinguished endowments independent of his art. In producing a work, he is placed in contact with jarring interests and conflicting passions; he may be talked down by the rude voice of authority, or undermined by intrigue; and it is necessary in every stage of rehearsal that he be a man of address, a good general, and an eloquent and ready orator, to triumph over his difficulties. Life in the orchestra is a great school of practical philosophy. In the long run, however, there is sympathy with a bold and original composer even in the orchestra; and Berlioz has found it, though the great labours required in the rehearsing of his works has produced ill-humour in some performers, and a disposition to cavil at merit which they cannot comprehend. Nor were the old composers of the Conservatoire much more liberal. Cherubini being invited to attend the performance of Berlioz' *Requiem*, replied that it was unnecessary for him to go " to learn what ought *not* to be done." He had hoped to have his own *Requiem* performed, and could not bear that it should be postponed in favour of another; hence the irritation of that celestial mind.

But events during 18 years have been so favourable to Berlioz, and the past has so well prepared him for the future, that he is enabled to look on incidents of this kind as pleasantries. He has by his system and doctrines confessedly outraged the professors of the Conservatoires, and had nothing to expect from them but the scourge as often as they could apply it. They lashed away as long as they could, but his powers of endurance fairly exhausted them. In Germany, within a few years, opinion on Berlioz has taken a most decided tone. Lobe, the editor of the *Musical Gazette*, and Schumann, the critic and composer of Leipsic, with Dr. Griepenkerl of Brunswick, have recognised with enthusiastic admiration the genius of Berlioz; and with the greater candour and generosity, since it has been at the expense of the German national supremacy in music. Neither the active friendship of the late Mendelssohn and of Meyerbeer, nor the personal attachment of Liszt and Ernst, nor the eulogies of writers, nor the transcendent romance of a career which has introduced Berlioz personally to most of the sovereigns of Europe, could, however, place him next in his art to Beethoven. A sense of power and achievement—which there is no resisting, because in fact, it is the truth—could alone do this. When the most experienced hearers find themselves strongly moved under the influence of music of which they can discover no trace or type in known composition, the mystery has but one solution: such originality is unquestionably genius.

.   .   .   .

The most halcyon days in the remembrance of the composer are those which he passed at St. Petersburg, where for three months, he was constantly at the head of great orchestras and grand choruses. The highest advantage which a composer can desire, namely the opportunity of having his works thoroughly and efficiently studied, was here at his disposal free of expense or trouble. The amateur ladies who formed the chorus attended punctually every morning to rehearse, the musicians were full of devotion and good will, the audience were courteous, brilliant, attentive, and enthusiastic. Criticisms on the productions and genius of Berlioz were written in the public journals by amateurs of high rank. In short, good music was *fashionable*; the composer was presented to the Emperor, and both himself and his art received all the distinction they deserved. Tempted by his first success in Russia he went on to Moscow, but music there was not in the same favourable state as at St. Petersburg. With what feelings a composer who has been fêted for three months

IRLANDE

9 Mélodies pour une et deux voix avec Chœur.

PAROLES DE THOMAS GOUNET,

MUSIQUE DE

HECTOR BERLIOZ

(N°)

Paris, chez Richault, Editeur, Boul.t Poissonnière, 26 au 1.er

(10,217 à 25 R.)

The Commissioners appointed by Her Majesty for the
promotion of the Exhibition of the Works of Industry of
all Nations to be holden in the year 1851. Do
hereby nominate and appoint M. Budroy

of _____ Funnel _____ to be

a Juror in Jury _____ for the purpose of awarding
Medals to the articles of merit in that Class

Exhibition Building
Hyde Park.

5th day of May 1851

Albert
President of the Royal Commission

Registered
illegible

No. 164   Delivered July 12th

CLASS X   *illegible signature*

in a city where his compositions afforded a daily occupation to the musical world and were produced with luxurious completeness, returns to the indifferent musical life of Paris or London, we may easily conceive. From being the centre of attraction and sympathy, to lose himself again in the busy crowd until the turn of events offers him some new chance of distinction, is a dreary change. Such alternatives of excitement and endurance compose the life of our symphonist, of whose greatness there cannot be a doubt, even had he written nothing more than that one piece, the *Offertory* of his *Requiem*.

It was after all the continental success we have described that M. Jullien engaged Berlioz to conduct his operas. The opening prospect was fair, and the temptation to visit a country that has always put the stamp on good music, strong. However, the gradual failure of operas at Drury Lane involved Berlioz in the general calamity. There had been no care to bring forward his music until the theatre was on the point of closing, and then it was done without any proper announcement; consequently, the audience were not collected which should have been to hear what, as a performance, must certainly be considered the finest ever heard in England. The band and chorus were immense; and there had been 16 rehearsals of the former, and more than 20 of the latter. The whole, however, passed away like a dream; not, however, without convincing us of the existence of a great musical genius, hereafter and under more favourable circumstances to be hailed with as general delight in England as elsewhere.

Chapter Six

THE disturbed state of the Continent put foreign tours out of the question for the next two years, and Berlioz remained in Paris, earning a precarious livelihood with an occasional notice for the press. He gave his whole attention in 1850 to the foundation of a Philharmonic Society on the English model, at which some of his works were heard, but unfortunately it only lasted for two seasons; he had, however, been at pains to offer honorary membership to Sterndale, Bennett, Macfarren, Davison, Benedict and Balfe.

Berlioz' son Louis had always wished to go to sea, and his father had entered him as an apprentice on a merchant vessel. He returned home from his first voyage in March 1851; he was then aged sixteen and a half. Mme. Adèle Suat, Berlioz' favourite and devoted sister, took a keen interest in the sailor boy's career, and was waiting to hear the news.

Paris, March 31, 1851.

Louis has arrived in the best of health, he is tall and strong and full of enthusiasm for his rough profession. I went and woke him up at Havre at six o'clock in the morning last Thursday, then, after settling all his present and future business with the shipowner and visiting his excellent Captain, we left again at eleven for Paris, where we arrived at five o'clock in the afternoon. But as a result of this awful journey I was all doubled up, tired and seedy, and have been in bed ever since. To-day for the first time I feel a bit better; I've suffered terribly from rheumatism of the pectoral muscle accompanied by vomiting, or rather by retching caused by excess of nervous pain. The run of a hundred and eighty leagues in a few hours, the cold I felt at night in the train, and loafing round the streets of Havre in the pouring rain and an icy wind are more than enough to account for it all.

As for Louis, I can only repeat, he is stronger than ever, and even handsomer; the sea air has made him lose the little red patches on his face; he is patient and brave, the Captain was quite satisfied with him. But if you saw his poor hands! . . . calloused and hard like a labourer's from being chaffed by ropes, etc. . . . I have paid for his next voyage in the same ship; he will start again in a few weeks' time, perhaps in a fortnight. I have just dressed him up from top to toe " like a gentleman," and it was indispensable not only for his stay in Paris but also for his shore incursions when he goes back to the Antilles. On his last trip he had several invitations from people who, on hearing that he was my son, wished to be polite, and he had to refuse, on account of his clothes.

He was particularly sorry not to be at the ball given by our Consul at Haiti, M. Raybaud, a very nice man who aroused his pride when he spoke of me. He was so happy, at finding in the Antipodes people who knew and respected his father's name. So I have been obliged to spend more than a thousand francs in two days at Havre and in Paris. But the shipowner, when I paid him the fee for Louis' next voyage, undertook to take him free on the one to follow. So starting from his third voyage, my poor boy will be able to live from his work, until he gets his pay.

I am telling you a lot about him, dear sister, but I am sure you will forgive me. His mother, you can guess, was very happy to find him so much changed for the better. Her condition is still the same. Thank you for the details you gave me about your children and the little entertainments you got up for them.

You have not forgotten, I hope, my commissions for Uncle Marmion. If he goes to London, it would be as well if he started at once looking out for lodgings there, for that will be the chief difficulty of his stay during the exhibition.

1851 was the year of the Great Exhibition in Hyde Park, and a few days after writing this letter, Berlioz, much to his surprise, heard that he had been selected to act as French representative on the musical jury. Camille Pal, his brother-in-law, was at once apprised.

Paris, April 15, 1851.

My dear Camille,

The Minister of Commerce has just appointed me a member of the jury that is to watch the interests of the French exhibitors in London. They cannot tell me precisely when the Commission is to start. However, possibly it may be early next month . . . The

French Government will pay for the trip but, like a prudent man, the Minister writes me that he is not yet in a position to state the amount that will be allowed for expenses. It will be very modest I fear. However, unless they prove excessively stingy I shall accept. I am the only musician on the Commission, I asked for nothing, I heard of my nomination through the newspapers; it is an honourable distinction and all my London friends are delighted about it. I am very much afraid it is not a sinecure; there will be very stormy debates between the Paris and the Berlin exhibitors (of musical instruments). They are all friends of mine, I shall be between the devil and the deep sea. Anyhow, I am determined to remain a Minos worthy of these more or less harmonious trials and not to do injustice. God alone knows (though I bet He knows nothing about it) where and how I shall find a lodging. Mr. Charles Dupin, whom I saw yesterday, is in complete ignorance as to whether the English organisation has thought of reserving us a dog-kennel in the Crystal Palace or elsewhere, and so far our Minister has not bothered his head about it. Of course he is very young! . . . only four days old . . .

Berlioz had kept in touch with his London friends during his absence. In a letter to Morris Barnett, on April 28, 1849, he wrote:

Forgive me asking for a line or two, as I know how much writing you have to do every day. But you absolutely must let me hear from you. I did hope for a time that you were coming to Paris to see the absorbing " Prophète," or at least that the " Morning Post " would send you; but I was wrong, and I don't know what has become of you, nor how you are. I look upon you as a very great friend, we simply cannot leave it at that—and not exchange a greeting from time to time; so I'll begin. " How do you do! " I often think of our long talks, cigars and excellent wines at Southampton Street; and it has often happened that, forgetting the countless Lilliputian ties that keep me in Paris, I suddenly decided to pick up my hat and a little money, and said: " Bah! I'm off to see Barnett." Then, at the end of my street, turning in again feeling very stupid and downcast at my small amount of liberty. No matter! If I don't see you, I don't forget you, and one of these days I really must go and knock at your door, even though the " Journal des Débats " and the " Gazette Musicale " should be seriously annoyed at my escapade. Oh, that fire might fall from heaven and rise from hell, and join in devouring these damnable articles! . . . What a dog's life our's is!

Hearing that Adolphe Sax was starting for London for the Exhibition, Berlioz gave him a letter of introduction to Barnett, a part of which he courageously wrote in English:

> *This is to introduce my friend Sax, who has come to London to exhibit his splendid instruments. " Be kind for him as you are, and anything more, for every one; as you are for me. I will be in London "[1] in a few weeks' time. I am a member of the Commission sent by the Minister of Commerce to make a report on the Exhibition. It will be a treat to see you again.*
>
> Paris, April 25, 1851.

The saxophone, one of several instruments named after their maker, was still a recent invention when Berlioz with singular caution remarked: " skilful composers will hereafter get admirable effects from saxophones . . . in combinations which it would be rash to try to foresee." It was not given to him to witness its ultimate destiny.

Friday, May 9, 1851.

> *My dear Morel,*
>
> *. . . Now I am leaving for London, the Minister of Commerce having had the idea (a singular one for a Frenchman) of choosing me as a judge on the merits of the different musical instrument makers, who are exhibiting their work in the Crystal Palace. I cannot get over my astonishment . . . Yesterday and the day before we had meetings of the Jury, and this evening I am off by train. I shall have a lot to do, as I am the only musician on the commission . . . There is talk of a huge musical enterprise in London, the direction of which would be left to me, at which the " Te Deum " would be heard.[2] If the money is there, I will write you to come and help me, either at the rehearsals in Paris or in London. We shall want a big staff and a clever one to carry the thing through.*
>
> *P.S. I don't know yet where I shall put up, but you can write me under cover, to M.A. Duchesne, 27 Queen Anne Street, Harley Street, London.*
>
> *Louis has gone off again and asks to be remembered to you.*

On arriving in London, Berlioz went straight to 27 Queen Anne Street,[3] and found it belonged to Francis Soutten, the

---

[1] These words in English were interpolated.
[2] The *Te Deum* had to wait another four years for its first performance, in Paris.
[3] Now No. 58.

musician, who at once arranged to put him up during his stay. At this address Soutten had in the previous year inaugurated what he called the New Beethoven Rooms, where chamber music was given. Later Berlioz describes what he heard on opening the door of his room leading on to the landing (page 93). The Exhibition had been open a week, and he was soon immersed in his duties, which proved arduous enough, and for a time compelled him to defer renewing acquaintance with the associates of his previous visit.

London, Sunday (May) 18 (1851).

My dear Gruneisen,

Excuse me if I have not yet paid you my visit. The business of the Jury at the Exhibition takes up all my time. That's what it is wanting to be a " just " Minos or Rhadamanthus; this would seem to prove that virtue never goes unpunished. But I shall snap my fingers at my judicial duties one of these days, and shall then be rewarded by coming and shaking you by the hand.

27 Queen Anne Street, Cavendish Square.

Berlioz afterwards found that he was able to go about a good deal. He met other Frenchmen, writers and journalists, who had come over to see the sights, and could exchange impressions with Jules Janin, " the Prince of Critics," sent here as special correspondent by the *Journal des Débats*. They were particularly struck by the perfect order and good humour of the people. Julius Benedict was living close by in Manchester Square, and Berlioz was delighted to find his old friend G. A. Osborne, the pianist and composer, settled down at 33 Devonshire Street, just off Portland Place.

George Alexander Osborne had known Berlioz for many years. Their friendship began in Paris in their student days, when both were struggling to earn a living. Osborne's Irish humour and happy-go-lucky disposition appealed strongly to Berlioz' temperament; they were often together. Shakespeare and Moore's poetry formed a further bond of sympathy. Osborne was present at the Odéon on the famous night in September 1827, when a company of Shakespearean actors took Paris by storm with their performance of *Hamlet*, the Irish girl Henriette Smithson playing the part of Ophelia. He says that: " never before nor since was a greater success achieved on the French stage or greater unanimity of highly eulogistic praise to be found in the press " . . . " Miss Smithson was much admired and sought after. I remember being at a public ball, and while walking with her leaning on my arm, we were stopped by Mlle. George, the great French tragedienne, who took my other arm, making me look like an urn with two handles as we paced up and down the room. Many were the winks and nods I received, one gentleman loudly remarking 'Look at that monopoliser of tragedy'."

Osborne used to visit at Berlioz' house after he had married Henriette Smithson, and had an intimate knowledge of their domestic relations. He knew of the liaison with Marie Recio, which began some eight years later. Osborne records that Berlioz' " married life was far from being a happy one, owing to the uncontrollable jealousy of the lady who eventually became his second wife. One evening after dining with me, we conversed on the usual painful subject, and as I saw but one remedy, I frankly told him of it. Much to my surprise he sat down and wrote a charming letter of adieu to the lady, which he left at her lodgings when walking out with me. Next day he told me that he had gone back to the house, took the letter from the servant and tore it up, his courage having failed him."

Osborne had also told us something of how Berlioz acquired his intimate knowledge of the orchestra. " It was his constant habit to go into orchestras and sit with the different performers watching them and turning over the pages for them. In this way he learned the capacity of each instrument. Besides which he got several instrumentalists to come to his house, where they played together little things which he wrote for them to see what they could accomplish. He also asked both Chopin and myself whether such and such passage could be played on the piano."

It was Orborne whom Berlioz took with him to St. Paul's for the Service of the Charity Children, which was to make so deep an impression upon him; he confirms Berlioz' narrative in every detail. Later in the season he gave his annual Soirée Musicale, at which Berlioz was present.

It was a brilliant affair in every way. As is usual with him, this elegant pianist had the reception he deserves. Besides his own compositions, he played several pieces by Chopin with marked distinction. He seems to play better every day.

Osborne inherited a taste for music from his father, organist and lay vicar of Limerick Cathedral; his mother was a McMahon, a cousin of the famous Marshal. When 19 years of age he had decided to qualify for his profession on the Continent. He went first to Brussels, where he stayed for a year at the house of the Prince de Chimay, and thence to Paris to study pianoforte and composition. In London his polished manners and attractive personality soon won him a host of friends, and innumerable pupils came to him for pianoforte lessons. He was always ready to joke about *La Pluie des Perles*, a piece of his which was very popular at the time.

Osborne's songs, as sung by his sister Mrs. Hampton, Berlioz thought charming. Bessie Osborne, as she then was, Berlioz had met in Paris when she was staying with her brother. Though an amateur, she had taken Paris by storm with her attractive voice and beautiful rendering of Irish melodies. It mattered not what famous singer there might be at a party, there was always a clamour for an Irish melody by Bessie Osborne. Her daughter married Henri Wieniawski the great violinist, and her grand-daughter is Lady Dean Paul, the clever composer, who writes under the name of Poldowski.

Thackeray wrote to Osborne one day saying that he was engaged in writing a book, and wanted his name for one of the characters, who could not be described as a hero, and certainly bore no resemblance to him. Still he thought it best to ask his permission first. Hence the name George Osborne in *Vanity Fair*.

Berlioz had long had by him a copy of Moore's *Irish Melodies*, and in his Memoirs he tells a pathetic tale of how he set the poem *When he who adores thee* to music, at a moment when he was distracted by his love for Henriette Smithson. He would never allow *Élégie*, as he called the song, to be sung at any concert. While in London he took the opportunity of getting from Leigh Hunt the history of the poem. Leigh Hunt explained that it was based upon the love of Robert Emmet, patriot and rebel, for Sarah Curran, the daughter of the great advocate. Apparently Berlioz was still puzzled to know what the " fault " was, of which Emmet accused himself in the first lines of the poem. Emmet's address to the judge before sentence leaves no room for doubt that he was referring to his own tragic failure. Berlioz sets out the conclusion of Emmet's address as a preface to *Élégie* in the collection of his songs.

Chapter Seven

WITH characteristic energy and enthusiasm Berlioz, soon after his arrival, started drawing up a scheme for a Musical Festival in the Crystal Palace, which should add lustre to this assemblage of the arts of all nations. The success of the Great Exhibition was to be marked by this solemn function as a crowning act. The omens seemed propitious. The vast spaces of the Palace would enable him to do things on a big scale, and employ large orchestral forces and choral masses. His knowledge of our English choirs convinced him that a splendid body of singers could be recruited from the choral societies of London, Liverpool and Manchester, assisted by the choruses from the two opera-houses. He hoped also to invite musical deputations from Paris, Brussels, Cologne and other centres, while the many distinguished artists on a visit to London could be counted on to lend their aid. As general director, he determined to work out plans for four concerts in August, rehearsals to occupy a month in advance. Stages erected in the Eastern Gallery would hold a choir of one thousand and an orchestra of five hundred. Expenses he calculated at £3,700 for the first concert and £1,500 for the three others. With tickets at the price of half a guinea big receipts were certain.

He of course would conduct, and he selected items for the programme which seemed to him appropriate. His own *Te Deum*, composed two years previously and as yet unheard, must begin the proceedings. Then would come a chorus from Gluck's *Armide* and an aria sung by Signor Mario, the great tenor. The *Fête at Capulet's* from his *Romeo and Juliet* symphony should be given, forty harps being added for a specially brilliant effect he knew they would give, (this is something the present writer is still waiting to hear at a London concert, if only with twelve harps, two invariably being drowned). After an aria by Mme. Cruvelli, was to come the Prayer from Rossini's *Moses in Egypt*, also with forty harps, then Berlioz' *Hungarian March*, an unaccompanied chorus *Chant des Chérubins* by the Russian Bortniansky, and, as a fitting conclusion, the Triumphal Chorus from Handel's *Judas Maccabaeus*.

Unhappily the plan failed to materialise. He conducted no concerts in London that year, and had to content himself with writing descriptive articles for the *Journal des Débats* and carrying out his duties as juryman at the Exhibition.

His stay afforded Berlioz ample opportunities of reviewing the state of musical affairs in London. The first article he sent to the *Journal des Débats*, contained an account of our musical institutions, which is valuable for the information it contains in summary form, and the light it throws on contemporary thought, while an early visit to the Great Exhibition found him an amused observer of what there passed for Chinese Music.

It will be noted that, despite their popularity, he did not regard promenade concerts as worthy of mention, although M. Jullien had performed the *Carnaval Romain* overture and two movements of the *Harold* Symphony since his visit here. Evidently he thought they could not be classed as "musical institutions."

MUSICAL INSTITUTIONS IN ENGLAND

England, and this is a fact little known on the Continent, has during the last few years established several institutions of great importance, in which music is not treated as a commercial speculation as in the opera-houses, and in which it is cultivated on a big scale, ably, conscientiously, and for its own sake. Such are *The Sacred Harmonic Society*, *The London Sacred Harmonic Society*, in London, and the Manchester and Liverpool Philharmonic Societies. The two London Societies, which perform oratorios in the large concert room of Exeter Hall consist of nearly six hundred singing members. The voices of these singers are not very beautiful, it is true, though they appeared to me to be much superior to the Parisian voices properly so called; but their ensemble produces an impressive and essentially musical effect; in fact, these choruses are capable of performing correctly such complicated works as those of Handel and Mendelssohn, that is to say all the most difficult choral music. The orchestra which accompanies them is only inadequate in point of numbers; having regard to the simple character of the instrumentation of oratorios in general, it leaves little to be desired in other respects. I heard a performance[1] by this well organised body of amateurs, aided by a small number of professionals, before a deeply attentive audience of two thousand, of the magnificent sacred poem *Elijah*, Mendelssohn's last work. Between such institutions and those which have got our workmen in Paris to sing once a year in public more or less worthless popular songs, there is a great gulf. I cannot yet speak to the merits of the Liverpool Musical Society. That of Manchester, now conducted by Charles Hallé, the model pianist, the musician " sans peur et sans reproche," is perhaps superior to the London Societies, if impartial judges are to be believed. The beauty of their voices is at least extremely remarkable, their musical feeling very much alive, the orchestra numerous and well trained; and as for the zeal of the *dilettanti*, it is such, that over and above the regular subscribers there are four hundred people who pay half a guinea each *for the reversionary right to buy* any ticket that a regular subsciber may find himself unable to use. Supported by such zeal, a musical institution must prosper, no matter how costly it may be . . .

Among the musical institutions of London, I must also mention the old Philharmonic Society of Hanover Square, which is so well known that I need not tell you about it.

As for the *New Philharmonic Society*[2], recently founded at Exeter Hall, which is just beginning so brilliant a career, you can understand that I must confine myself to a few details. In my position as conductor of the Society, it would ill become me to sing its praises. I may mention however that the directors of the enterprise have provided me with the means of performing masterpieces under splendid conditions and the possibility (almost without parallel up to now in England) of having an adequate number of rehearsals. The orchestra and the chorus together form a personnel of two hundred and thirty executants, which include all the best English and foreign artists in London. All are possessed of unquestioned skill, coupled with great zeal and love of art, without which the best talents can often only produce mediocre results.

There are also in London several Quartet and Chamber Music Societies, of which the most flourishing at the present time is called the *Musical Union*. It was founded by Mr. Ella, a distinguished English artist, who directs it with a care, an intelligence and a devotion beyond all praise.[3] The object of the *Musical Union* is not merely to make known quartets but all fine instrumental Chamber Music, to which are sometimes

---

[1] At the Sacred Harmonic Society on Nov. 17, 1847.

[2] The reference to the *New Philharmonic* was added to the article in the following year, when Berlioz included it in his *Soirées de l'orchestre*.

[3] Berlioz and several foreign Commissioners of the Exhibition were Ella's guests at one of the matinées in June.

added one or two songs, belonging almost always to the productions of the German school. Mr. Ella, though a violinist of talent himself, has the modesty only to be the director and organiser of these concerts, without taking any part in them as executant. He prefers to add to the most accomplished virtuosi of London celebrated foreigners who happen to be there for a short stay, and so he has been able this year to include MM. Deloffre, Hill, Webb and Piatti, the celebrated violinist Sivori and the extraordinary double bass player Bottesini. The public readily accepts a system which assures it at the same time both an excellent performance and a variety of style which cannot be got by always keeping the same artists. Mr. Ella does not confine his attention to the performance of the masterpieces which figure in the programmes of these concerts; he also wants the public to understand them. Accordingly, the programme of each matinée, sent in advance to the subscribers, contains an analysis or synopsis of the trios, quartets and quintets which they are to hear; in general it is a good analysis, appealing to the eye as well as the mind, by adding to the critical text musical extracts, the theme of each piece, the most important musical figure or the most striking harmonies or modulations. One could not do more. Mr. Ella has adopted as a motto for his programmes these words in French, of which unhappily, we ourselves show very little appreciation, by the learned Professor Baillot: " It is not enough that the artist should be prepared for the public, the public must be prepared for what they are going to hear."

Unhappy operatic composers, if you have genius and emotion you can always rely on your audience preparing to listen to your works by stuffing itself with truffles and champagne and coming to the Opera to digest! Poor Baillot was dreaming[1] . . .

I must also mention the *Beethoven Quartett Society*. This Society exists solely for the purpose of giving regular and fairly frequent performances of the quartets of Beethoven. Each evening's programme consists of three; never less, and nothing else. Generally they belong to one of the three different periods of the composer's work; and it is always the last, that of the third period (the period of Beethoven's compositions alleged to be incomprehensible) which excites the greatest enthusiasm. You see there English people following the fanciful flight of the composer's thought in little pocket scores printed in London for this purpose; which might mean that several of them can read the score after a fashion. But I confess to doubts about the knowledge of these enthusiasts

[1] Baillot, the great violinist of the classical school, gave chamber music concerts in the 'twenties, at which Beethoven's quartets were heard in Paris for the first time. Berlioz described to his sister the emotion felt by him and his friends when, in the Spring of 1829, they heard the posthumous quartet in C sharp minor.

since I looked over the shoulder of one of them and caught him with his eyes fixed on page four while the performers were at page six. The amateur no doubt belonged to the school of the King of Spain whose fad was to play the first violin in Boccherini's quintets and who, being always behind the other players, used to say to them when the hullabaloo became too serious: " Go on, I shall soon catch you up! "

This interesting Society, founded if I mistake not ten or twelve years ago by Mr. Alsager, an English amateur who met with a tragic end, is now directed by my compatriot M. Scipion Rousselot, who has lived in England for many years. A witty man of the world, a skilful cellist, a clever composer, an artist in the best sense of the term, M. Rousselot was fitted, better than many others, to carry on this enterprise successfully. He has associated with him three excellent virtuosi, all full of zeal and admiration for these extraordinary works. The first violin is no other than the Austrian Ernst,[1] more thrilling, more dramatic than ever. The second violin is Mr. H. C. Cooper, an English violinist, whose playing is always irreproachable and perfectly clear, even in the playing of most complicated passages. He does not try to shine out of place like many of his rivals, and only gives his part the relative importance assigned to it by the composer. The viola is played by Mr. Hill, also an Englishman, one of the leading viola players of Europe, who besides owns an incomparable instrument.[2] Finally, the violoncello is in the safe hands of M. Rousselot. These four virtuosi have already performed the entire set of Beethoven's quartets some twenty times. More than that they do not fail to have long and careful rehearsals before each public performance. So you can understand that this quartet party is one of the most perfect that can be heard.

The meetings of the Beethoven Quartett Society take place at what are called the Beethoven Rooms. I had an apartment, for a time, in this very house.[3] The drawing-room, capable of holding at most two hundred and fifty people, is therefore frequently let for small concerts; there are many such given. My apartment being situated above the main staircase, I could easily hear the whole performance by simply opening my door. One evening I heard Beethoven's trio in C minor being played. I opened my door wide. Come in, Come in,

---

[1] Berlioz said, " Liszt, Ernst and I are, I think, the three greatest vagabonds among musicians, who have ever been pushed out of their country by a restless temperament and the desire to see things for themselves."

[2] Henry Hill played on a viola by the early English maker Barak Norman; he also wrote the analytical notes.

[3] Formerly No. 27 Queen Anne Street, and now No. 58. This house, with its open staircase and fine double drawing-room, decorated in the Adam style, is still standing. The common assumption that Berlioz was describing the old Beethoven Rooms at 76 Harley Street, where the Society had held its meetings in 1848, is incorrect.

welcome, proud melody! How fine and beautiful it is . . .
Where did Beethoven find these countless phrases, one more
poetical in character than another, all different, all original,
without even that family likeness which one recognises in the
work of the great masters famous for their prolific production?
And what ingenious developments. What unexpected movements! . . . How this unwearied eagle flies . . . How he
spreads his wings and hangs poised in his heavenly harmony!
He darts into it, is lost, ascends, comes down again, disappears
—then returns to the point of departure, an eye more brilliant,
on stronger pinions, scorning repose, trembling athirst for the
infinite . . . Well played! Who was it took the piano part?
My servant tells me it is an Englishwoman. A real talent
and no mistake! . . . Ah! What is that! A grand aria by a
prima donna?—John! *Shut the door*, Shut the door, quick,
quick. Ah the wretched creature! I can still hear her. Shut the
second door, the third; is there a fourth? . . . At last . . . I
breathe again . . .

The songstress down below reminds me of one of my
neighbours in the rue d'Aumale, Paris. Having taken it into
her head to become a real *diva*, she worked with might and
main to force the sound of her voice, and she is very robust.
One morning, a milkwoman passing under her window to go
to market, heard her piercing shrieks, and she said with a
sigh: " Ah! marriage is not all a bed of roses! " About the
middle of the afternoon, passing the same place on her way
back the sympathetic milkwoman heard the transports of the
indefatigable singer again; " Ah! My God! " she cried,
crossing herself. " Poor woman! It is three o'clock, and her
baby is not born yet! "

CHINESE MUSIC AT THE GREAT EXHIBITION

I wanted to hear the famous Chinese *The small footed Lady*,
as she was called on the placards and the English advertisements. My interest in the matter related to the divisions of
tones and Chinese tonality. I wanted to know if, as said by so
many people they are different from ours. After the conclusive
experience I have had, in my view there is none. This is what
I heard. The Chinese family, two women, two men and two
children sat on a little stage in a Saloon of the *Chinese House*
at Albert Gate. The sitting opened with a song in ten or
twelve couplets, sung by the *music master* to the accompaniment
of a little instrument with four metal strings like a guitar. To
play it he used a bit of leather or wood, instead of the quill
used in Europe to pluck the strings of the mandoline. The
finger-board of the instrument is divided into compartments,
marked by frets set closer and closer together as they approach

the sound-board, exactly like our guitars. Owing to the lack of skill of the maker one of the last frets was badly placed and produced too high a sound, just like a guitar when it is badly made. But this division none the less produced results in entire conformity with those of our scale. The accompaniment to the song was such as to lead to the conclusion that the Chinese have not the faintest idea of harmony. The air which was grotesque and abominable from every point of view, like any vulgar romance, *finished on the tonic* and never left the tonality nor the mode indicated from the beginning. The accompaniment consisted of a rhythmic figure lively enough and always the same, on the mandoline, which was scarcely if at all in tune with the voice. The most awful thing was that the young woman, to increase the charm of this curious concert, quite regardless of what her master was playing, persisted in scratching with her nails at the *open* strings of another similar instrument during the whole of the piece. It was like a child in a drawing-room, where music is going on, amusing herself by striking the keys of the piano at random; in a word, a song accompanied by a little instrumental discord. As for the Chinaman's voice, I have never heard anything so strange in my life—hideous snorts, and groans, very much like the sounds dogs make, when they wake up, stretch their paws and yawn with an effort. All the same, the burlesque melody was quite perceptible, and could have been noted down . . . This was the first part of the concert.

In the second part, the rôles were inverted; the young woman sang and her master accompanied her on the flute. This time the accompaniment did not produce any discordant effect, but followed the singing in unison quite well. The flute resembles ours except for its greater length, and the mouth-hole pierced almost in the middle instead of near the top of the tube. Further, its sound is sweet enough and pretty well in tune, or rather pretty well out of tune, and the performer played nothing outside our scale and tone system. The young woman, in comparison with her master is blessed with a heavenly voice, a mezzo soprano, similar in timbre to the contralto of a boy whose voice is on the point of breaking. She sings fairly well, comparatively speaking. I kept on thinking of one of our cooks in the country singing " Peter! my friend Peter " while washing up. The melody in a clear tonality, I repeat, consists neither of *quarter* nor *half quarter tones*, but is based on our diatonic scale, and seemed to me a little less extravagant than the *romance* of the man singer, yet it is so curious, so intangible and strange in rhythm, that I should have had a good deal of trouble to fix it on paper, had I wanted to. Of course I do not regard this *exhibition* as typical of the actual state of music in the Celestial Empire, in spite of the *rank* of the young woman, a very high rank indeed, if the director of the troupe, who spoke passable English, is to be believed. The Cantonese and Pekinese singing ladies *of rank*, who remain at home rather than come here and shew themselves in public for a shilling, must, I suppose, be as superior to this one, as the Countess Rossi[1] is superior to the Esmeraldas at our fairs. The more so as the young lady is perhaps not so *small footed* as she would have you believe, and her foot, a distinctive mark of women of the upper classes, might well be a natural foot, a very plebian one in fact, to judge by the care she took not to shew more than the point of it.

Berlioz' own son Louis, ever present in his thoughts, had gone away on a second voyage, his father not having satisfied his longing to go to sea by entering him as an apprentice on a merchant vessel at the age of sixteen. His mother was now lying paralysed and blind in her house at Montmartre, and though Berlioz was separated from her, he continued to visit her and provide for her support.

> *M. Louis Berlioz,*
> > *apprentice on the ship " Félix," Captain Duhait,*
> > *stationed at Guadeloupe French Antilles.*

> *My dear Louis,*
> *I am writing you a few hasty lines to send you greetings, and to let you know that I am in London and very busy indeed, The Universal Exhibition, the competition of all nations, and above all the huge Crystal Palace where everything is exhibited, are marvels of which I shall not attempt to give you any idea . . .*
> *Your mother is fairly well, before starting I left her money for two and a half months; I should hope the Minister will not dock me of my salary at the Conservatoire during my absence, but I can scarcely hope for as much. How are you? Did you write me on your arrival? Did you have a good voyage out?*
> *I am anxiously awaiting news of you. If your letter reaches Montmartre it will be sent on to me here. You had better address everything to Montmartre, as I do not know if I shall stop in London another whole month. Probably I shall be at Lille on June 1st. to hear the " Lacrymosa " of my Requiem which is to be performed at the " Northern Festival "; I have just had an invitation from the Lille Committee.*

---

[1] Henriette Sontag, the famous singer (see p. 110).

HENRIETTE SONTAG

EXETER HALL

Do you still like the sea? I was not ill crossing the Channel; the weather was splendid.

Try to keep all right, do your duty and take care of yourself; please do not expose yourself to the sun as you did last year; do not eat too much fruit. I should like to send you some money, but I am afraid to do so, too many letters get lost. I will keep it for you till you come back; you will want a coat, another pair of trousers and various odds and ends. I should like to see you and kiss you. Poor dear boy, I am awfully fond of you and I am sure you are fond of me. Your great-uncle Marmion[1] came to Paris where I saw him, then he came over here and we were looking for each other for three days without managing to meet.

Good-bye, dear child, I have too many jobs to do, and worn out as I am I must go on.

Monday, June 1, 1851.
London, 27 Queen Anne Street, Cavendish Square.

---

[1] A colonel in the Dragoons: he fought under Napoleon.

Chapter Eight

A MID the varied incidents marking Berlioz' stay in London, nothing left so profound an impression on his mind as his visit to St. Paul's, to attend the Annual Meeting of the Charity Children. He received an invitation from John Goss, the Cathedral organist; Thursday June 5, was the appointed day.

> 27 *Queen Anne Street, Cavendish Square,*
> *London.*
> *June 21,* 1851.

My dear d'Ortigue,

I have already made a report in M. Ducroquet's favour; so he has reason to be pleased with me. I can't say as much for the young man who plays on his organ, curse him! He regales us every day with two or three dozen polkas, not to speak of cavatinas out of opera-bouffes; no doubt he thinks the English are imbeciles! . . .

Try and read my second article in the " Débats "; if it hasn't appeared to-day in Paris, you must look out for it every day till it does. I describe the unique impression made upon me lately in St. Paul's Cathedral by the choir of 6,500 charity school children who meet there once a year. It is incomparably the most impressive, the most Babylonian ceremony at which up to now it has been my lot to attend. I still feel excited when telling you about it. It is a part of my dreams come true and a proof that the power of musical masses is still absolutely unknown. On the Continent, at all events, they have no more idea of it than the Chinese have of our Music.

By the way, have a look too at my article of the 31st *May, you will find the story of my visit to the Chinese singer and her music master. You will see what to think of the silly inventions of some learned theorists on so-called music in quarter tones. There is nothing stupider than a learned man.*

Tell Mr. Arnaud that I shall be delighted to set a series of his poems on Joan of Arc to music, if I too can manage to " hear

*voices." Let him write in short strophes; long couplets and fine
verse are both fatal to melody. It must be in the form of a popular
legend, quite simple and dignified, a succession of pieces or songs.*

*Good-bye; I am obsessed by musical instruments and still more
by their makers.*

*France is carrying the day, without question against all Europe.
Érard, Sax and Vuillaume. All the rest are merely tin kettles,
penny whistles, and fiddle-de-dees.*

P.S. My opinion of the exhibitors is for your private ear.

In the result all three of them obtained the highest award for
their respective instruments—a Council Medal. A similar
honour fell to M. Ducroquet.

The second article he sent to the *Débats* described the Service
at St. Paul's, and the Great Exhibition.

THE CHARITY CHILDREN AT ST. PAUL'S.

I was in London at the beginning of June when a cutting
from a newspaper falling into my hands by chance, I saw that
the *Anniversary Meeting of the Charity Children* was to take place
at St. Paul's Cathedral. I at once set out to get a ticket, and
after writing several letters and taking different steps I at last
obtained one by the kindness of Mr. Goss, the organist of the
Cathedral.

By ten o'clock the approaches to St. Paul's were crowded
with people, and I had some trouble in getting through. When
I got to the organ loft reserved for the choir, composed of
men and boys to the number of seventy, I was given a copy
of a bass part which they asked me to sing with the rest, also
a surplice which I had to put on, so that my black coat should
not clash with the white costumes of the rest of the choir.
Disguised thus as a cleric, I awaited the performance with a
sort of vague emotion, roused by the spectacle. Nine almost
vertical amphitheatres, sixteen tiers high, had been put up for
the children, under the dome and in the choir in front of the
organ. The six under the dome formed a sort of hexagonal
circus opening only East and West. From the latter opening
stretched an inclined plane ending above the main entrance;
it was already covered by a huge congregation, who were able
in this way to see and hear everything perfectly even from
the furthest seats. To the left of the gallery where we were, in
front of the organ, there was a stand for seven or eight trumpets
and drummers. On this stand a large mirror was placed so that
the musicians might see the reflection of the choir-master

beating time in the distance, in an angle under the dome; whence he controlled the whole of the massed choirs. This mirror also acted as a guide to the organist whose back was turned to the choir. Banners planted all round the vast amphitheatre—the sixteenth tier reached almost to the capitals of the columns—marked the place of each school, and bore the names of the parishes and districts of London to which they belonged. As the children came in and filled the amphitheatre from top to bottom, the sight reminded me of the phenomenon of crystallization under a microscope. This crystal compound of human particles was of two colours, the dark blue of the boys on the top tiers, and the white of the girls on the lower. Further as the boys had brass plates or silver medals on their jackets, these glittered as they moved like a thousand intermittent sparks on the dark background. The appearance of the girls' seats was still more curious; the green and pink ribbons worn by these little white maids, made this part of the amphitheatre look exactly like a snow-covered mountain with blades of grass and flowers peeping out here and there. Then there were the different hues among the congregation, the crimson throne of the Archbishop of Canterbury, the richly decorated benches of the Lord Mayor and the aristocracy, and high up at the other end the gilded pipes of the great organ; imagine this magnificent church of St. Paul's, the largest in the World after St. Peter's, framing the whole scene, and you will still have only a very faint sketch of this incomparable sight. The magical effect was enhanced by the order, the quietude and the serenity which reigned everywhere. No stage setting however admirable can ever approach the reality which even now appears to me like a dream. As the children, in their new clothes came to their seats with happy serious faces, without noise but with a certain pride, I heard my English friends saying to each other: " What a scene! What a scene! . . ." and I was deeply stirred when, the *six thousand five hundred* little singers being seated, the ceremony began.

After a chord on the organ, there burst forth in gigantic unison the first hymn sung by this unique choir;

> *All people that on earth do dwell*
> *Sing to the Lord with cheerful voice.*

It is useless to try and give you an idea of such a musical effect. It compares with the power and beauty of the finest vocal masses you have ever heard, just as St. Paul's compares with a village church. I may add that this hymn, with its broad notes and sublime style, is supported by superb harmonies which the organ gives out without drowning it. I was agreeably surprised to hear that the music of this hymn, for a long time attributed to Luther, is by Claude Goudimel, choir-master at Lyons in the *XVI* Century.

Though I was trembling and felt a sense of oppression, I held up, and managed to control myself well enough to be able to take part in the psalms which were next chanted by the professional choir. Boyce's *Te Deum* (written in 1760), a piece without character, calmed me down.

With the Coronation Anthem in which the children joined the small professional choir from time to time, with solemn exclamations such as: *God Save the King!—Long live the King!—May the King live for ever!—Amen! Hallelujah!*[1] I began again to be electrified. I stopped several times, in spite of my neighbour,[2] who kept on pointing to the bar we had got to in his part, thinking that I had lost my place. But when I heard the psalms in three time by J. Ganthony, an old English master (1774), sung by all the voices, with trumpets, drums and the organ—a truly inspired composition with its grand harmonies, my feelings overcame me, and I had to use my Music as Agamemnon did his toga, to hide my face. After this during the sermon preached by the Archbishop of Canterbury one of the ushers took me round—I was still *lacrymans*—to different parts of the church, to see the spectacle in all its aspects. He left me among the smart people near the pulpit, as it were at the base of the crater of the vocal volcano. And when the eruption began again, for the last psalm, I must admit that the effect was twice as great there as elsewhere. As I went out, I met old Cramer, who in his excitement, forgetting his perfect command of French, began calling out to me in Italian; *Cosa stupenda! stupenda! La gloria dell'Inghilterra!*

Then Duprez . . . Ah! The great artist who, during his brilliant career roused so many people to enthusiasm, that day received payment of his debt of gratitude, but that debt was paid not by the French but by the English children. I have never seen Duprez in such a state; he stammered, he wept, he began to ramble; while the Turkish Ambassador and a handsome young Indian[3] passed near us, cold and sad as if they had just heard their dancing dervishes howling in their mosques.

The children do not know music, they have never seen a note in their lives. Every year for three months they are taught the hymns and anthems, for the *Meeting*, mechanically with the aid of a violin. They learn them by heart.

Berlioz' allusion is to J. B. Cramer, widely celebrated as pianist and composer of the *Studies*, and long a notable figure in

[1]The " Coronation Anthem " and the " Hallelujah " chorus.

[2]G. A. Osborne.

[3]The *Times* speaks of " two eastern chiefs whose conspicuous and magnificent attire was the object of general observation."

English musical life, then eighty years of age, while Gilbert
Duprez was principal tenor of his day at the Paris Opera.
Duprez told Berlioz he had come over expressly to hear his
young daughter Caroline sing at Her Majesty's, where she had
made a successful début, and won high praise for her finished
art.

The Annual Meeting of the Charity Children,[1] transferred to
St. Paul's in the time of George III, always proved a great
attraction to foreign musicians on a visit to London. Many
years before Haydn had had an emotional experience similar
to that described by Berlioz. He listened in silence till he could no
longer contain himself, and exclaimed loud enough to be heard
by all around him, " Well, never till now did music make upon
me the impression I get from this simple religious and powerful
performance." General regret was felt when it was ultimately
decided to discontinue the meetings. The last was held in June,
1877.

THE GREAT EXHIBITION

I left St. Paul's still intoxicated by the music and wandered
down, for no particular reason, to a Thames steamboat. Once
on board I was subjected to a twenty minutes' drenching
downpour. I landed, wet through, at Chelsea, and having
nothing to do there, I walked back and tried to get to sleep;
but after such a day sleep was out of the question. The tune
of *All people that on earth do dwell* kept on running in my head.
I was in St. Paul's again and saw the church revolving round
me. I had the curious illusion that all was changed into
pandemonium—the scene in Martin's well-known picture;
instead of the Archbiship, Satan sat on his throne; instead of
thousands of the faithful and the children being grouped
around him, the fiery glances of demons and the damned
gleamed through the visible darkness, and the iron amphitheatre on which these millions were seated vibrated in a
terrible way, and gave forth frightful harmonies.

At last, worn out by these continuous hallucinations I made
up my mind, though it was scarcely dawn, to go out and walk
towards the palace of the Exhibition. In a few hours' time I
was due there for my duties as juryman. London still slept;
none of the Sarahs, Marys, Kates, who every morning wash
the doorsteps were to be seen sponge in hand. A gin-sodden
old Irishwoman smoked her pipe, huddled up alone at the
corner of Manchester Square. The cows lay ruminating

[1] William Blake's poem *Holy Thursday* gives another picture of the scene.

listlessly on the thick sward of Hyde Park. The little three-master, that plaything of a sea-faring people, rode drowsily on the Serpentine. A few lights shone from the high glass windows of the palace open to *all people that on earth do dwell*.

The watchman, on guard at the entrance of this " Louvre," who was used to seeing me at all sorts of untimely hours let me pass in. At seven in the morning the deserted interior of the palace of the Exhibition was a sight of peculiar grandeur— a vast solitude, no sound to break the silence, soft lights falling from the transparent roof, dry fountains, silent organs, motionless trees, a harmonius display of rich products brought from all corners of the earth by a hundred rival peoples. Ingenious works, the products of peace, instruments of destruction recalling war, all the causes of movement and noise appeared at the time to hold mysterious converse in the absence of man, in that unknown tongue which one hears with the *ear of the spirit*. I settled down to listen to their secret dialogue, thinking I was alone in the palace; but there were three of us, a Chinaman, a sparrow and I. The *slits* of eyes of the Asiatic had opened before their time, or perhaps, like mine they had not closed at all. With a little feather brush he carefully dusted his beautiful porcelain vases, his hideous grotesques, his lacquer, his silks. Then I saw him take a watering-pot, go and draw water at the basin of the glass fountain, and coming back, tenderly water a poor faded flower, Chinese doubtless, which stood in a wretched European vase. Then he came and sat down near his shop, looked at the gongs hanging up, and moved as if he were going to strike them; but as he remembered he had neither brothers nor friends to wake up, his hand which held the hammer of the gong dropped, and he sighed. " *Dulces reminiscitur Argos*," said I. Assuming my most gracious manner, I went up to him, and thinking that he understood English said, " *Good morning, sir*," full of an unmistakably kindly interest. His only response was to get up, turn his back on me, open a cupboard and take out some sandwiches and begin to eat without noticing me, with a rather contemptuous look on his face for such *barbarous* food. Then he sighed again . . . He evidently was thinking of his own succulent sharks' fins fried in castor oil with which he regaled himself in his own country, of soup made of swallows' nests, and those famous wood-louse jams for which Canton is famous. Faugh! The thought of such rude cookery makes me sick, and I slipped away.

Passing near a big " 48 " cannon, cast in Seville, which seemed, as it faced Sax's shop near by, to defy him to make a brass instrument of the same calibre and voice, I frightened a sparrow hidden in the jaws of the brutal Spaniard. " Poor survivor from the massacre of the innocents, fear nothing, I will not denounce you; far from it, here! . . ." I drew from

my pocket a piece of biscuit which the usher at St. Paul's
had given me the day before, and scattered crumbs on the
floor. When the palace of the Exhibition was built a flock
of sparrows had chosen as their home one of the big trees
which now adorn the transept. They persisted in stopping
there in spite of the threatened progress of the construction
work. These birds could scarcely imagine they would be caught
in such a cage of glass and iron trellis-work. When they
realised it, their surprise was great. The sparrows sought an
escape by flying to the right and the left. Fearing they might
damage some of the fragile exhibits, it was decided to kill
the lot, and it was done with pea-shooters, twenty different
kinds of trap and treacherous *nux vomica*. My sparrow, whose
retreat I had discovered and did not betray, was the sole
survivor. He is the Joash of his people:

I'll save him from the fury of Athaliah's rage.

As I uttered this striking line, improvised at the moment, a
noise not unlike the sound of rain was heard in the vast
galleries; it was the jets of water and the fountains which the
keepers had just set playing. The crystal castles, the artificial
rocks, vibrated under the shower of liquid pearls. The police-
men, the good unarmed " gendarmes," respected by everyone
with so much reason, came to their posts. Mr. Ducroquet's
young apprentice went up to his master's organ, and thought
of the new polka with which he was going to regale us; the
ingenious manufacturers of Lyons came to complete their
fine display of goods; the diamonds, prudently hidden during
the night, reappeared glittering in their cases; the big Irish
Clock in *B flat minor*, which commands the Eastern Gallery,
persisted in striking, one, two, three, four, five, six, seven,
eight strokes, quite proud at differing from her sister in the
church[1] in Albany Street, with its harmonic resonance of a
major third. The silence had kept me awake, these noises lulled
my nerves; the desire to sleep became irresistible. I was just
going to sit down in front of the Erard grand pianoforte,
that marvellous exhibit of the Exhibition; I was leaning on its
rich covering and was going to sleep, when Thalberg struck
me on the shoulder, and said: " Eh, my good fellow! The
jury is assembling. Come along! Look sharp: To-day we have
got to examine thirty-three musical boxes, twenty-four
accordions and thirteen bombardons! "

How to eliminate the sparrows was a problem indeed, for it
was clear that shot-guns could not be used in a glass-house. So
Queen Victoria appealed to the Duke of Wellington—" Try
sparrow-hawks, Ma'am," was his laconic reply.

[1]Holy Trinity.

A battered old elm tree which stood inside the Exhibition, may still be seen in Hyde Park, opposite Knightsbridge Barracks; while the crystal fountain offers a somewhat exiguous display in the Central Hall of the Palace,[1] happily long since set to crown the heights of Sydenham.

The pianist Thalberg was one of the members of the musical jury class Xa; among the others were Sir Henry Bishop (chairman), Sir George Smart, Sterndale Bennett, Cipriani Potter, Dr. Henry Wile and Chevalier Neukomm. When Thalberg's opera *Florinda* was produced that year at Her Majesty's, Berlioz excused himself from coming to the work that interested him. He was there on the first night, and sent a frank account of it to the *Journal des Débats*: he found but little to admire.

Berlioz remarks upon what he felt was the singular practice of inviting the jurors of five or six different classes to form a *group*, to whom the awards already made by each class were submitted for revision by a majority of votes. One day he found himself with other musicians, called upon to decide as to the propriety of awards made to various makers of surgical instruments! When the jurors of the Paris Exhibition, following the English precedent, adopted the *group* system, Berlioz felt bound to admit its moral efficacy, though the reason for it escaped him.

[1]Alas, it was burnt down in 1936.

Chapter Nine

B ERLIOZ found time in the evenings to visit the two Italian Opera-houses. Seeing an announcement in the papers of a performance of *Il Franco Arciero* (Italian for *Freischütz*), he went to Covent Garden,[1] and his impressions were the subject of one of his articles to the *Débats*:

Just a word about Covent Garden to commend the care with which the public is reminded that there, as at masked balls, *a decent attire is indispensable*. One evening recently they gave *Freischütz*. I was curious to see what sort of a figure certain recitatives of my acquaintance might cut with Italian words. The Covent Garden management had come to Paris in a great hurry the previous year to ask me for them. I arrived dressed up to the nines, white tie, white waistcoat, black dress-coat, patent leather boots, my costume lacked nothing. Unhappily a fancy in trousers, of a very dark colour however, had taken the place of the classical black. It was quite enough to get myself stopped as I went in and be shewn the door most politely by an attendant. It was suggested to me as a consolation that I should take a seat in the sixth tier among the gods . . . I am not proud, so up I went. The overture admirably played, was encored, despite the fact that Mr. Costa introduced an untimely ritardando in the midst of the most furious excitement of the coda, and despite the use of a modest big drum, a single one, and an honest ophicleide with which he thought it was his business to enrich Weber's orchestration. After the first chorus, I listened attentively, as I was anxious to know whether the recitatives were more or less effectively done than they were in Paris. But I listened in vain, I did not recognise a bar. All was changed, there was even in several places a piano accompaniment, with the rustle of the violincello proper to recitatives in Italian opera-bouffes. What did it all mean ? They had, however, last year,

[1]The present Opera House, erected to E. M. Barry's design, was opened in 1848. The older building had been burnt down two years before. John Flaxman's bas-reliefs, partly reinstated on the new facade, invite admiration for their classic grace discernible under a thick coating of London grime.

at the first performance of *Freischütz*, put on the bills a name
which left me in no doubt; the English papers had also printed
it. The result of my enquiries showed that the recitatives,
bought and paid for by the management, the composer of
which had been named to the English public by the Press in
chorus, in reality had never been sung at all at Covent Garden.
They too, had been shown the door at the outset and sent to
the devil by an employé at the opera-house, who offered to
write others. No doubt the poor recitatives had not got on
black trousers!

Berlioz might have added that the book of words, on sale in
the House that night, contained the unequivocal statement:
" the music by Weber (with recitatives by Hector Berlioz) as
represented at the Royal Italian Opera, Covent Garden."

He saw *Fidelio* twice at Her Majesty's,[1] and once at Covent
Garden. Again in the *Débats* he wrote:

It was first given at Lumley's opera-house, an impersonation
by Mlle. Sophie Cruvelli. This young and still rather incorrect
singer showed great qualities of sensibility, energy and musical
intelligence. Her splendid voice, sonorous and thrilling
throughout its range, shewed up marvellously especially in
the wonderful air in the first act and in the quartet in the
prison scene. I was really moved and carried away . . . Sims
Reeves (Florestan, who is here called Fernando[2]) scarcely
managed the difficulties of the famous air in which Haitzinger
has left such stirring memories in Germany and France. So
this piece passed almost unnoticed. Reeves has the fault
common to English singers whose intonation is not irreproachable; he often sings sharp.

It had been advertised that the prisoners' chorus in the 1st
Act would be performed, not only by the whole of the chorus,
but by all the *members* of the opera-house, Calzolari, Gardoni,
Massol, Poultier, Coletti, etc. It is quite true they appeared,
but without their assistance contributing much to improve
the performance of this sweet sad piece. They scarcely seemed
to know more than two or three notes of their parts each.
They should have been introduced in the great finale, given
time to learn it well, and urged to put into it all the entrain
and enthusiasm of which they were capable, with which after
all the music overflows. It is exactly what they were not asked
to do. The finale produced a mediocre effect; fire, assurance
and volume of tone were lacking. Reversing the order of

[1]The site of Her Majesty's Theatre is now occupied by the Carlton Hotel and
His Majesty's.
[2]It was at Covent Garden that the name Ferdinando was substituted for Florestan;
at Her Majesty's it was merely Italianised to Florestano.

things at Covent Garden, Mme. Castellan sang the part of Fidelio correctly, but without much fire, it is too high and too tiring for her, and Tamberlick electrified the whole house in Florestan's air. He was made to repeat it amid uproars of applause. Well done, this is a rendering! It is alive, vibrant, woeful, distracted; it tears at your heart strings; *c'est Beethoven tout entier à sa proie attaché*[1] . . .Tamberlick is the only singer to my knowledge who, since Haitzinger, has made this sublime piece intelligible. Further the grand finale was dashed off with explosive feeling, thanks to the bite in his high chest notes and the enthusiasm which possessed him. Formes was excellent as the gaoler, and Tagliafico did well in the perilous role of the governor. Both overtures[2] are always encored at Covent Garden, so keen is the English public on Beethoven when it is well played.

When in Paris Berlioz had never failed to note the occasions on which conductors sought to embellish the works of great masters by amending their orchestration, and in like manner when in London he expressed his condemnation of the practice.

That composers are great masters, armed with great authority, that they are called Mozart, Beethoven, Weber or Rossini, matters little. Mr. Costa[3] has for a long time thought fit to give them lessons in instrumentation, and I say it with regret, Balfe has followed his example. The two orchestras include 3 trombones, an ophicleide, a piccolo, a big drum and cymbals; in their opinion such things are there for use. In Mozart's masterpiece, during the supper scene, while Don Juan's private band is playing the naïve music of the *Cosarara*, an incredible solo on the ophicleide has been introduced (at Her Majesty's Theatre), which clashes in the most curious way with the occasion and the style of the piece. The bovine snorts of the instrument disfigure the delicate instrumentation of Mozart, as would mortar flung on a picture by Raphael. The result is as ugly as it is incredible; for in the Devil's name, was not Don Juan a man of taste, and if one of his people had thought fit to come and play him Martini's[4] music on the ophicleide during a meal, the elegant Spaniard would certainly have told Leporello to show the noodle the door.

[1]cp. *C'est Vénus toute entière à sa proie attachée*—Racine's *Phèdre*.
[2]Berlioz tells us of the practice in London of performing *Leonore* No. 3 as an *entr'acte* before the second act of *Fidelio*. This is surely the most appropriate place. In recent years a German conductor thought better to give it as an interlude to cover the change of scene before the close of the second act; a veritable anti-climax after the ecstatic joy of the duet, which should lead straight to the triumphant finale.
[3]cp. page 64.
[4]Vincenzo Martini y Soler.

As for Mr. Costa (at Covent Garden) he has actually introduced the trombones and the ophicleide in old Marcellina's Air in Rossini's *Barber*; and to make the entry of the four instruments stand out more—the effect just there sounds like the chandelier falling into the stalls in a general lull—the violins are always made to play *pianissimo* up to this point, and suppress the little accents of *rinforzando* marked by Rossini in the incidental phrase which alternates with the tune. The sudden attack of the brass is the more devastating, and makes you jump in your seat, when you hear it, and wonder if the ceiling has collapsed . . . What an admirable and skilful contrivance! . . . In the finale of the opera he has, of course, added the big drum and cymbals and the four big brass instruments: that is only too true. He has done as much in that of *Don Juan*, he has added the big drum and cymbals and the ophicleide in the *Freischütz* Overture; the big drum, the cymbals and the same dear ophicleide in the finale of *Fidelio*— *they are stuck in everywhere!*

Reading these comments in the Press, Balfe being a good fellow would just laugh them off, but they were scarcely a tactful prelude to Berlioz' association with Costa in the production of his opera *Benvenuto Cellini* at Covent Garden two years later. Berlioz then realised this well enough.

Don Juan at Her Majesty's has the advantage of having a Zerlina such as there never has been, Mme. Sontag. It is impossible, I think, for the liveliest imagination to conceive a more complete realisation of Mozart's ideal. Ingeniousness, grace, charming awkwardness, instinctive coquetry, everything one looks for, everything one has dreamed of for this delicious *bricconcella* united with the most incomparable perfection of singing.

He also saw *The Marriage of Figaro* at Her Majesty's.

I saw a performance of Mozart's *Figaro*, but it was a brazen version—trombones and ophicleide blazing away.

Mme. Cruvelli played the page, and for the first time in my life I heard this part sung in an intelligible fashion.

Mme. Cruvelli however does it with a little too much stress on the passionate side; she makes too big a boy of Cherubino; she makes him out to be almost a young man. Mme. Sontag *was* Susanna. It seemed scarcely credible that such a talent should exist, even if you have felt its charm. Here is a singer who understands the art of delicate nuance, who commands the whole gamut of expression, and knows how to use it!

Manibus date lilia plenis.

Henriette Sontag, remarkably gifted both as singer and actress, was born in 1805. She had had the great distinction of being asked by Beethoven, when she was only nineteen, to take the soprano parts—and what parts they are—at the first performance not only of the Ninth Symphony, but also of the Mass in D. She was a comely creature and very attractive, and princes, diplomats and aristocrats vied with one another in paying her court. Lord Clanwilliam, English Ambassador at Berlin, pursued her so persistently, that to indicate his habit of following Sontag he earned the nickname of *Lord Montag*. Her brilliant operatic career came to a sudden end when she met a young Sardinian diplomat, Count Rossi, fell in love, and decided to give up her profession to become his wife. It was a really happy marriage. When, however, the political troubles of 1848 affected their fortunes, she decided to return to the stage she had left some eighteen years before, her husband this time resigning his position. He might have retained his post as Minister, had he consented to a formal separation from his wife. Lumley made her a splendid offer to appear at Her Majesty's, where Berlioz heard her. She was no longer young. W. Ganz saw her in all her roles as he was engaged at the Opera House; he says: " she sang with great charm, and her face as she sang was a pleasure to look upon; she was still very pretty."

Berlioz went to Covent Garden for a special performance of Mozart's *Magic Flute*. As he thought there was no prospect of ever hearing the work in Paris, he took the opportunity of describing his own impressions of Mozart's music, and gave a detailed account of the opera.

> The large and religiously attentive audience were unaffected by the absurdity of the libretto. They do not go to the Opera to hear the words, it is even good form to say they bother very little about the story . . . The public wish to pay homage to Mozart's genius . . . The only merit of Schikaneder's stupid book is that it gave Mozart the opportunity of putting into music the calm grandeur and veiled sublimity believed to have been inherent in the cult of Isis . . . At the earnest entreaty of the bankrupt manager Mozart consented to set the book to music for the sum of 300 florins, which he never paid him. He even swindled him out of his rights in the score by having several copies made which he sold to his colleagues in Germany and elsewhere. Poor Mozart avenged himself by telling Schikaneder he was a knave and inviting him to dinner . . . In the overture, the most famous and

entrancing example of the fugal form in instrumental music, you find none of the vulgar tricks which the contrapuntists so often use. Here there are real ideas, unflagging inspiration, a tissue of harmony and melody which is a model of pure art . . . I do not believe the stories of the impossible speed at which Mozart is said to have composed it, for the simple reason that a copyist could not have written it down in the time . . . The overture was played by the Covent Garden orchestra with finish and precision, though the tempo adopted by Mr. Costa was rather lacking in animation . . . There are three different styles in the music; the passionate, the buffo and the ancient religious . . . In Tamino's delightful air there are certain phrases which recall the *Marriage of Figaro*, and so rob it of much of its originality. The interruptions of the melody by the orchestra, which takes part in an attractive dialogue, are generally resented by singers. Mario, whose voice is better suited than most to do it well, gave the air in rather a luke-warm fashion. He apparently finds the style of it less sympathetic or less familiar than that of the modern Italian operas . . . The composer has impaired the exquisite beauty of Pamina's single air by a vocal exercise of two bars, which one is astonished to find there. Mlle. Grisi sang her small part with resignation. It did not give sufficient scope for her talent . . . The Queen of the Night has two airs, the eccentric form of which invariably attracts the public. Amid beauties of the first order vocal exercises rising to the F. in alt are introduced . . . But, Mozart had a sister-in-law, Constance[1] Weber, a diva, whose exceptional voice ascended to one doesn't know where; willy-nilly she had to shine and be given the chance of using her high notes—a fine reason for a master to spoil his finest inspirations by such incongruities. Divas possessing the high soprano register are not of this opinion. Mlle. Zerr may be the exception, but she uttered the little cries of an angry hen with a happy audacity which brought down the house. The public is always the same in the face of difficulties successfully overcome whatever their absurdity. What would have happened if Mlle. Zerr had stopped when she came to the vocal exercises and substituted a dance on a tight rope ? I like to think the public would have been logical enough to applaud with equal warmth; the difficulty would perhaps have been greater, and they would have had the added charm of the risk run by the artist . . . The attractive pieces Papageno has to sing, so popular in Germany, straight-way ensured the success of the whole work . . . Ronconi and Mme. Viardot entered into the spirit of the duet of Papageno and Papagena with rare wit and sense of comedy. Lastly there are the marvellous numbers in the second act in which

[1] Josepha Weber. Berlioz not having a reference book by him in London, gave her name incorrectly as Constance.

Mozart uses what I call the ancient religious style . . . All
are of an incomparable beauty and maintain an immense
elevation of style and thought . . . They are the Egyptian
pyramids of music defying time and feeble imitations. Especially
admirable are the sovereign majesty and impressive calm
of Sarastro, to whom all in the Temple of Isis do obeisance.
Never did pontiff of any ancient religion equal him in
grandeur, serenity, strength and sweetness combined. The
burthen of his song is the infinite goodness of the divine
powers and the charm of virtue; all about him thrills in
harmony with his voice. The mysterious echoes of the monument give answer. To hear his voice is to tread with him
the sacred pavements, to breathe strange perfumes in an
atmosphere suffused with new and paler lights. Forgotten
is the earth, its troubled passions. As he sings he himself falls
into sublime ecstacies. In calm and grave accents his voice
assumes a grander note, then subdues its tone and is still.
There is a deep and mysterious silence, it is the threshold
of the infinite.

Nothing is more difficult to attain than the exact nuance
of expression needed for this music, in spite of its extreme
simplicity. A shade too much force in the voice, the least
acceleration of the rhythm, and the charm is broken . . . No
singer in the part had ever quite satisfied me, but Formes
who sang it here seemed to me to understand it better than
them all, and got within an ace of a perfect rendering I
almost forgot to mention the remarkable fact without precedent
since they put an old masterpiece at Covent Garden. *Mr.
Costa this time added nothing to Mozart's orchestration.* He allowed
the composer to dispense with cornets, two horns and even
the big drum, cymbals and the ophicleide, instruments which
one was beginning to think of prime necessity in these operas.
He confined himself to adding four bars to the priests' chorus
in the Second Act; let us hang out the flags!

At a performance of Mendelssohn's *Son and Stranger*, introduced by Benjamin Webster at the Haymarket Theatre between
two farces, Berlioz heard Willoughby Weiss, " a very good
English baritone whose acting is full of humorous spirit," and
Miss Louisa Pyne, " a soprano with a voice of great range and
beautiful timbre, whose talent appears to entitle her to better
parts than those in which she appears." Alfred Mellon was the
conductor.

He mentions that Mme. Charton Demeur had an ovation at a
Philharmonic concert. " She sang the great scene from *Freischütz*
with a breadth of style, a sensibility, a dramatic élan, a certainty
of intonation, and a fidelity which won her besides the applause

of the audience, the support of all true artists, astonished at hearing a celebrated piece, which is usually done so badly, so well rendered . . . She is indeed a remarkable singer who may well succeed in the passionate style, as she has in the light and ornamental."

Mme. Charton Demeur amply justified his belief in her powers, and was chosen by him to create the part of Dido in his opera *The Trojans*, when at long last it was performed in Paris (in a truncated version).

Chapter Ten

BERLIOZ suddenly remembered that he had not as yet written to his favourite and much-devoted sister, Adèle Suat, and imparted to her the unhappy situation in which he now found himself in London.

(London), July 1851.

My dear Adèle,

I am seizing the moment's rest which is left us to-day to let you have news of me. I have been in London for a month and a half, fully occupied with the stupid job of examining the musical instruments sent to the Exhibition. There are days when I am utterly discouraged and I am on the point of returning to Paris. You can have no idea of the abominable drudgery which is my special duty. I have to listen to wind, wood and brass instruments. My head splits as I listen to hundreds of wretched things, one more false than the other with perhaps three or four exceptions.

Apart from this boring task my stay in London is very agreeable; I get invitations from everywhere; from the Lord Mayor, the Mayor of Birmingham, my fellow countrymen, without counting the polite attentions of which the English are so lavish. Then the operatic managers, the concert givers, who have to be satisfied as far as possible, and the exhibitors who have explanations to give me. It is only on Sundays that I can breathe and I go for a stroll in the country.

In the midst of all this I have to find time to write long articles for the " Journal des Débats " ; I have already done three, one of which only has appeared. So you will not be astonished that I missed my uncle who came over here for only three days. He wrote me addressing his letter to No. 19 instead of No. 27 in my street, this meant a day's delay in getting his note and when I went to his hotel he had just left.

As for our meeting in the Crystal Palace, there was not much chance of that, it is too huge and too crowded.

The Minister of Commerce pays me well enough for my stay in England, though with curious stinginess they make us pay our own travelling expenses. Consequently please tell Camille not to send either to Paris or here the note which he writes me every two months. I shall let him know when I return to France.

For the first time to-day the warm weather has put in an appearance; I was afraid I should not see any Summer this year. Now the London parks and the squares are charming; as for the surrounding country it is delightful and has a richness of vegetation which we can see nowhere on the continent. I tell you nothing of what I see here that is curious or interesting, you can see all by reading my letters in the " Journal des Débats " . . .

I am expecting a letter from day to day from Louis who is now at Guadeloupe.

I have good news from Henriette; that is, her condition is still the same.

Good-bye dear sister.

My love to your husband and your children.

P.S. I shall be here for a fortnight more, at the very least.

During the last few weeks of his visit Berlioz, when able to escape from his duties at the Exhibition, penned further articles for the *Débats,* including another experience of Chinese music, and a personal observation on the subject of the musicians at that time to be seen in the London streets.

CHINESE SOIRÉES MUSICALES ET DANSANTES.

Now listen to a description of the *Soirées musicales et dansantes* given by Chinese Sailors on board the junk they brought to the Thames; and believe it if you can.

When you have got over the inevitable first feeling of horror, the fun of it all gets the better of you; you laugh, you laugh consumedly, you burst with laughter. I have seen English women end by falling in convulsions on the bridge of the celestial ship; such is the irresistible power of the oriental art. In the orchestra there is a big gong, a little gong, a pair of cymbals, a kind of wooden box or bowl placed on a tripod which is struck with two sticks, a wind instrument rather like a coco-nut, this is just blown into and makes a howling sound—Ho! Ho!; and lastly a Chinese violin. But what a violin! It is a big bamboo tube six inches in length, in which is stuck a very thin wooden stalk about a foot and a half long, it looks rather like a hollow hammer with the handle driven in near the head of the mallet instead of in the middle. Two fine strings of silk are stretched, no matter how, from the upper end of the handle to the head of the mallet. A fabulous bow, pushed or drawn across the two strings, makes them vibrate. The two strings are discordant, and the sound which results is awful. Yet the Chinese Paganini, with a seriousness justified by the success he obtained, holds his instrument on his knee, and uses the fingers of his left hand at the upper end of the double strings to vary the intonations, as in playing the violoncello, but at the same time does not observe any division relative to tones, semitones or any interval at all. This produces a continuous series of scratchings and feeble mewings and gives the idea of the pulings of a new-born infant of a ghoul or vampire.

In the tuttis, the hub-bub of gongs, cymbals, violins and coco-nut is more or less frantic, according as the man of the wooden bowl (who at least would make an excellent drummer) accelerates or slackens the rolling of his sticks on the box. Sometimes even, at a sign from this virtuoso, who is conductor, drummer and singer combined, the orchestra stops for a moment, and, after a short silence, strikes a single blow with good effect. The violin goes on mewing by itself. The tune passes successively from the conductor to one of his musicians in the form of a dialogue. These two using the head voice, mingled with some chest or rather stomach notes, appear to be reciting some legend of their own country. Perhaps they are singing a hymn to their god Buddha whose statue with fourteen arms adorns the interior of the large cabin of the ship.

I shall not try to describe the jackal cries, the death rattles, the turkey gobblings, in the midst of which in spite of close attention, I could only discover four *perceptible notes* (*d, e, b, g*). I must admit the superiority of the *Small-footed Lady* and her music master. Evidently the singers of the Chinese house are artists, and those of the junk are only bad amateurs. As for the dancing of these strange fellows, it is on a par with their music. Never have I seen such hideous contortions. They looked like a troupe of devils twisting, grimacing, jumping, to the hissing of all the reptiles, the roaring of all the monsters, the metallic din of all the tridents and all the cauldrons of hell . . . It will be difficult to convince me that the Chinese people are not mad . . .

On another occasion Berlioz pointed to laws in force in China from time immemorial as worthy of admiration for the protection they afforded to composers' works. To disfigure, or to interpret them in an unfaithful manner, to alter their text, feeling or spirit was not permitted, and was the subject of severe penalties, e.g. the loss of an ear, or for a second offence, of both ears.

LONDON STREET MUSICIANS.

There is no city in the world, I am convinced, where so much music is consumed as in London. It follows you even in the streets, and that is sometimes not the worst of its kind; several talented artists have found out that the lot of the itinerant musician is incomparably *less laborious and more lucrative* than that of the orchestral musician in an opera-house. Work in the streets only lasts two or three hours a day, in the opera-house eight or nine. In the street you have fresh air, and can breathe, change from place to place, and only play a short piece from time to time; in the opera-house, you have to put up with a stuffy atmosphere, the heat of the gas, and remain seated and playing continuously, sometimes even during the intervals.

At the opera moreover a second-class musician scarcely gets £6 a month; the same musician if he starts his career in the public streets is almost sure to pick up double that sum in four weeks, and often more. In this way it is possible in the London streets to listen with real pleasure to little groups of English musicians, white like you and me, who have thought it advisable to black their faces to attract attention. These mock Abyssinians accompany themselves on the violin, guitar, tambourine, a pair of drums and castagnets. They sing short songs for five voices, which are quite pleasant in point of harmony and often original in rhythm and melodious enough. More than that, they are lively, which shows that they are not displeased with their task and are happy. There is a shower of shillings and even half-crowns after each of their pieces. Besides these peripatetic troupes of true musicians, you may hear a handsome Scot, dressed in the curious Highland costume, and followed by his two children also wearing plaid and kilt, play on the bagpipes the favourite air of the Clan Macgregor. He too is lively and gets excited at the sound of his rustic instrument; and the more the bag-pipes murmur, sputter, bawl and frisk, the more his gestures and those of his children become rapid, proud and menacing. You would think that the three of them, these Gaelic chiefs, were going to conquer England.

Then you see coming forward, sad and sleepy, two poor Indians from Calcutta, in turbans and dress which once were white. Their only orchestra is two little drums shaped like barrels, of which dozens can be seen at the Exhibition. They carry the instrument on their stomachs suspended by a cord, and strike it softly on both sides with the stretched fingers of each hand. The feeble noise which results is in rather curious rhythm, and by its continuity, resembles that of a quick tick-tack of a mill. One of them then starts singing, in an Indian dialect, a pretty little melody in *E* minor, one covering a sixth, (from *E* to *C*) so sad in spite of its lively movement, so painfully suggestive of exile, slavery, discouragement, absence of the sun, that one is seized, listening to it, by an access of home-sickness.

Berlioz was well acquainted with the history of the Clan Gregor. When a student at the Villa Medici, he had submitted to the authorities in Paris, as evidence of his industry at Rome, an overture entitled *Rob Roy Macgregor*, introducing the old Scottish air *Hey, tutti, taitie*, now better known as *Scots, wha hae.* It is true he had afterwards decided to discard the work, when he found the leading themes served him to better purpose for his symphony *Harold in Italy.*

In the matter of sacred music Berlioz found " nothing very interesting to record " during the latter part of his stay. He mentions however that he was present at Westminster Abbey at a *Purcell Commemoration.*[1]

> A small choir of mediocre voices with organ accompaniment sang hymns, anthems and motets by the old English master. A small and reverential congregation attended the service. It was cold, stagnant, sleepy, slow. I endeavoured to feel admiration, but only experienced the opposite sensation. Then the recollection of the childrens' choir at St. Paul's Cathedral flashed on my mind, I make an invidious mental comparison and went out, leaving Purcell to slumber with his faithful adherents.
>
> One Sunday Sir George Smart was kind enough to do me the honours of St. James's Chapel of which he is organist. Alas! music has deserted this habitation since the kings and queens have ceased to live in the palace. A few singers with no voice, eight choir boys with too much, a primitive organ, that is all one heard. This chapel was built by Henry VIII., and Sir George shewed me the small door by which the king came to return thanks to God and sing *Hallelujahs* composed by himself, every time he invented a new religion or had a wife's head cut off.

My dear Camille (Pal),
> *I am leaving here the day after tomorrow . . .*
> *I was beginning to get very tired of all this business, the more so as kind M. Buffet, Minister of Commerce, finding that our stay in London was getting too long, announced that from July* 15

---

[1] The Annual Purcell Commemoration took place on the last Thursday in June, the choir being " strengthened by the attendance of many members of the Purcell Club."

onwards he would not pay us any more. In spite of this strange proceeding I did not want to quit my post before the end of my task as member of the jury.

It will only finish tomorrow. And if I had allowed myself to give it up, I could see that it would have involved considerable harm to the French exhibitors, who, in the result, have been treated with conspicuous fairness. So the Minister will drive into bankruptcy those of the jury who have done their duty best; last week there were only twelve of us; to-day I am alone. The musical task has been the toughest and the longest.

Good-bye, I am expecting news of you at any moment. Kind regards to Mathilde. I do not know if we shall see each other this Autumn. I should like to.

It was during this visit that the project was formed of founding a new orchestral society in London, of which Berlioz was to be offered the post of conductor.

Chapter Eleven

THE following year brought Berlioz his greatest triumph in London. He was engaged to come here in March, and conduct the concerts of the New Philharmonic Society which had just been formed. This venture was not, as the name might suggest, a rival to the old Philharmonic; its principal object was to bring forward new or unknown works of merit, which the elder association did not condescend to notice. It was intended to foster the rapidly growing taste for music in this country, and appeal to musical amateurs in general, by charging moderate prices for admission (from half a guinea down to half-a-crown). Exeter Hall was chosen as the *locale*, and an orchestra of 110 executants, the largest ever collected together in London, had been engaged.

The names of the leading instrumentalists in the country, many of them soloists, figured in the list: Sivori (leader), Henry Hill, H. C. Cooper, J. T. Willy,[1] J. W. Thirlwall, N. Mori, Pollitzer, Kreutzer (1st. violins); Jansa, John Loder, Love, Marshall, Perry, W. Ganz (2nd violins); Goffrié, Westlake, Trust, Waud, Vogel, Webb (violas); Piatti, Rousselot, Reed, Rogé, Goodban, Paque, Hausmann (cellos); Bottesini, Rowlands, Winterbottom, Pickeart, Pratten (double bass); then there were Rémusat the flautist, Barret and Crozier the oboe players, Henry Lazarus (clarinet), 12 harpists including Wright and Trust; Charles Harper, Standen, Hooper, Jarrett (horns), Thomas Harper (trumpet), Arban, Koenig (cornet), Cioffi, Winterbottom (trombone), Prospère (ophicleide), Édouard Silas, and afterwards W. Ganz (antique cymbals), T. P. Chipp,[2]

---

[1] John Thomas Willy gave the first performance in England of the *King Lear* Overture, then newly published, at one of his promenade concerts at the Princess's Theatre in December, 1840.

[2] At his house in Great Portland Street, T. P. Chipp shewed Ganz the large "Handel drums" as he called them, they dated from Handel's time, which he used for the oratorios at Exeter Hall. Their other name "Tower drums" was based upon the belief that one of them was made from the skin of a lion in the menagerie at the Tower of London.

and Ista (drums). A chorus of similar size directed by Frank Mori, the young composer, had also been engaged. The programmes of the six concerts, which included Beethoven's Choral Symphony and various works by Berlioz, aroused the greatest expectations. Frederick Beale was manager; of him we shall hear more.

Just before arrangements were concluded, Berlioz had said to General Alexis Lwow: " Paris is impossible now, and I think that next month, I shall go back to England, where there is at least a real and persistent *wish to like* music. Here every place is taken; mediocrities devour each other, and one watches the dog-fight with as much anger as disgust."

Auguste Morel heard the news soon after.

Paris, February 10, 1852.

My dear Morel,

. . . *Beale has engaged me to organise and conduct six big concerts in London at Exeter Hall, rather too large a place, I think . . . I am to have considerable personnel* (300 *performers for all the concerts and additional ones when I need them for particular works). At the first we shall do five pieces from my " Requiem "; there is some talk also of doing Beethoven's Choral Symphony; it was once murdered by Costa, and has not been heard in London since. There will be a lot to do. I am very sorry not to have you next me in the battle, for it will be one. Beale who conceived the idea is firmly supported by all the young generation of English artists, and by very rich amateurs who are tired of always hearing the same repertoire at the Hanover Square concerts, or at least I hope so.*

The pieces from the *Requiem* were not given.

The dimensions of Exeter Hall (since re-placed by The Strand Palace Hotel) were:—76 ft. broad, 131 ft. long, 45 ft. high. It held more than 3,000 people, without discomfort. A great improvement had recently been made to it by the construction of a new roof, upon more correct acoustic principles, which materially added to the effects of the music. The narrow frontage on the Strand consisted of a lofty portico formed of two handsome Corinthian pillars, with a flight of steps from the street to the Hall door. The word " Philadelpheion," in Greek characters over the entrance indicated its dedication to charitable uses, though the " No Popery " placards, so conspicuous below, could scarcely be said to inculcate brotherly love.

The London engagement clashed with another momentous event, Franz Liszt's revival of *Benvenuto Cellini* at Weimar. The Paris failure of 1838 was to be avenged in significant fashion, and Berlioz could not be there.

The author of this book has been entrusted with the publication of a letter which sets out Berlioz' anticipations before starting for London and· his apprehensions lest the works he was to conduct should receive scant rehearsal.

Paris, February 11, 1852.

Dear Sister,

I was to have started for Weimar tomorrow, and here I am. This is what has happened.

I have perhaps already told you that my opera " Benvenuto Cellini," translated into German, has been in rehearsal at Weimar under Liszt's direction for the last four months. It was fixed for the 16th of this month, the Grand Duchess's birthday, and the date still holds good. I was going to hear it, and be present at the dress rehearsal, and afterwards I was going to have a benefit concert which would have brought me in quite a nice sum. And now Liszt tells me that our two principal singers, the Tenor and the Prima Donna, are ill. The doctor can't promise any improvement for a fortnight or three weeks. So everything is upside down; if in spite of anticipation they get well soon enough to be able to sing on the 16th, I should hear of it too late. I shall not even be able to hear the second or third performance because I have other much more important business which requires my presence in London at the end of the month. A celebrated English entrepreneur and music publisher etc., Mr. Beale, has asked me to organise and act as conductor to a big new musical institution, which is to begin by giving six huge concerts in the biggest hall in London (Exeter Hall). The cost of the six concerts alone will be 70,000 francs. After several letters we have come to an agreement; I am to get a thousand francs a concert, and remain in London to conduct them all, from the beginning of March to June 15. Beale is known as a man of honour and for his great wealth, so I hope this time to be paid, to say nothing of other delightful results for myself if the business succeeds; for I shall get fixed up in England, or at least be on the way to finding a place there. The moment I have the luck to be taken up in England, I shall be earning money quickly in one way or another. It will be a second edition of my old struggle with the old guard in their old positions. Beale's prospectus has made a big stir, and that has fluttered them already. The very idea of the innovations of which they know I am capable, and the slap in the face of this invitation to a Frenchman to conduct the biggest musical enterprise ever yet attempted in London of course exasperates them. Fortunately, if I have enemies in London I have also plenty of friends. I have given Beale his instructions and it looks to me as if he was really inclined to carry them out. He wants to do everything in a handsome way. I am afraid of one thing only, the haste shewn in all musical matters in England and the artists' hatred of rehearsals. Their affection for what is nearly right, but not quite, for scratch performances, may ruin everything, as it is a question of learning a new and very difficult repertoire. That is the only point upon which I don't feel quite at my ease . . .

Berlioz had of course been in correspondence with Franz Liszt on the details connected with the production of his opera, and explaining his enforced absence from Weimar.

My dear Liszt,

  . . . Adieu; there was no need to recommend Joachim to me, I have known him and appreciated his talents for a long time past. I am leaving in a few hours' time. You will have already seen in the Paris newspapers some account of the " New Philharmonic Society." There is a devil of a shindy in London, and when I get there I shall have my hands full with the whole of " Old England," their fury is at boiling point. The Andersons, Costas and others are irritated beyond measure. Provided Beale lets me have the necessary rehearsals, their opposition only amuses me . . .
Paris, Tuesday, March 2. (1852).

Berlioz accompanied by Marie Recio arrived in London on Thursday March 4, and drove to 10 Old Cavendish Street, where he had taken rooms over the shop of Nurse, the carver and gilder. He lost no time in getting to work, the first orchestral rehearsal being called for the following Monday at Caldwell's Rooms, 20 Dean Street, Soho. A special feature in the policy of the new society was that no expense should be spared in the matter of orchestral rehearsals; such a thing was at that time unknown in the practice of our older institutions. For England it was a great innovation. My father in his diary provides a valuable note of what was done. A youth of eighteen, he had been engaged as one of the second violins. Berlioz proved to be a wonderful conductor, his beat was clear and precise, and he took infinite pains to get everything right. All the members of the orchestra were intensely enthusiastic and anxious to please him. As Berlioz was about to start the *Queen Mab* Scherzo of his *Romeo and Juliet* Symphony, he turned to my father and said: " Ganz, I want you to play the antique cymbals with Édouard Silas in the Scherzo," here used to get a particularly delicate effect. Berlioz had brought these little silver cymbals with him from Paris. This was a great honour, as Berlioz records with particular appreciation that at St. Petersburg they were played by Romberg and Maurer, the two conductors of the Imperial Orchestra. Three further orchestral rehearsals were held, as well as several separate ones for the Choir. Berlioz, we know, firmly believed that, to obtain a faithful interpretation of modern works, separate practices for different sections of the orchestra should precede full rehearsals. One afternoon he asked Ganz and Édouard Silas to meet him at Robert Addison's, the music publisher, at 47 King Street, Golden Square, to try over the passage for the little cymbals. When they got there, they found that players of the tambourine, triangle, kettle drums and big drum had also been invited for, what seemed to them strange, and unusual, a sectional rehearsal of the percussion department. At the concert Berlioz had the young men near him, so that the sound of the little cymbals should not be lost.

London, March 17, 1852.
10, *Old Cavendish Street,*
Oxford Street.

Dear Sister,

I have not had a moment to write you since I arrived; I got here on the 4th. I had a lot of things to settle before leaving Paris, and I obtained three and a half months' leave from my duties as Librarian. M. Bertin was sorry to see me go, because of the importance my articles have assumed, now that political writing is a nullity.[1] Nevertheless, he realised the impossibility of my declining the proposal which had come from London, it was in every way too important.

[1] The *Journal des Débats* was out of favour with the new regime resulting from Louis Napoleon the Prince President's *coup d'État* of the previous December. A strict Press cencorship had been instituted, which extended even to foreign publications. Travellers landing at Boulogne-sur-mer found themselves relieved of their copies of the *Illustrated London News* and even of *Punch*.

As a matter of fact, I have got the rarest kind of entrepeneur, honest, clever, charming and rich, supported by three other capitalists ten times richer than himself. On my arrival he paid me £50 in advance (1,250 fr.) and I have no doubt I shall be paid with the same regularity every month. My position here, musically speaking, is also a very good one; I am in for a struggle with all the old gang in London, it is true, but I am well armed, I am a born fighter, and all the young English musicians are interested in backing me up.

I have an admirable orchestra, a select choir, and everything is going as well as could be up to now except for the solo singers: I shall never be able to put life into them. Marble statues if they could sing would sing as these people do. Our first concert will be on Wednesday next.

Every day all my time is taken up with rehearsals and a thousand and one things that have to be done, visits to my colleagues on the press, etc. Before leaving Paris I had a letter from Louis dated from Havana; he is quite well and says he will be back very soon. I sent him a letter to Havre telling him what to do as soon as he arrives. He will come over and visit me either here, or at Folkestone (when I shall go to meet him) before re-embarking and after having been to Paris to embrace his mother.

As for your ideas on cock-fights and other English matters, please excuse my not answering. You know about as much of the state of things in this country as you do of the Antipodes. Your opinions date from the time of the Empire . . .

Good-bye, a rehearsal is on in a moment, and I must close.

Frederick Beale was the manager. The capitalists were Sir Charles Fox (the famous engineer of the Great Exhibition of 1851), Sir Morton Peto (who constructed the leading railways in this country) and Thomas Brassey (railway contractor to the Great Northern Railway). Dr. Henry Wylde was also a guarantor.

Louis Berlioz was away on his third voyage; he had left in January touching at Plymouth on the way out.

The rehearsals had now been carried through to Berlioz' satisfaction, and in the first programme the names of Gluck and Mozart, Beethoven and Weber testified to the faith that was in him.

PROGRAMME of the 1st Concert, March 24, 1852.

PART I.

Symphony in C.	Jupiter	*Mozart*
Selection from	" Iphigenia in Tauris "	
	(for chorus)	*Gluck*
	Air of Thoas, Chorus and	
	Dances of Scythians.	
Triple Concerto	MM. Silas, Sivori and	
	Piatti	*Beethoven*
Overture	Oberon	*Weber*

PART II.

Dramatic Symphony	Romeo and Juliet	*Hector Berlioz*
	(Part I.)	

1. Introduction. Combats—Tumult—Intervention of the Prince. Prologue: Choral Recitative. Strophes : Contralto Solo. Scherzetto: Tenor Solo and Semi-Chorus.
2. Romeo Alone. Sadness. Distant sounds of revelry. Grand Fête at Capulet's Palace.
3. Capulet's Garden in the stillness of night. Chorus of Capulet youths quitting the Fête. Love Scene.
4. Queen Mab. Scherzo.
Soloists: Miss Dolby and Mr. Lockey, and Chorus.

Fantaisie for double bass		*Bottesini*
	Signor Bottesini	
Overture	William Tell	*Rossini*

Conductor M. HECTOR BERLIOZ.

The evening was a triumph for Berlioz. Mozart's *Jupiter* symphony displayed the fine quality of the orchestra, skilfully trained to present a masterly *ensemble*. Not a point was lost or clouded, and in the swift movement of the fugal finale the players reached the " acme of execution." Berlioz' interpretation was faultless in clarity, balance of phrase and rare nobility of style. The selection from Gluck's opera created a perfect furore. Any objection purists might have felt at finding the bass solo given to a dozen men's voices was answered by the spirit and animation of the performance, and the whole selection was unanimously redemanded. *Iphigenia in Tauris* was a work of which Berlioz was passionately fond. He well knew what he was about; in his Memoirs he explains how some vocal music can be sung with far greater effect by a highly-trained chorus than by a conventional soloist. The overture to *Oberon* played with rare impetuosity and finesse ended amidst an uproar of applause, and a general recall of Berlioz. The Dramatic Symphony of *Romeo and Juliet,* his masterpiece in the poetical vein, made a deep impression. The novel form of the work with its immense variety of idea and effect and its vivid orchestral colouring completely captivated the hearers. The chorus did their part with a will. After the excitement of the *Fête* at Capulet's, enhanced by the sound of the twelve harps effectively placed in front of the violins, came the lovely music to the *Scène d'amour.* This was felt to be the most beautiful passage in the Symphony. The gaiety and verve, the elfin grace of the exquisite *Queen Mab* Scherzo also aroused the keenest delight. The whole work was played with marvellous precision; the audience followed each movement with the closest attention, and applauded the composer to the echo, calling him back again and again.

The Literary Gazette noted that " the Hall was filled. The effect of so vast an assemblage, 1,500 we understand, all in evening dress, may be imagined."

The next day he wrote an enthusiastic letter to his friend d'Ortigue.

March 25.

My dear d'Ortigue,

I am writing you a line so that you may know that I had a pyramidal success last night. Recalled, I don't know how many times, and applauded both as composer and conductor. This morning I have read in " The Times," " The Morning Post," " The Morning Herald," " The Advertiser " and other papers dithyrambs such as have never been written about me before. I have just written M. Bertin to tell our friend Raymond of the " Journal des Débats," to make a hotch-potch of all these articles so that at least the thing may be known. There is consternation in the camp of the " Old

Philharmonic Society." Costa and Anderson are drinking the bitter cup to the dregs.

I could only get one of your ladies passed into Exeter Hall; the other managed to get in too (by paying I fear). Anyway don't worry. All goes well. I've got a rattling fine orchestra and an admirable entrepreneur (Beale) who spares no expense. Since yesterday he has been half mad with delight. This success is a great event for music here as well as for me.

Good-bye, the best of greetings. Go and see Brandus, if you have time and ask him to get the pith of the English papers for his " Gazette." I assure you it is really odd, quaint.

He also wrote off to Franz Liszt:

I have just had a most glorious success at Exeter Hall, and that at the very time when you were conducting the second performance of " Benvenuto " at Weimar. The New Philharmonic Society has a very large and magnificent orchestra; 20 first violins, 18 seconds, etc. . . . and it all goes like a good quartet.

I have been asked here for details, which I cannot give, about the resurrection of our Lazarus at Weimar.

John Francis Barnett the composer, then a boy of thirteen, (whom the present writer knew in later years as a shy retiring little man) used to recall how he was fascinated at this concert by the delicate charm of the *Queen Mab* Scherzo of the *Romeo and Juliet* Symphony. " The day after," he said, " I saw Berlioz walking down Regent Street. I noticed how deep and poetical was the expression of his features. There was also a look of pleasure on his face, such as one might expect after his artistic triumphs the previous night."

Berlioz wrote in reply to full particulars sent by Franz Liszt from Weimar:

Dear and excellent friend,

This morning I was at Exeter Hall at nine o'clock, and left at five like a drowned rat. I slept two hours, and now as a complete change I am answering your letter.

I found it on my table on coming in, it was a pleasure and relief. The details you give are most interesting, I might even say astonishing. What did you do to get all the instrumental rumpus

*there in my score? . . . Well, you must have the power of Moses,
and your baton, when it strikes the walls of the theatre, can make
the instruments emit waves of sound, just as his rod drew water
from the rocks. On the other hand, what could have frightened
the Tenor in Cellini's air? If he cannot sing that, what can he
sing? Is it the high C in the middle? That bar could easily be
altered. I rather think this proves that Mr. Beck belongs to the big
school of singers who don't sing. Fortunately you are well able to
hold your own . . .*[1]

*The fragments of the " Flight into Egypt," a mystery attributed
to Pierre Ducré, an imaginary " master of music," are the result
of a little joke I played on our honest Dogberrys the French critics.
I let them hear the " Farewell of the Shepherds " of this old master
twice, and when they had thoroughly spread themselves about the
old school and pure and simple style, I let out my name.*

*I am very sorry that Joachim is not here yet, we were counting
on him for the second concert at least. Now the ranks are filling up,
so that I don't know how I can place him . . . Good-bye, don't
forget to make a speech to your orchestra, thanking them in my name.*

London, April 12,
  10, *Old Cavendish Street,*
    Cavendish Square.

Joseph Joachim, then a young man of twenty, arrived soon
after from Weimar, where he had taken part in the performances
as leader of the orchestra. He was anxious to thank the composer
personally, for " the stimulating ideas " his music had aroused.
When Berlioz met him, he was depressed at having so little
do in London, and not having the opportunity of playing with
a big orchestra. Berlioz told him about his experiences at the
Service of the Charity Children the year before, and said he
meant to go again. This time he took Joachim with him to St.
Paul's, as well as G. A. Osborne. All three donned surplices,
and sang in the choir.

---

[1] In the French there is a pun on the name Beck " tu as bec et ongles."

Chapter Twelve

THE news of what had happened on March 25, had gone round the town, and the Hall was crowded in every part for the Second Concert.   But Berlioz included no work of his in the programme.

PROGRAMME of the 2nd Concert. April 14, 1852.

PART I.

Overture	Anacreon	*Cherubini*
Recit & Aria	" One hope and one joy " (Iphigenia) Mr. Alexander Reichardt	*Gluck*
Chorus	Chant des Chérubins	*Bortnyansky*
Concerto in F Minor	for Pianoforte M. Alexandre Billet	*H. Wylde*
Liebeslied	" Mein Herz das ist " Mr. Alexander Reichardt and Chorus	*F. Gumbert*
Symphony in C Minor		*Beethoven*

PART II.

Overture	Magic Flute	*Mozart*
Operatic Masque	The Island of Calypso	*Edward Loder*
	Soloists: Mrs. Sims Reeves, Miss Dolby, Mr. Sims Reeves, Mr. Weiss.	

Conductor:
M. HECTOR BERLIOZ

Beethoven's fifth symphony in C Minor was " *the* performance of the night." The overwhelming climax of the last movement literally took the audience by storm and drew forth tumultuous demonstrations of approval. Bortnyansky's *Chant des Chérubins* Berlioz had heard in St. Petersburg, where the Russian choral singing had made a deep impression upon him. He brought away some of the music, and introduced it here as he had done in Paris. Dr. Henry Wylde conducted his own Concerto.

Some of the critics said that the performance of Loder's work, which came at the end of the programme, was not satisfactory, and attributed it to insufficient rehearsals. So Berlioz wrote a letter to the composer.

April 15, 1852.

To Mr. Loder of Manchester.

Sir,

I think it my duty to offer you some explanation on the subject of the performance of your beautiful work at the Second Concert of the New Philharmonic Society. You were absent, but be assured I neglected nothing to secure for it a good rendering. Some faults, however, by no means numerous, were remarked upon in the performance of the last part. We might have had to deplore more serious accidents; Mr. and Mrs. Reeves, entrusted with the parts of Telemachus and Eucharis, not having been present at any orchestral rehearsal. At the first (with wind instruments and double quartet) I had to sing as well as I could, the airs and recitatives, while conducting the orchestra. At the second, with eighty musicians, Miss Dolby and Mr. Weiss alone attended. At the third with half the orchestra at Blagrove Rooms,[1] I was again obliged to sing the parts of Eucharis and Telemachus, Mr. and Mrs. Reeves having again failed to put in an appearance.

These two artists only rehearsed once, with me at the piano, on the same day as the Concert, and the orchestra was therefore obliged to accompany them without having heard them.

You will understand therefore why the band occasionally lacked confidence in the recitatives.

All the same, the only grave error we have to regret was not committed by the orchestra. I was on the point of refusing to conduct

[1] At 71 Mortimer Street: musicians will remember them better as the Cavendish Rooms and their use, till pulled down, for operatic and other rehearsals.

the performance of a work of such importance, in such strange conditions. The fear of seeing my conduct misconstrued restrained me. It is the first time in my life I was ever placed in such a position. You see I was forced to submit and it is I alone, I assure you, who have been compromised.

Sims Reeves was ready with his reply. He resented the whole blame being placed on his shoulders. He explained his absence from the first rehearsal on the ground that he had not received any notice of it, from the second that he was indisposed, and from the third that he had heard nothing whatever of it. Then, with a touch of sarcasm, " Were the *fautes peu nombreuses*, which elicited a chorus of condemnation from the press, committed by us only ? Did our non-attendance at rehearsal make the band falter in the recitatives and songs of the other artists ? Did it give unsteadiness to the choristers ? M. Berlioz says that the only *grave error* was not committed by the orchestra, but with due deference I must observe that it appears to me a very *grave error* to perform a work from first to last without any successful attempt at accent or colouring, and this was certainly the case with the execution of Mr. Loder's *Calypso*, and will be so whenever a conductor (however excellent his merits) consents to give a new and *bel ouvrage* to the public with only one full band rehearsal."

The Cantata was regarded as not equal in interest to his earlier works, notably *The Night Dancers*, an opera which made his name.

The composer Spontini had died the year before, and Berlioz, while paying a tribute to his memory, thought he could induce the London public to reverse their earlier verdict of indifference to *La Vestale*, a work he himself profoundly admired. He therefore was anxious that Spontini's widow should be present, and sent an invitation.

> 10, *Old Cavendish Street,*
> *Cavendish Square,*
> *London, April* 20, 1852.

My dear Érard,
     I have just got away from the first rehearsal of the selection from " La Vestale " which we are performing at our Third Concert, at Exeter Hall, Wednesday next, the 28th, at 8 o'clock.

The wonder and admiration of the musicians cannot be described. As there has been a kind of anti-Spontini faction at work in London for the past twenty-five years, they had come full of prejudice. I think I am going to give them all a rude lesson. The effect will be immense, we have a choir of 120, and an enormous orchestra. Staudigl is singing the High Priest, Mme. Novello, Julia; for Licinius I have Reichardt a young German tenor, I am teaching him his part and he will do.

So try and come with Mme. Spontini and be at this triumph, which will be twenty times more important than any on the continent. Come and see the smashing of a cabal a quarter of a century old! It is a joy you don't get every day.

Come! do come!

Staudigl was of course the famous bass singer, very popular in England at the time. He might have told Berlioz how he had taken the part of the High Priest when the opera, given at Covent Garden in German in the summer of 1842, and conducted by my grandfather, Adolphe Ganz, aroused the admiration of *The Times*, which commented on the indifference of the public.

Alexander Reichardt enjoyed considerable popularity here in the fifties, both in opera and in oratorio. Berlioz described his style and voice as a tenor of the first water, sweet, tender, sympathetic and charming. Though a good musician, he is responsible for the song " Thou art so near and yet so far," which had a great vogue.

A letter written that evening to Henry Jarrett,[1] the orchestral superintendent, shows Berlioz' attention to practical matters. The " deputy " system was evidently in force at that time.

Tuesday evening, 20.

My dear Jarrett,

I have your attendance sheet before me. But I see the signature of Mr. Winterbottom, and he was not there.

I leave you the business of notifying those you want on Thursday.

But on Saturday the four singers are expected, try and get Sivori and 6 or 7 other first violins, 6 second violins, 4 violas, 4 violin-cellos, 4 double bass, 1 flute, 1 oboe, 1 clarinet, 2 bassoons, 2 horns.

[1] In later years, as agent to Mme. Sarah Bernhardt, he won her respect for his inexorable firmness and honesty.

Thursday next we shall have to get Mr. Wright. 1. *Rémusat;* 2. *The second oboe;* 3. *The second clarinet;* 4. *The second, third and fourth bassoon;* 5. *The horn who was not there to-day;* 6. *The trumpet who was not there to-day;* 7, *Second and third trombone;* 8. *Arban and Philips;* 9. *Chipp and Ista;* 10. *Ganz and Silas;* 11. *Thomson (for the tambourine);* 12. *Hughes (bass drum); at least* 6 *first violins,* 6 *second violins,* 3 *violas,* 5 *violoncellos,* 4 *double bass.*

As to instruments, we want 2 *pairs of drums,* 1 *cymbals,* 1 *triangle,* 1 *tambourine,* 1 *big drum,* 1 *harp.*

For Thursday we also want a tamtam (Gong). Beale promised me one. But keep your eye on it.

Berlioz called a fourth rehearsal on the morning of the Concert.

During this week lively interest was aroused in musical and legal circles by the strange case of Mlle. Johanna Wagner (niece of the composer). The rival opera-houses both claimed to have secured the " exclusive " services of the celebrated singer. Lumley and Gye printed challenging advertisements in the newspapers. Then came Gye's announcement that she would definitely make her London début at Covent Garden on the following Saturday as Fides in the *Prophète*. Marie Recio at once asked Berlioz to try and get seats, and he sent a note[1] to Davison (in English),

Mon Cher Davison,

Can you have two places for us in your Box for the Wagner's Début?

If I have not an answer to-morrow, I will understand an impossibility.

Thousand friendships,

Your,

H. BERLIOZ.

The day before the performance Lumley applied *ex parte* to Vice-Chancellor Parker, and obtained an injuction restraining her from appearing at Covent Garden. She had the consolation of finding herself the central figure in a leading case.

---

[1] Davison's Memoirs incorrectly ascribe this to the year 1856.

PROGRAMME of the 3rd CONCERT April 28, 1852

PART I.

Overture	Fingal's Cave	*Mendelssohn*
Dramatic Symphony	Romeo & Juliet (Pt. 1)	*Hector Berlioz*

Soloists:
Miss Dolby and Mr.
Alexander Reichardt
and Chorus

Chorus & Air de Danse	Armida	*Gluck*
Concertstück for pianoforte	Mme. Pleyel.	*Weber*

PART II.

Overture	Euryanthe	*Weber*
Selection	La Vestale	*Spontini*

Chorus of Vestals, with Solo
Contralto: Grand Vestal. Duet:
Julia and Licinius. Aria: Julia.
Finale: Pontiff and Double Chorus.

Soloists:
Mme. Clara Novello, Miss A.
E. Byers, Mr. Reichardt and
Mr. Staudigl.

Overture	Egmont	*Beethoven*

Conductor:
M. HECTOR BERLIOZ.

A second hearing of the *Romeo and Juliet* Symphony deepened the impression previously made. The public was evidently delighted with the work, and greeted each movement with immense applause. As a further illustration of the beauties of Gluck's music, Berlioz chose the *Jardin des plaisirs* scene from *Armide*, a favourite of his. This was much liked. His expectations however, as to Spontini's *La Vestale* failed to materialise. Dr. Wylde conducted the *Euryanthe* overture.

Mme. Pleyel shewed herself to be a consummate artist and played Weber's Concertstück with great éclat; she had an enthusiastic reception. After the concert she is said, according to a story recorded by one writer (not, however, a contemporary), to have taken exception to the way in which the orchestral accompaniment was done, even suggesting that the conductor had set out to spoil the effect of one of her solo passages. J. W. Davison, who exhausted his vocabulary of superlatives in speaking of her playing, states specifically that " M. Berlioz conducted the concerto with the greatest judgment, and the orchestra accompanied it to perfection." In none of the other papers is there a suggestion of any deficiency in the accompaniment, with one exception. The eminent Mr. Chorley writing at the time said, " the fine orchestra by no means administered the support to Mme. Pleyel in Weber's Concertstück which a *solo* player has a right to expect." There the matter stands.[1] But there are two interesting sidelights. W Ganz in his diary records that next month she gave a concert of her own with orchestra; Berlioz was not asked to conduct. Liszt at the time was the recipient of confidences from both of them. She would naturally turn to him, for had he not said she was not *la plus grande,* but *le plus grand pianiste du monde.* In a letter written a week after the concert, she tells Liszt of her triumphs at the Musical Union, but says not a word about the New Philharmonic. It is perhaps strange that if she had any cause of complaint against Berlioz she should not have mentioned it to her confidant Liszt.

Over twenty years before, Berlioz had been deeply involved in a tender passion for this lady, his *Ariel* as he named her. Introduced to him by her timid admirer Ferdinand Hiller, Camille Moke, as she then was, had straightway transferred her affections to Berlioz. He won the Rome scholarship, and left for Italy after she had agreed to marry him on his return. In his Memoirs he tells a wonderful tale of his fury, he was at Florence at the time, when he heard in a letter from her mother that she was about to be married to another. There was no time to be lost; he bought a pair of pistols and a chambermaid's full

---

[1] The Rev. J. E. Cox's *Recollections* of these concerts, composed eighteen years later from " desultory jottings," with " the advantage of continued reference to the *Athenaeum,*" are so largely a paraphrase, where not a mere transcript, of Mr. Chorley's language, that he can scarcely be said to add anything by way of independent testimony.

rig-out as a disguise, stuffed into his pockets two little bottles of laudanum and strychnine " for refreshment," and started off for Paris, with the fixed idea of shooting the daughter, her mother and her intended, and then blowing out his own brains. He says that his cries, as he sat in the carriage, must have frightened the coachman into the belief that he was a devil condemned to carry about a bit of the true cross. A letter to Horace Vernet indicates that at Genoa, whether accidentally or by design, he fell off the ramparts into the sea; it then occurred to him that it might mean his losing his Rome Scholarship. He managed to cool down, and soon forgot the lady and her treachery. She married M. Pleyel, the pianoforte manufacturer.

She had real grounds for resentment in the fact that Berlioz had introduced her, without disguise, into a fantastic tale he published called *Euphonia*, merely reversing the spelling of her name Camille.

> And yet in spite of her great and brilliant talent Ellimac apears to me endowed with a vulgar organisation. Shall I tell you ? She preferes ornate music to the transports of the heart and soul; the world of dreams eludes her; she heard your symphony one day in Paris from beginning to end without shedding a tear; she thinks the *adagios* of Beethoven *too long*! . . . (Elamef fo nam!) The day when she confessed this to me I felt an icy chill in my heart. Still more!—a Dane—born at Elsinore, she owns a villa, built upon the very ground and *with the sacred stones taken from Hamlet's castle* . . .and she sees nothing particular in that . . . She mentions the name of Shakespeare without a tremor; he is no more to her than a poet, like so many others . . . She laughs,—she laughs, poor unfortunate—at Ophelia's songs, which she finds very *indelicate*, nothing more. (Elamef fo epa). Oh pardon me! (raed sey sit soumafni). But in spite of all I love her, I love her; and in the words of Othello, whom I should imitate if she deceived me: " *Her jesses are my dearest heart-strings.*" Perish glory and art! . . . She is my all . . . I love her . . .
>
> I think I see her swaying motion, her great sparkling eyes, her air of a goddess; I hear the voice of Ariel, quick, silvery, thrilling . . . I seem to be near her; I speak to her . . . Her head is resting on my shoulder, we softly murmur intimate confidences.

In the sequel which includes a love scene in an aeroplane, the hero is tricked and abandoned, and after many curious incidents, interspersed with bitter jibes and the worthlessness of the heroine, the tale ends in a climax of horror, only equalled in the imagination of Edgar Allan Poe.

Unlike the lady, Émile Prudent, a clever French pianist, who was giving a concert at the Hanover Square Rooms the day after the New Philharmonic, asked Berlioz to conduct the orchestra. Sivori and Piatti played duets.

Jetty de Treffz a light soprano, whose popularity is evidenced by a Baxter print of the day, sang Schubert's *Schifferlied*, and Alexander Reichardt charmed everyone with Berlioz' beautiful song *l'Absence*. The orchestral numbers were Auber's *Zanetta* and Beethoven's *Prometheus* overtures, with Mendelssohn's *Wedding March* as a cheerful ending to the concert. My father played in the band.

It will be observed that, when he comes to tell his friend d'Ortigue about the third New Philharmonic Concert, Berlioz makes no mention of Mme. Pleyel, while his subsequent allusions to her are couched in rather captious language.

London, April 30, 1852.

My dear friend,

. . . The night before last our third concert took place and the second performance of the first four parts of " Romeo and Juliet." It was all played with a dash, a delicacy, and an insight unknown in this country. The orchestra, at some moments, surpassed in powerful effect anything I have ever heard. The piece of the " Fête," which was less satisfactory the last time, was played as it has never been played before anywhere. And would you believe it, in the Introduction the Solo on the trombones was interrupted, after its third passage, by a volley of applause!

As for the rest of it, I wish you had been there to hear it. The papers go on praising me up, except the " Daily News," whose musical critic is Mr. Hogarth, an excellent old fellow whom I had hitherto regarded as a great friend· of mine, but who for some years has been acting as secretary of the Old Philharmonic Society. " Inde Irae." There is also Chorley in the " Athenaeum," who is a bit of a " Scudo " because he couldn't get out of Beale, the " Scudi " he asked for the English translation of the new works we are giving, (confidential please! . . .) But that doesn't affect the general success, and I am at the hub of things. I am now preparing Beethoven's Choral Symphony which, up to now, has never been done here, but only " done in." Would you believe it, almost all the critics are

*against " La Vestale," of which we performed the most beautiful
parts on a grand scale? I was weak enough to feel well nigh
heartbroken at this " lapsus judicii " . . . although I know that
there is nothing beautiful, ugly, false or true for every man, and
that the understanding of certain works of genius is inevitably
denied to whole peoples . . .*

*I am almost ashamed at such a success. All of this of course
between ourselves.*

*" The Musical World " has translated an excellent article from
a Leipzig paper on the third performance of " Benvenuto " at
Weimar. Liszt has sent me another one, but I don't know what it
says.*

Scudo was a Parisian musical critic, particularly hostile to
Berlioz. Mme. Spontini, the widow of the composer, had come
to London expressly for this concert, and presented Berlioz with
the bâton[1] which " her dear husband had used, to conduct the
works of Gluck, Mozart and his own."

To Stéphen de la Madelaine he wrote:

London, May 1.

*Everything is going on well; the third Concert which I conducted
at Exeter Hall was splendid. It seems to me I have never yet had
such a decided success, or such a fine performance. We were giving
" Romeo and Juliet " for the second time. I wish you had been here
to see the warmth of the huge public, its close attention, its
interruptions . . . There was a public for you! As a contrast to all
this; I still see, a trembling apparition, two or three old men who
did not know what to look for, and were annoyed because they could
make absolutely nothing of it all.*

Berlioz' son Louis, then nearly eighteen, had returned from
Havana, and was at Havre. The instability of the boy's character
was causing his father much anxiety, and wrote to him in rather
stringent terms.

London, May 3.

*You tell me you are going mad. So you are. You must be
mad or an imbecile to write me such letters; and this on the top
of the daily and nightly fatigue I have to endure here. In your last*

---

[1] This was customary with conductors at the time. The author possesses a short,
black bâton that Spontini presented to Adolphe Ganz, who frequently conducted
his operas.

letter from Havana, you told me that when you got back you would
have a hundred francs on you, and now you owe forty!!! Who told
you to pay 15 *francs to get a box of cigars through the customs?*
Couldn't you have thrown them overboard?

Here is half a hundred franc bank note; you will get the other
half when you tell me you have received this one. You can stick them
together and get the money from a money changer. It is a common
precaution to take when sending money through the post.

I am now writing to Mr. Cor and Mr. Fouret to find out about
your approaching departure. You can guess I don't pay the slightest
attention to your stupid nonsense. You have started on a career
chosen by yourself; it is hard work, I know, but the worst is over.
You have only a five months' voyage to finish, after which you will
take a six months' course in hydrography in a French port and you
can then earn your living.

I am working to put by the necessary money for your expenses
during those six months.

I have no other means of helping you.

What is this you say about being in rags? You have only been a
month and a half at Havana and everything you have is done
for. You have not a shirt to your back. Do you need a dozen shirts
every five months? You must take me for a fool!

I advise you to weigh your words when you write to me; your
style does not suit me. If you think that life is a bed of roses, you
will soon find out that it is not. In any case and in a word I do not
mean to start you on any career other than what you yourself have
chosen. It is too late. At your age, you ought to know the world well
enough to behave differently.

When I get a sensible letter telling me of the receipt of the half
note, I will send the remainder as well as my instructions. Till
then, stop at Havre.

Good-bye

In spite of the sharp tone he adopted, Berlioz was well aware
of his inability to teach his son habits of economy. " We are
such good friends that half the time when he is going into his
accounts I burst out laughing, as if it were a great joke."

During his absence in London, Joseph d'Ortigue replaced him
on the *Débats*, and helped him in other ways, as appears from
this letter.

My dear friend,   London, *May* 5.

The last few days I have not had a moment to write to you; and I am answering you to-day on leaving a rehearsal of Beethoven's Choral Symphony, and at the moment of leaving there to begin another for the vocal part of the same work . . .

Mlle Moulin was at the Second Concert. I gave her two places; but her mother is, I believe, away from London. The total effect, I say again, was much superior to that at the first concert, and the performance much better. I retained the tambourine[1] part, because I had a skilful artist to play it and he played the little solos with great delicacy and with an excellent effect of distance, which wasn't like what we heard in Paris; because the pianissimo of the drums in this hall, being almost inaudible, the rythmic contract would have been lost if the drummer were left to play alone. No, it's exactly what I wanted; but whether it be the tambourine or the violin you must know how to play it.

Do you want to do me another favour ?

Go to Amyot's the publisher, rue de la Paix, and to Charpentier's, rue de Lille, and ask if one or other of them would care to publish a stout volume of mine in octavo of 450 to 500 pages, it is very funny, satirical and varied in style, and is entitled " les Contes de l'orchestre." It contains short stories, tales, novels, caustic comments, criticisms and discussions—music only comes in incidentally and is not treated theoretically—biographies and dialogues, which are carried on, related or read out by the members of an anonymous orchestra during the performance of bad operas. They only pay serious attention to their duties when a masterpiece is given. The work is divided into soirées; most of the soirées are literary, beginning with the words: " A very dull French or Italian or German opera is going on " ; the drums and the big drum attend to their business, the rest of the orchestra listen to such and such reader or speaker, etc.

When a soirée begins with the words: " The opera is ' Don Juan,' or ' Iphigenia in Tauris,' or ' The Barber ' or ' La Vestale,' or ' Fidelio '," *the orchestra does its duty in earnest and no one reads or talks. The soirée consists of nothing but a few words on the performance of the masterpiece . . . I am finishing the book, see if you can find a publisher for it.*

The book was published in the autumn of that year as *les Soirées de l'orchestre;* it was a striking success.

---

[1] In the scene entitled *Tristesse de Roméo* in the *Romeo and Juliet* Symphony.

Chapter Thirteen

A T the next concert the Hall was packed to overflowing for Beethoven's Choral Symphony. Till then, owing to inadequate preparation, it had never been properly understood in England. With the advantage of numerous rehearsals, Berlioz was able to achieve a result which surpassed all expectations. The performance at the concert was masterly, completely realising the grandeur and beauty of the immortal work, and the effect on the audience was electrical. Berlioz was called back again and again amid perfect storms of applause. Of the singers in the Symphony, Clara Novello was in her best voice, Sims Reeves rather off colour, and Staudigl in magnificent form.

PROGRAMME of the 4th CONCERT May 12, 1852

PART I.

Symphony in D Minor	No. 9 (Choral)	*Beethoven*
	Soloists:	
	Mme. Clara Novello, Miss Williams, Mr. Sims Reeves and Mr. Staudigl.	

PART II.

Concerto in G Minor		*Mendelssohn*
	Mlle. Clauss.	
Scena	" The Knight of Leon "	*Wylde*
	Mr. Sims Reeves.	
Overture	Der Freischutz	*Weber*
Song	" O ruddier than the Cherry "; Mr. Staudigl	*Handel*
Wedding March		*Mendelssohn*
	Conductors:	
	M. Hector Berlioz and Dr. Henry Wylde.[1]	

[1] Dr. Wylde conducted the second part of the Concert.

This critics were agreed in regarding the occasion as historic. J. W. Davison in *The Times* sketched the story of the treatment hitherto accorded to the Symphony in terms distinctly un-flattering to the Society for which it was written. In contrast thereto he dwelt upon the liberality of the managers of the younger institution, who called seven rehearsals instead of the time-honoured "one." The performance under Berlioz was signalized by Davison as the greatest triumph so far achieved by The New Philharmonic Society. In particular he noted:— "The time of the allegro was indicated to a nicety, and amidst all its exciting crescendos and overwhelming climaxes the majesty of the movement was never lost sight of. In the scherzo the trio, for the first time in his remembrance, was played as fast as it should be . . . The instrumental opening of the last movement brought out the force of the stringed instruments, the basses especially, with tremendous effect . . . The concluding passages were taken with enormous rapidity and the Symphony ended amidst volleys of applause that made the walls echo again." Explaining the success in the *Daily News*, George Hogarth observed that he had always considered the Hanover Square Rooms "a place quite unfit for the production" of the work: while Howard Glover, the Irish composer, writing in the *Morning Post*, said it was the best orchestral performance ever heard in this country. Never before had he heard so much accent and true expression from an English orchestra. He praised Berlioz' poetic reading of the score and the consummate skill with which he conveyed his ideas to the orchestra. Every nuance of expression was clearly indicated and promptly realised. Berlioz' deep reverence for Beethoven's music was well-known, and the unsurpassable band was animated by an enthusiastic determination to render the work ample justice.

As early as 1829, and well in advance of his time, Berlioz wrote that after reading the score of the Choral Symphony carefully, while he did not pretend that he could appreciate it in its full scope, he had "no hesitation in considering it the culminating point of the composer's genius." He had to wait till he came to London for the opportunity of conducting it.

George Grove heard the Choral Symphony for the first time at this concert. He confessed, with a sincerity which commands our respect, that he "could make very little of it."

Writing again to d'Ortigue, Berlioz says :

My dear d'Ortigue,   *London, May 22, 1852.*

Please excuse the delay in answering you. I have been fully occupied these last few days finishing my book. It is finished and I am now engaged in polishing it up.

. . . You mention the expenses of our concerts here; they are indeed enormous, and the entrepreneurs are losing money this year like all the other musical institutions in London. But they knew beforehand that it would be so, and they make so little secret of it, that, in the programme of the last concert, Beale let the public know (mind you say nothing about it to the French) the expense which was occasioned by the rehearsals of Beethoven's Choral Symphony, an expense which has swallowed up more than a third of the subscription.

Nevertheless he regards this outlay as initial outlay and his intention is still to go on next year, at the same time getting rid of an individual in the enterprise who bothers us. I will explain the details when I get back.

The Choral Symphony which had never managed to go well here produced a miraculous effect, and I had a very great success as a conductor. I was recalled after the first part of the concert. It was such an event that many people doubted if we should be able to carry through this terrible and marvellous work with flying colours.

The same evening Mlle. Clauss played Mendelssohn's G Minor Concerto with admirable purity of style, expression and finish; she had to repeat the adagio. This child is now considered in London to be the leading lady pianist (who is also a musician) of the age, in spite of the intrigues of the Pleyel lady. Don't fail to mention Mlle. Clauss and the Beethoven Symphony in your next article.

Thanks very much for tackling the publishers. If you have time go and try another . . .

Write me as soon as you can. I am going to begin the rehearsals for our fifth concert in which only an overture of mine will be given. At the sixth the two first acts of " Faust " will be played.

In view of the expenses involved, it was now decided to limit the number of rehearsals; so he sent instructions to Jarrett the orchestral superintendent.

My dear Jarrett,

I am really unlucky! There is always something which prevents our dining together. Still I hope that your indisposition is not

MME. CAMILE PLEYEL

W. GANZ

serious. We must rehearse the orchestra and solo singers on Monday next at Blagrove Rooms, or tomorrow if it is impossible on Monday, for we absolutely must have two rehearsals. It was agreed with Beale. Don't forget in your notice that this time we need the 2 cornets, 4 bassoons, 2 harps, 1 side drum (Ista), 1 big drum, 1 cymbals, 1 triangle (Silas).

Again:

Saturday, 2 o'clock.

We want the 8 harps for Monday and we shall never be able to get them all in at Blagrove Rooms. We want the 4 bassoons and the 2 cornets and all the rest.

My father in his diary notes that he attended a rehearsal at Blagrove Rooms on Monday, May 24. These letters were therefore written two and three days previously. The 8 harps were to take part in Berlioz' version of Weber's *Invitation à la Valse,* which the Russian Ballet has used once more with delightful effect in the *Spectre of the Rose,* the scenario based on the poem of Théophile Gautier. Berlioz' insistence on the presence of the four bassoons indicates beyond question the particular orchestral balance he had in mind in his works, as clearly appears in the French full scores; yet the German edition consistently disregards his directions, specifying only two bassoons.

PROGRAMME of the 5th CONCERT May 28, 1852

Part I.

Symphony in A (No. 4)		*Mendelssohn*
Romanza	" All' età dell " innocenza; M. Fedor	*Mercadante*
Concerto in D Minor for pianoforte	M. Edouard Silas	*E. Silas*
Recitation & Air	The Gnome of Hartzburg Miss Louisa Pyne	*Henry Smart*
Overture	Les Francs Juges	*Berlioz*

PART II.

Concerto for Violin	Signor Sivori	*Mendelssohn*
Overture	Leonora	*Beethoven*
Song	" Arm, Arm ye Brave "	
	M. Holzel.	*Handel*
Invitation à la Valse		*Weber*

Conductor:
M. HECTOR BERLIOZ.[1]

J. W. Davison, in *The Times*, said the performance of Mendelssohn's Italian Symphony was beyond praise, and for the first time in England the tempo of every movement was correctly taken, Berlioz conducting in masterly fashion. The overture to *Les Francs Juges*, an early opera he was compelled to discard, with its sonorous phrases for massed brass and abrupt contracts between plaintive notes of the oboes and harsh ejaculations of the strings, all so clearly conceived in terms of the orchestra, was strangely impressive. Performed with faultless precision it was received with " tumultuous applause." The accompaniments to Signor Sivòri in the violin concerto were done with a delicacy and correctness without parallel in this country.[2] Sivori had been the first to play this concerto in London 6 years before. Eight harps came in with brilliant effect in the *Invitation à la Valse* a remarkable specimen of Berlioz' ingenious orchestration.

Franz Liszt was kept informed of what was passing.

London, June 7, 1852.

My dear friend,

I don't know what is happening in Paris so can tell you nothing about it. Mlle. Clauss, in whom you take an interest, has won immediate recognition here; now that she has been taken up I think she ought to come over to London every year. There is another pianist " Diva " of our acquaintance who is strangely put out by the girl's success . . . She[3] (the Queen of Pianists) is playing

---

[1] Berlioz conducted the whole programme.

[2] When writing about Berlioz, after his death, Mr. Chorley remembered that " he had never rehearsed or even perused Mendelssohn's violin concerto " before conducting it.

[3] Mme. Pleyel.

one of your big pieces at our last concert the day after tomorrow. Mlle. Clauss played another (the one on " Don Juan ") with great success at one of the matinées of the Musical Union.

Mlle. Clauss was only 17 years of age; Berlioz had done a great deal to help her when she made her debut in Paris two years previously. Young Edouard Silas, who missed nothing of what was happening, and visited both these ladies, gives an amusing account of his call upon Mme. Pleyel, where he remained for two hours. " When I got there, she came in and said: 'I must take off my bonnet, it interferes with my smoking.' thought I had misunderstood her; but when she presently brought out a box of big strong cigars, her meaning became clear. She offered me one, took one herself, lay down on the sofa and exclaimed: ' now play me something.' I soon saw that I had found more than my match in the consumption of big and strong cigars. Mme. Pleyel is a fine woman, an excellent pianiste, has led rather a wild life and has all sorts of scandals attached to her name, but—I liked her, nevertheless."

PROGRAMME of the 6th CONCERT June 9, 1852

PART I.

Choral Symphony (No. 9)		*Beethoven*
	Soloists:	
	Mmc. Clara Novello,	
	Miss Williams,	
	Mr. Reichardt and Mr.	
	Staudigl.	

PART II.

Selection from Cantata	" Prayer and Praise "	*Dr. Wylde*
Fragments from Faust		*Hector Berlioz*
	Soloists:	
	Mr. Reichardt and Mr.	
	Staudigl.	
Solo pianoforte	Prophète	*Liszt*
	Mme. Pleyel	
Chorus	" Blessed be the home "	*Benedict*
Overture	Jubilee	*Weber*

Conductor:
M. HECTOR BERLIOZ.

Upwards of 2,000 persons assembled for this, the last concert of the season, and the evening was marked by scenes of indescribable enthusiasm. The two chief works were conducted by Berlioz, the rest of the programme being left to Dr. Wylde. The Choral Symphony went even better throughout and the soloists also distinguished themselves. The work had never been properly appreciated before Berlioz' visit, and it was felt that honour was due to the new society and their admirable conductor, for having removed the stigma from the English public, for whom Beethoven had composed his incomparable work. The audience was enraptured with the selection from the *Damnation of Faust*, which went with immense verve and distinction, and at the end every one joined with hearty goodwill in giving Berlioz a terrific ovation. They were loth to let him go.[1]

Mme. Pleyel again found herself in the same concert hall as Berlioz. This time she decided to dispense with an orchestral accompaniment, and played as a solo, Liszt's brilliant transcription of the skating scene in the *Prophète*, with Rossini's *Tarantelle* as an encore. The orchestra, disregarding the slight she had put upon them, politely joined in the applause.

Berlioz determined that his sister Adèle should be the first to learn of the brilliant conclusion of the season.

London, June 11, 1852.

Dear Sister,

I am writing you in haste to say that I do not know exactly when I shall get back to Paris, I am still excited by a success, the like of which, so the English tell me, has never been seen in London.

Our last concert was a triumph. The excerpts from "Faust" were encored, and repeated amid storms of applause, then the huge audience called me back I do not know how often; they threw me laurel wreaths, and the cheers of the orchestra and the chorus, etc., and the newspapers—a regular furore. Yesterday I wanted to write to you—impossible. First I slept half the day, then visits did not

---

[1] " The Literary Gazette," June 12th, 1852:— " The gigantic symphony was given as only it could then be given, with strength vocal and instrumental, directing genius and amplitude of space . . . Its overpowering bursts of harmony, its exquisitely fantastic delicacies, were noted and received with perfectly riotous applause . . . Berlioz' *Faust* fairly carried the audience out of their senses; they were in perfect raptures . . . It was a proud night for Berlioz. Seldom has a composer received in this country such unmistakable homage or had his genius so inequivocally recognised. The greetings when he left the orchestra seemed fairly to overwhelm him."

leave me a free moment. To-day it has been almost the same thing . . .
Good-bye, I am afraid I shall miss the post, I will write you
at greater length from Paris if I do not stop on here.

Joseph d'Ortigue had also to be told.

London, Saturday, June 12.

My dear friend,
Just a line to tell you that our last concert took place last
Wednesday with amazing success, a huge crowd and big receipts.
I was recalled four or five times. Two pieces from " Faust " were
encored amid storms of applause; the English papers say that there
is no parallel in London for such a striking musical success—it is
stupendous. After the chorus of the Sylphs, they threw me a laurel
wreath; so it is a victory crowned with laurels, as the soldiers say,
oak leaves, roses, roses, all the way. I wanted to leave yesterday
and then tomorrow. But I shall stop for a few days more, unless
I can get through the business, visits, dinners, letters of thanks etc.,
sooner than I expect.
However this long stay has worried me financially. I have so
much rent to pay in Paris, my son's expenses who is there now, etc.,
that the luxury of living in London when I have nothing more to do
there would break me. Indeed, it is not really a luxury; for it is
a mistake to leave England at the moment when I see so many
things in the air.
A simple-minded amateur from Birmingham, who was sorry not
to have been able to engage me this year to conduct the provincial
festival, said:
" It is unfortunate for us, for it seems that Mr. Berlioz is far
superior to Mr. Costa."
How I shall miss my magnificent orchestra, and the choir. What
beautiful voices the women have! I wish you could have heard
Beethoven's Choral Symphony which we gave for the second time
last Wednesday! . . . The whole thing, and the size of Exeter
Hall make a grandiose and impressive effect.
Once back in Paris I shall soon have to forget these musical
delights and take up my stupid task of critic, the only thing left
me to do in our dear country.
I think I shall fix up an arrangement tomorrow for an English
edition of my book. Mitchell will undertake it.

Mme. Moulin has mentioned your commission about that overcoat. I'll attend to it. I will put it on and the Customs House can't say anything.

Ten days later Berlioz was back in Paris. Still full of his London exploits, he bethought him of his friend Lecourt, a barrister, a clever amateur cellist, and a loyal supporter of his living at Marseilles. " A few years ago, he travelled 450 miles to hear the first performance of one of my works."

Paris, June 22, 1852.
My dear Lecourt,

I have got back from London and had an altogether extraordinary success exceeding anything I had had in Russia and Germany. In addition I prepared and gave two performances of Beethoven's Choral Symphony, which still struck most amateurs and artists as a sort of very disagreeable Enigma. It aroused tempests of enthusiasm. Indeed, the performance by our huge orchestra and our big choir in the vast spaces of Exeter Hall took quite a different turn to that of the Paris Conservatoire, good as that may be. Moreover we had excellent soprano and alto voices which were simply marvellous in the grand finale. In Paris they have no idea of the voices of these English women; and still less of the intelligence of these choral singers who in three sittings, learn the most complicated works by heart. As for the orchestra, it was in full force; but it included many French, Italian, German and Belgian artists, such as: Barret, Rousselot, Rémusat, Rogé, Pickaert, Sivori, Piatti, Bottesini, Cioffi, Jansa, Arban, the brothers Molinauer, etc.

To sum up I had a magnificent season in every respect, and have given the old 'uns a good shake up, the jolly boys who love each other like Bérenger's beggars.[1]

. . . Oh! The (" Romeo and Juliet ") Symphony went splendidly in London! The adagio made a great impression! And you weren't there; and yet I do beg of you, my gallant Crillon, please don't go and hang yourself.[2]

[1] Les gueux, les gueux,
Sont les gens heureux;
Ils s'aiment entre eux
Vivant les gueux!

[2] Cp. Henri IV's famous injunction to his henchman: " Go and hang yourself, my gallant Crillon! Arques was a victory, and you were not there."

Astonished to read in Lecourt's reply that he, of all people, should not know the *Romeo and Juliet* symphony, Berlioz wrote:

Paris, July 12, 1852.

. . . Joking apart, so you know nothing of Romeo? I do ask you to sit down patiently and hatch out the adagio, and if sooner or later you don't see Shakespeare's two lovers come forth, if you don't see the moonlight shining through the trees in Capulet's garden, if the duet sung by the violins and cellos, if the interminable farewells at the end, if all the palpitations, if all the embraces, if the devastating forte in E in double chords, do not wring your heart-strings, then the truth is you are a triple bound member of the Institute.

The London success led to an American proposal, which he imparted to his sister.

August, 1852.

Dear Sister,

. . . Did I tell you that I had had an offer of 25,000 francs to go and spend five months in New York and let them hear my works there? The entrepreneur who made the proposal was present at my last London success, and he was beside himself. He wanted absolutely to carry me off on the spot. He intends to come back next year and make me another offer . . .

Telling Franz Liszt about it, Berlioz said:

I did not accept; but if I am ever tempted to do so by a more attractive offer, it will only be in the hope of being able on my return to give up my job of musical critic—my shame and despair.

It was a constant matter of bitter complaint that in this way alone could he earn a living, his music and his concerts in Paris bringing in little or nothing.

During the winter he found that his London hopes rested on a somewhat frail basis, as he told Morel.

My dear Morel,   *Paris December* 19, 1852.

*. . . But this must not make me forget our great and solemn
functions in London! . . . You should have seen the huge audience
at Exeter Hall, carried away by the pieces from " Romeo " and
" Faust "! . . . then those cheers of our big orchestra! . . . Ah!
I thought of you very often on coming back at night to supper with
those Englishmen, they have got real enthusiasm,—rum—iced
champagne galore! What a strange, but what a great people! They
understand everything! Or at least you can find people there who
are capable of understanding everything.*

*Well, Beale after having told me a month ago that I was to be
re-engaged next season wrote me a week ago that he had just retired
from the Committee, because Doctor Wylde (my Assistant Conductor
who got people to put up the money for the New Philharmonic
Society) had managed to prevent them engaging me. He was so
laughed at last year by the artists, the public and the press, that he
wants next year, he says, to have his revenge by choosing a less
inconvenient Partner.*

*He wants to have old Spohr engaged. Of course I could not, to
oblige the man Wylde, conduct in a nonsensical way, that is to say
as he conducts himself. He only wants a one-eyed, or a blind
associate and I did not even wear spectacles.*

*This is fatal . . . but neither I nor my London friends can do
anything. They are now talking of other projects of course in
England; it will soon be settled. Here there is nothing doing,
nothing whatever. My book " Soirées de l'orchestre " is a success;
it is getting a good deal talked about. I will send you a copy . . .*

*Good-bye, my dear Morel; it is one o'clock in the morning and
my candle is burnt out. Louis asked me the other day to remember
him to you, he is at Havre where he is to finish his course of
hydrography. He has got back from Havana.*

Berlioz did not believe in working at night: sleep he found
an absolute necessity. " If I had to be guillotined at nine o'clock
in the morning, I should still want to sleep on till eleven."
Back in Paris his hopes were still centred in London.

Paris, Sunday (December) 27, (1852).
My dear M. Duchesne,

*. . . As for me doing any music in Paris, that will never happen
again. I am content with London where I have good friends and a*

splendid orchestra and an admirable public. They are busy at the moment arranging three concerts there for me in April. I don't know if they will succeed in getting over certain obstacles which have just occurred through a Doctor Wylde who is a professor at the conservatoire, a friend of a millionaire, and an imitator of Handel. I will let you know the upshot of the little intrigue which is worthy of Paris . . .

Henry Wylde, a Cambridge Doctor of Music, was a man of numerous and varied activities, teaching harmony for a time at the Royal Academy of Music, and subsequently founding a new institution styled the London Academy of Music. For nearly a generation he held the Musical Professorship at Gresham College. A novel feature of the New Philharmonic Concerts was his adoption of John Ella's idea of providing the audience with analyses of the works to be performed, with thematic illustrations.

Chapter Fourteen

THE next year was to see Berlioz' only appearance at a concert of the old Philharmonic Society, and a single performance of his opera *Benvenuto Cellini* at Covent Garden.

The previous November, when Berlioz was at Weimar for a week and *Benvenuto Cellini* was performed twice, one of the visitors he met there was Mr. Chorley, critic of the *Athenaeum*. The latter says, " I was present at that performance, the excitement of which was remarkable—almost amounting to a contagion not to be resisted." He however eluded the danger quite successfully, though he appears to have become friendly with the composer. In January he inserted a note in his paper: " We are glad to hear a rumour that the *Benvenuto Cellini* of M. Berlioz may be one among the novelties given at *Her Majesty's Theatre* during the coming season," so Berlioz then communicated with him.

> 19, *Rue de Boursault*,
> *February* 8, 1853.

My dear Chorley,

I have read the few lines you had the goodness to slip into " The Athenaeum." Your news is probably (as they say in the game of Boston) only " a call "; but it is the expression of a kindly wish on your part, and regarding it in that light I thank you. In any case, I am going on getting ready and I am patiently or impatiently correcting the work of the translator of my book of " Benvenuto." What a nuisance it is to have to be translated! I had as lief be dragged[1] before a Court Martial—excuse the wretched pun!

Once again I have been let in, that is to say chucked out, by the " Officials," on the occasion of the Emperor's Marriage. I was summoned by H.M's Secretary Colonel Fleury, who informed me almost officially that my " Te Deum " was to be performed.

[1] In French " traduit."

However, 24 hours beforehand the Minister of the Interior made other arrangements for the musical part of the ceremony: summoned the Director of Fine Arts (M. Romieu) who summoned his Musical Director (M. Auber) who summoned his Conductor of the Orchestra (M. Girard) who summoned his Chief Copyist (M. Leborne) and they shamelessly disinterred all the old stuff in the Opera Library to have it performed after one rehearsal at the Ceremony at Notre Dame. Three pieces from a Lesueur oratorio, two pieces from a Cherubini mass, a piece from a mass by Adam (all the " Fathers of the Church "), plus a march from the Ballet " Vulcan's Nets " by Schneitzhoeffer, and a plain chant instrumented with violins etc., by Auber!! . . . What do you think of the omelette, of the olla podrida? . . . That is how the trick was done. Now I am told in the Minister's office that I shall be amply compensated, and that my " Te Deum " will be performed at the Coronation Ceremony. I don't believe a word of it. It is only another piece of humbug. They will have an arrangement made of one of Musard's quadrilles, unless they can find something worse.

But enough of these villainies. After a series of letters, which followed in rapid succession, news from London ceased altogether. Consequently I don't know what is in preparation in the matter of concerts. Beale has stopped writing to me. I only know that they are engaging artists for the New Philharmonic Society. They have even written on the subject to musicians in Paris.

Vieuxtemps has had big successes, Sivori has had a big success, Mlle. Clauss will soon have her second big success. Hiller has had slight successes, others have had no successes, and they are all losing a lot of money. You see everything is for the best in the worst of all possible worlds.

Good-bye, that's all my news.

Schneitzhoeffer as a composer of ballets was not unknown to Londoners. Thackeray had referred to his *Sylphide* in *Pendennis* published three years before. Harry Foker is speaking to Blanche Amory about Taglioni between mouthfuls of "souprame of volile "; " ' She's clipping in the Sylphide, ain't she ? ' and he began very kindly to hum the pretty air which pervades that prettiest of all ballets, now faded into the past with that most beautiful and gracious of all dancers. Will the young folks ever see anything so charming, anything so classic, anything like Taglioni ? "

At the Paris Opera in the old days the composer was generally called Chênecerf, " his real name not being susceptible of pronunciation in any human tongue." To settle matters, says Berlioz, he had printed on his visiting cards: " Schneitzhoeffer pronounced Bertrand."

Berlioz knew that Liszt would be interested to hear that *Benvenuto Cellini* was to be produced in London.

Paris, March 4, 1853.

My dear Liszt,

. . . Now I must tell you that Beale and I are exchanging letters every two days on the subject of " Benvenuto " for which he has found, he says, a royal road into Covent Garden. Yesterday I sent my terms (as they say in London) and I am awaiting an answer from Gye, the manager of Covent Garden. As usual they appear to want to put it on at once, in double quick time, without waiting to take breath. However I pointed out the necessity of at least copying the parts for the chorus, the orchestra and the principal rôles—that takes time; and I insisted on the copying being done in Paris under my own eyes.

In his newly published book *Les Soirées de l'orchestre* speaking of opera rehearsals at Her Majesty's and Covent Garden, Berlioz had said: " what is deplorable is to see the devilish haste of the English opera-houses in the preparation of all their performances becoming a habit, and even turned by some people into a special talent to be wondered at. ' We have put on this opera in a fortnight,' is said on the one hand—' And we did it in ten days! ' is the reply—' Good work! ' the composer would say if he were present."

His son Louis was again causing trouble. Adèle had to know.

Paris, March 5, 1853.

My dear Adèle,

Thanks for your good and friendly letter, I had one from Louis at the same time. So the crisis is past, he begs my pardon, he admits all his faults, which he puts down to his headstrong character . . . But in fact what is done is done, he has thrown my money into the gutter, he has paid for three months without learning anything whatever . . . I don't know what will become of him, I am going to give him the rest of the month to make up for lost time, and afterwards if he cannot pass his examination, there is no room for hesitation. Admiral Cécile advises us to ship him on a frigate for three years . . . I have told his mother everything . . . and she is moaning over it. But she herself is so ill that her mind is much enfeebled. She now needs a third woman to look after her, she has to be carried from her bed and carried back. Electrical shocks had no effect, and Robert[1] whom I put in touch with her doctor was of opinion that no further recourse should be had to this treatment.

In the midst of all these sad worries, there is a mass of business which is always just on the point of being settled, but never is settled. Here I am in correspondence with Covent Garden Theatre in London. They have heard of the Weimar success, and want to put on my opera " Benvenuto." When they asked me my terms, I told them £200 (5,000 francs), and for the last three days I have been waiting for their decision; I also stipulated for singers who suit me, so as to have the parts properly filled, and that the copying should be done under my own eyes in Paris. So I am in a state of suspense, not knowing if all these conditions will be accepted.

On the other hand Liszt writes me to send him at once the new modifications which I have made in the work, because the King of Saxony is coming to Weimar at Easter and they want to let him hear " Benvenuto." Then there is my Italian translator, whose blunders I have to correct (at Covent Garden they only sing in Italian) and my printers who overwhelm me with proofs; happily there have been no articles to do for three weeks, but for that I don't know where I should be. You can well imagine that to cover all these expenses I have had to earn money as best I could. I have sold several manuscripts to a Paris publisher for what he was willing to give me; now in addition I am going to make up my mind to sell " Faust." It is a very big work, and he will give me all the less on that account and because it will cost more to publish. There is a question of a second edition with illustrations of my book " Les Soirées de l'orchestre," I don't yet know what this will bring in.

I don't know if I have told you the business of the " Te Deum " which was to be performed at the Emperor's Marriage and which was not done, through an intrigue of officials. The Emperor does not interest himself in any way in all these musical matters; the salaries at the Conservatoire have just been reduced by a third.

---

[1] Dr. Alphonse Robert, his cousin. They went together to Paris as medical students in 1821.

Napoleon the Third's attitude towards music may be judged by Pasdeloup's story which Berlioz used to tell with keen relish. The famous conductor had recently conducted a concert at Court in a room adjoining the one in which the audience was seated; the door of the music room being open. Pasdeloup began a symphony, the Emperor came in and, hearing the noise, hastened to have the door shut.

Worried and ill with bronchitis at the end of the month, Berlioz sold the copyright of the *Damnation of Faust* to Charles Simon Richault the publisher, for 700 francs (£28). Small though the sum was, the full orchestral score and parts thus became available for use in years to come. Under the French system the composer retained his interest in the performing rights.

To Ernst, the violinist, then in London, he wrote:

Paris, April 7, 1853.

My dear Ernst,

. . . I have been ill for several days and cannot go out; yesterday and the day before I hadn't even the strength to write to you . . . I am probably going to London; the manager of Covent Garden would like to put on my opera "Benvenuto Cellini," and if the terms I have just sent him are accepted, I shall still have to start afresh with the torture of rehearsing the singers . . . I remembered you the other day to Miss Helen Hogarth, who had come over to Paris with Mlle. Clauss. The New Philharmonic Society is in for a real " frost "—thanks to Lindpaintner, and Doctor Wylde, who has determined I should not be re-engaged this year. That's why Beale retired. But you don't know about this doctorial intrigue and it would take too long to tell you . . . Heine has just written one of his most delightful impieties in the " Revue des Deux Mondes " entitled " The Gods in Exile." It is sparkling with wit and admirably written. By the way, do you know that you write excellent French. Who the devil gave you permission ? It's indecent!

Heller[1] is all right and begs to be remembered; he has some pupils and is beginning to give his lessons pretty regularly. Good-bye, I feel my head turning round through writing you these four short pages.

[1] The composer Stephen Heller, a man of singular charm, delightful humour and keen literary instinct, who was to prove a congenial companion to Berlioz during his closing years.

It was while lying ill in bed that Berlioz indulged his humour in a characteristic quip, which he knew must ensure him the enmity of one prominent member of the musical world. M. Panseron had sent him a prospectus announcing in vulgar French, the opening of a musical studio where amateur composers could have their songs corrected for a fee of 100 francs. Berlioz promptly printed the prospectus in full in the *Journal des Débats*, merely adding a heading, set in thick type :—

CONSULTING ROOM FOR SECRET MELODIES

A. Panseron,
Professor of Singing at the Conservatoire
Member of the Legion of Honour.

Émile Prudent, the pianist, was also in London, so his help was enlisted.

April 9, 1853.
19 *Rue de Boursault.*

My dear Prudent,

. . . Since you left I have had a fresh proposal from Mr. Gye to produce " Benvenuto " at Covent Garden. The business is now settled and the copying is going ahead; in a week or ten days' time I shall send the parts for the principals and the chorus so that rehearsals can begin. As you know some one at the theatre, will you please find out the exact number of women and men in the chorus at Covent Garden so that I can get the corresponding number of chorus parts copied. How many first Sopranos, Contraltos, first and second Tenors, first and second Basses ?

So we shall probably meet in London in a month's time. Please add to the information which I am asking for, some details as to the troupe of singers now assembled in London. With what did they open the Covent Garden Season ? Has Tamberlick arrived ? Ronconi, Formes, Tagliafico ? I know nothing about it all. I have written to Mme. Julienne on the subject, but have not yet had a reply. As for Mr. Gye he answers laconically like the business man he is. I can get nothing out of his letters . . .

When Berlioz arrived he found Émile Prudent in the thick of the London Season, " literally pestered with invitations to appear at concerts and requests to give lessons. He played at Drury Lane and Exeter Hall, at Court and in fifteen to twenty aristocratic drawing rooms. Between two successes, he was off to Dublin; then back again to teach his chief compositions to ladies enamoured of *le Réveil des Fées* and *la Chasse*. He did it all like a typical Frenchman who would be sorry to know a word of a foreign language, and when a beautiful English girl enraptured with one of his pieces exclaimed ' Very nice! ' he replied— ' No madame, not this year,' thinking she had asked him if he was coming to Nice."

The business side of the Covent Garden production needed attention.

> *My dear Mr. Gye,*
>
> *The copying of the singers' and chorus' parts will be finished tomorrow, Saturday; I shall take a day or two to verify the work and correct the mistakes there are sure to be; and I shall at once send you on the parcel.*
>
> *I have found out the number of your chorus, and I hear that it does not exceed more than 65 persons. I thought it was much more. It is a pity especially for the Second Act, for the Finale and the Song of the Sculptors. If you think you can increase the personnel without too much expense, do so; it will certainly materially affect the success of a work in which the choruses play so big a part. If not, we will try to make the best possible use of what you have.*
>
> *I shall draw upon you on Monday or Tuesday for £32 for the translator, and for the account for the copying which I shall send you and of which I don't as yet know the exact amount.*
>
> *They are also working at extracting the orchestral parts and everything makes me think that it will be done well and quickly.*
>
> *I shall not start for London until they have got on a bit with the vocal rehearsals of " Cellini," and I would ask you to let me know.*
>
> *Do you think it would be proper for me to write to Mr. Costa? Have you nothing to tell me on the subject? Has there been any discussion with him about my work and who is to conduct? You know I shall follow your advice in this matter.*

> 19 *Rue de Boursault,*   *April* 15, 1853.

Berlioz and Marie Recio arrived in London on May 14. He again took lodgings in Old Cavendish Street, this time at No. 17, at Mrs. Elizabeth Turnour's the dressmaker. The news of his coming and of his intention to remain here for some weeks reached the ears of the Philharmonic Society. The New Phil-

LOUIS BERLIOZ

L'HOMME ORCHESTRE

harmonic no longer requiring his services, the directors of the older institution relented, and decided to abandon their former policy of ignoring him. He was invited to conduct the first part of one of their concerts on the 30th of the month, and was given the choice of such of his works as he wished to be heard. His reply is interesting:—

My dear Mr. Hogarth,

I thank you as well as the Directors of the Philharmonic Society for having so kindly thought of me for one of your concerts. I gratefully accept your proposal and offer you my " Symphonie Fantastique" which has never been heard in London, and a " Légende" for Tenor and female chorus, " The Repose of the Holy Family."

The Symphony has five movements and lasts an hour in all. The " Légende" lasts five minutes. But I cannot promise to perform this symphony with a single rehearsal; at least two with full orchestra are needed, and arduous ones at that.

See if it is possible to let me have them.

Further eight additional artists beyond those included in the Philharmonic Society's orchestra are required. They are (1) Two Cornets (2) Two harps (3) Three drummers (4 in all) although there are only two pairs of drums (4) An ophicleide. The drummers are used for a piano effect in four parts at the end of the adagio and should know how to play a " soft roll" well.

As for the Tenor, certainly the best available is needed, but I think it would be an advantage if he sang in English. The meaning of the words and their clear enunciation would increase the effect of the piece. I haven't an English translation, but this could easily be made. Eight women's voices will suffice for the small chorus at the end which should not actually be sung in the Hall but in an adjoining room.

Kindly let me have an answer to these different questions. I shall only start for London on the 15th or 16th of the month.

May 4, 1853.   *19 Rue de Boursault.*

P.S.   If this Programme does not suit I would suggest the " Harold" Symphony in 4 parts with Viola Solo, and the Chorus of Souls in Purgatory from " The Requiem," I rather think, however, that choruses are barred in the Hanover Square Rooms, for reasons I quite understand.

The secretary of the Society was instructed to write that the rehearsals asked for were impracticable. Thus the London public was deprived of an unique opportunity of hearing Berlioz conduct his most characteristic work.

The pieces chosen were the *Harold* Symphony, the *Repose of the Holy Family* from the *Flight into Egypt* (a first hearing), and the *Carnaval Romain* overture. The performance of these works after the customary single rehearsal, was so admirable as to draw from the composer expressions of unbounded surprise. The *Harold* Symphony, however, met with some marks of disapproval on the part of a few members of the audience, which were instantly suppressed. Gardoni, who sang the solo in the second number, was the star tenor from Her Majesty's. Berlioz was not asked to conduct Beethoven's C Minor Symphony, which was left in the capable hands of Mr. Costa. Ten guineas was the fee paid to the visitor.

Edouard Silas describes the "great treat and great joy" Berlioz' works gave him, and confesses that never had music produced such a touching effect upon him as that from the *Flight into Egypt*. Berlioz, himself, heard it for the first time.

The Press was full of praise, in particular the critic of *The Morning Herald* admitted to having changed his views since 1848: "The ear had become familiarised with a new and unprecedented style so wondrously unlike that of any other master." Opposition and objection had had their day. Berlioz had in great measure outlived both.—"No one can deny the presence of a musical poet, one burning with rapid and exacting passages."

He determined that Paris should know of his London success.

> 17 *Old Cavendish Street, London.*
> *June* 1, 1853.

My dear Brandus,

The day before yesterday I reappeared for the first time before the English public at the 4th Concert of the Philharmonic Society of Hanover Square. It was a risky business. The Classical School had turned up in full force.

" Harold " was played with astonishing spirit and precision. It was the same with the " Carnaval Romain." I was tremendously applauded in spite of the fury of four or five intimate enemies who, I am told, shrivelled np in a corner. My new piece in the old style

(*the "Repose of the Holy Family"*) *deliciously sung by Gardoni produced an extraordinary effect, and he had to repeat it. I had never heard it, even at the piano; I can assure you it is very nice.*

Davison was delighted and came to embrace me after the concert, he has not written anything yet, yesterday's "Morning Herald" had a splendid article by a writer as yet unknown to me. Write a few lines for Sunday's "Gazette" if you can manage it. Mention Sainton, first violin at Covent Garden, who played the viola solo in "Harold" in distinguished style.

Bottesini also had a success . . . All my friends here say that the success at the "Old Philharmonic Society" was immensely difficult to obtain. There was a packed house, and I was pleased to notice that a great part of the audience came for me alone, as a third of them went away after my last piece.

We are now working on "Cellini" at Covent Garden as far as it is possible to do so. The choruses are already certain, but the principal singers have still a lot to learn. The complete failure of "Rigoletto" compelled Gye to produce five works in succession to keep his repertoire going, this of course took up time and my singers have so far only reached their fifth rehearsal. I think the work can scarcely be performed before the 25th or 30th of the month. Tamberlick, I feel sure, will be splendid. Here is the cast: Cellini—Tamberlick; the Cardinal—Formes; Fieramosca—Tagliafico; Francisco—Stigelli; Bernardino—Polonini; Teresa—Mme. Julienne; Ascanio—Mme. Nantier-Didiée.

Harris[1] has a great idea for the setting of the Roman Carnival, I am even afraid that he will overdo it and that he may hinder the performance of the big finale. But I am keeping my eye on it. Everybody is friendly. The chorus applaud like mad at the rehearsals. Let's hope for the best.

Davison's critique appeared the next day, so Berlioz sent his thanks.

June 3.

Dear Davison,

I haven't time to come and grasp your hand and thank you for the fine article in "The Times," but you can well understand the pleasure it has given me. It is a splendid preparation for the big affair at Covent Garden. The singers are beginning to understand their parts and I hope we shall be ready to start in a fortnight.

---

[1] Augustus Harris, the elder, whose brilliant capacity for stage management passed to his son, the famous Sir Augustus.

A resounding failure on its first performance in Paris fifteen years before, *Benvenuto Cellini* had been put on the shelf until it was revived by Franz Liszt, the ardent champion of all that was advanced in music. Staged at Weimar in the spring and the autumn of the previous year, it had had a decided success. Accordingly in the eyes of the powers that be at Covent Garden there seemed every likelihood of the success being repeated here. The conditions were in many respects favourable. The stir Berlioz had made at the New Philharmonic Concerts was still talked about in London, and he himself was to superintend the rehearsals and conduct the opera at Covent Garden. He admits he had an excellent cast. To Princess Sayn-Wittgenstein he wrote, " I have the best possible Benvenuto (Tamberlick). It is the voice I dreamt of when I wrote the part."

Berlioz had numerous rehearsals, and superintended every-thing with the greatest care. My father is able to add some interesting details. Although only a young man of nineteen he coached both Mme. Didée and Tamberlick in their parts. Mme. Nantier-Didiée, a contralto of distinction, was introduced to Ganz by Auguste Tolbecque the eminent violinist, a friend of Berlioz in his student days. She was staying at Tolbecque's house, 28 Rutland Street, off the Hampstead Road. A further entry says: " May 22: After church, to Mme. Didiée. M. Berlioz there; tried over Mme. Didiée's part in his opera *Benvenuto Cellini*, which is to be produced at Covent Garden under his direction. He beat time, and I accompanied this difficult music at sight." My father was introduced to Tamber-lick, by Tagliafico. " June 13: to Signor Tamberlick, there at 10 o'clock. Studied *Benvenuto Cellini* with him. The music is frightfully difficult, and mostly in syncopated rhythm, but Signor Tamberlick surmounted all the difficulties through his good musicianship. I could not hear much of his voice as he sang mostly sotto voce. Still I noticed it was excellent, especially his high notes." Tamberlick soon knew his part by heart. As Berlioz remarked: " What a fine fellow he is! How quickly he under-stands! "

After a full rehearsal with the orchestra at Covent Garden, Berlioz decided to tighten up the finale of the opera:

My dear M. Tamberlick,   *Friday evening.*
   Be so good as to bring Tagliafico with you tomorrow morning

(I don't remember his address). I have made a cut in the finale of the last act and it is absolutely necessary that he should rehearse the alteration with me.

Till tomorrow 11 *o'clock at the opera-house.*

Everything was now ready. Berlioz' friends wanted to attend one of the final rehearsals of the opera, while Davison commented upon the bad policy of not inviting the press.

Chapter Fifteen

THE first and only time *Benvenuto Cellini*, announced as " Grand Opera, semi-seria," was heard at Covent Garden was on Saturday, June 25, in the presence of Queen Victoria and Prince Albert, and the blind King and the Queen of Hanover. " The Queen remained until the last note of the last chorus." In spite of the excellence of the performance it stood no chance against organised opposition. "A small yet well-disciplined band of malcontents," observed *The Atlas*, " were scattered over various parts of the house," and kept up an intermittent accompaniment of hissing throughout the evening. Edouard Silas, who was present and liked the work very much, says there was a strong cabal among the public, " part of it behaved most disgracefully, they hissed even the beautiful overture of the *Carnaval Romain*. Marie Recio, who came to our box, told us before the curtain went up that there would be opposition by Italians belonging to the other house, Her Majesty's; she maintained also that people were paid to hiss." Berlioz found some consolation in the outburst of resentment which this conduct provoked on the part of all musical London.

Ferdinand Hiller, an old intimate of his student days, was in London, and attended the performance at Covent Garden. He went to see Berlioz next morning at his lodgings, and found him depressed and ill in bed.[1] He was suffering from bronchitis when he came here, and he had worked so hard to achieve a happier result. The same day he sent a letter to Gye withdrawing his work, (a translation of this was printed in the *Illustrated London News*).

For the full story, told by one writer, not a contemporary, that there was a supper party after the opera from which all but one of the invited guests were absent, there seems to be no real foundation. Tamberlick, however, gave a dinner at Hampstead to the whole of the cast. He could afford it. " It is not his fault if he has a voice of gold! " said Berlioz.

Sir,

Permit me to thank you for the care you have bestowed in the production of my opera " Benvenuto Cellini." Unfortunately, I must, at the same time, beg of you to consent that it shall not be repeated, as I cannot again expose myself to such acts of hostility as those which we had to undergo last night, to the great amazement of the impartial public, and the like of which can scarcely have been witnessed in the annals of civilized theatres. I regret infinitely to have exposed you, and the distinguished and kind artists who took part in the execution, to so much trouble and annoyance by accepting your offer to produce my work.

Receive etc.,
HECTOR BERLIOZ.

Berlioz remained in London for another fortnight, and was overwhelmed by demonstrations of sympathy, which took the practical form of a subscription list for a testimonial concert. This was only abandoned owing to the lateness of the season. The two hundred guineas which had been collected, he felt himself constrained to refuse, when offered him as a present, and he was much gratified when it was then proposed to devote the sum to bringing out an English edition of the *Damnation of Faust.*

Franz Liszt and his friends received a full account of what had happened.

Paris, July 10, 1853.

My dearest Liszt,

The kind and charming terms of your letter gave me greater pleasure as I was still rather depressed by the after-taste of what I have just had to endure at Covent Garden. You will already have heard that a determined, angry and furious cabal of Italians had been organised to prevent the performance of " Cellini." The scoundrels, assisted by a few Frenchmen who had come from Paris, hissed from first to last. They even hissed during the performance of the " Carnaval Romain " overture, which had been applauded a fortnight previously at Hanover Square. They were ready for anything; and the presence of the Queen, of the Royal Family of Hanover who came to hear the performance, the applause of the great majority of the public, nothing could restrain them. They were sure to continue the following evenings, consequently I had to withdraw my work the next day. They even had Italians to stand

and hiss in the wings. However that may be, I was not put out for an instant, nor did it result in my making the slightest mistake: a thing that seldom happens to me with scarcely a single exception. My singers were excellent and the performance of the chorus and the orchestra may be reckoned among the finest. The work has gained much by this trial, several details in the score have been improved, slight effective cuts made and stage effects added. I shall be obliged to send you on the last two acts so that your slow copyist may put in all the changes. This is to tell you what has happened. Tamberlick's acting and singing as Benvenuto was thrilling and splendid in every way, especially admirable was his rendering of the last song " On the wildest mountains"; and his recitative when he shows the molten statue coming out of the broken mould and reads the Latin inscription:

Si quis te laeserit ego tuus ultor ero,

the inscription which actually appears on the Perseus at Florence, and which I make him throw in the teeth of those railing at him in the last scene.

The Fieramosca (Tagliafico) had a real success, and the public called for an encore of his song in the second act, but the cries of the cabal prevented me repeating it. The Ascanio was charming (Mme. Didiée); she was allowed to sing her song again. The big finale on the Colonna Square in spite of its complexity was done perfectly and very clearly. So you must now add to the title of the score: fell through for the second time on July 25, etc. Please note that some English newspapers in speaking of the last performances at Weimar, said that they took place under the direction of the " valiant Liszt." Well, may this fresh defeat of your protégé not detract from your valour. I assure you that " Cellini " is worthier than ever of your protection and sooner or later, I hope, it will do honour to its patron. Several English papers were all at sea on the subject, but the great majority gave it their energetic support and stigmatised the cowardly intrigue, as it deserved. That is to say " The Morning Post," " The Illustrated London News," " The Musical World," ' 'The Atlas"; " The Times " was pallid enough though it told the truth about the cause of the scandal. The artists of Covent Garden and the New Philharmonic Society wanted to give me a proof of their sympathy, by joining together to the number of two hundred in organising, without any outlay on my part, a huge concert at Exeter Hall; they formed a committee and opened a subscription list for tickets for the concert, which soon reached nearly £200 (5,000 francs); but as they could not get Exeter Hall at a time when it was possible to give the concert, the plan had to be abandoned; later on, the instrumentalists had to leave London to attend the Norwich Festival. Then the subscribers announced they would not take their money back, and the committee decided to apply the amount collected to bringing out an edition of " Faust " with English text. It was an attractive idea and quite an artistic one; it would have been in the nature of a more direct protest, had the committee voted for the publication of " Benvenuto " instead of " Faust," but one never thinks of everything.

Gye (manager of Covent Garden) nevertheless wanted to keep a copy of the damned opera. Has he an idea at the back of his head for later on? I don't know. When I left he requested me to write him a fresh score on a more dramatic and less absurd book than that of Cellini . . . It would require almost biblical simplicity to accept the proposal in the actual state of things and having regard to the Italian influence existing at Covent Garden. To end my tale of woe, I must tell you that at the Old Philharmonic at Hanover Square, " Harold," the " Carnaval " and above all the piece by Pierre Ducré: " The Repose of the Holy Family," produced an immense effect. This little scene which Gardoni sang very well was encored, it is one of the best things of a simple kind that I have written . . .

The Italian hegemony at the Opera regarded itself so well established that, as he told Brandus:

They are calling out about the invasion of Covent Garden by foreigners—because Mme. Julienne a Frenchwoman, Mme. Didiée a Frenchwoman, Tagliafico a Frenchman, Zelger a Belgian, Formes a German, Stigelli a German, are playing in the opera by a Frenchman. Between ourselves I am sure that there is a serious future for the score (in Germany and later in France). I am almost sorry to have composed it, because of the impossibility of my analysing it. I should write an odd sort of article about it. Whatever be its fate now, and whatever the ill luck it owes to the book, in my opinion the music is new and of indomitable vitality.

Berlioz gives an account of it all in his Memoirs. After describing the " cat-calls and hisses " he proceeds:

Public opinion, if not my own, put at the head of this cabal, comic in its fury, Mr. Costa, the conductor at Covent Garden, whom I had several times attacked in my articles on the subject of the liberties he took with the scores of the great masters, in cutting, instrumenting and mutilating them in every way. If Mr. Costa is the culprit, which is quite possible, he took care in any case skilfully to lull my suspicions by his eagerness to help me during the rehearsals.

The artists of London, indignant at this villainy, wished to express their sympathy for me by putting down their names to the number of 230, to take part in a " Testimonial Concert," which they invited me to give with their gratuitous services at Exeter Hall, but which nevertheless could not take place. The publisher Beale (to-day one of my best friends) brought me in addition a present of two hundred guineas offered to me by a group of amateurs at the head of which figured the name of the celebrated pianoforte makers Messrs. Broadwood. I did not think I ought to accept this present, so opposed to our French notions, though I realised the real kindness and generosity which had suggested the idea. Everybody is not Paganini.

The allusion is to Paganini's famous gift in the winter of 1838. In bad health and discouraged by the failure of *Benvenuto Cellini* at the Paris Opera, Berlioz nevertheless determined to give two orchestral concerts. He conducted at the second. Paganini, his voice completely paralysed by laryngitis, was there with his boy Achille, and heard the *Harold* Symphony for the first time. At the end he came forward gesticulating wildly and murmuring in inarticulate language. He dragged Berlioz back on to the platform, fell on his knees, and kissed his hand. Two days after Achille came round to Berlioz' house, and found him ill in bed. He handed him a letter from his father, and ran out of the room, saying there was no answer. The letter contained a banker's draft for 20,000 francs. " Louis! Louis! " cried the bewildered Henriette as she ran to fetch their boy, playing in the next room. " *Come here, come with your mother and thank God for what He has done for your father!* " Together they knelt at the bedside, the astonished child folding his little hands at her bidding. This gift enabled Berlioz to devote himself wholeheartedly to the composition of his masterpiece, the *Romeo and Juliet* Symphony, which he dedicated to Paganini.

The King of Hanover, who had been present at Covent

Garden, was to receive Berlioz when on his autumn tour in Germany, where he was in some measure compensated for the London failure by a succession of triumphs.

> *On arriving at my first rehearsal the orchestra received me with a flourish of trumpets and loud applause, and I found my scores garnished with laurels like prime hams. At the last rehearsal, the King and the Queen came at nine o'clock in the morning and remained till one o'clock in the afternoon when it ended. At the concert, terrific cheers and cries of encore etc. The next day, the King sent for me and asked me for a second concert, which takes place the day after tomorrow—" I did not believe," he said, " that it was possible to find new beauties in music, you have undeceived me. And then your conducting! I cannot see you (the King is blind), but I feel it." When I said how happy I was at having so musical a listener: " Yes," he added, " I owe much to Providence, who has granted me a taste for music as a compensation for what I have lost! "*

The excitement of the four hours' rehearsal was shared by Joseph Joachim and Johannes Brahms, who only a few days before had been acclaimed by Schumann as the long expected musical genius. When he reached Leipzig, Berlioz hastened to let Joachim know of Brahm's success there.

> *He made a great impression on me the other day at Brendel's with his scherzo and his adagio. Thank you for having introduced me to the daring young fellow, who with all his shyness has taken it into his head to do something new in music. He will have a lot to put up with.*

This is how it struck Brahms—" Berlioz, Pohl etc., were there, and, before I forget it, Schloenbach, Giesecke and all the literary notabilities (or nonentities ?) of Leipzig. Berlioz' praise was so exceedingly warm and hearty that the rest meekly followed suit. Yesterday evening at Moscheles he was just as friendly. I have much to thank him for."

The visit to Leipzig was also memorable for the first performance of the *Flight into Egypt*.[1] That the work appealed to young Brahms is evident from what he wrote to Clara Schumann

---

[1] This became the second part of the sacred trilogy, *The Childhood of Christ*.

two years later (November 6th, 1855). " The impression which Berlioz' *Flight into Egypt* made upon you is exactly what I should have expected. After all one is too easily inclined to call such simplicity forced and affected in one who, like Berlioz, is otherwise so hard on one's ears. I have heard it frequently and it has always made a delightful impression upon me. It is actually the work of Berlioz of which I am fondest."

On another occasion he expressed a liking for the *Death of Ophelia*, the second number of *Tristia*, and he chose the *Harold* Symphony when conducting orchestral concerts in Vienna.

Berlioz continued to keep his sister informed of his son's movements; he had volunteered for service in the French Navy with the temporary rank of midshipman. He passed an examination at Cherbourg with flying colours.

> *Louis has written from the Shetland Isles; he is very happy and asked me to write to Edinburgh. He has been out shooting and had invitations from all the municipal and military authorities at the ports where he landed; in fact he is " going strong."*

In the autumn he wrote to her from Leipzig:

> *I found a letter here from Louis. He is still in the neighbourhood of Calais. He often goes to Yarmouth. He has had invitations to several balls and evening parties, especially in England. I am very glad he should have the chance of picking up the ways of the polite world. He is really a fine fellow in his sailor's uniform. His poor mother is still in a sad state.*

Berlioz left London on July 9. The day before, he wrote letters to Michael Costa, Prospère Sainton, leader of the Covent Garden orchestra and a member of the Committee for the testimonial concert, and Smythson, the chorus master at Covent Garden. The Committee also included Frederick Beale, J. W. Davison, Ella, Holmes, Osborne, Julius Benedict, Frank Mori, Chorley, Gruneisen, Molique and Henry Smart. The letter to Costa is unpublished.

> *My dear Mr. Costa,*
> *Several of my friends lately got up a big concert for me at Exeter Hall, and I hear that the artists of the Covent Garden orchestra generously offered to take part.*

Unfortunately the concert cannot take place; but I am none the less deeply touched by the evidence of sympathy which these gentlemen have given me on this occasion. Will you be my spokesman, and assure them that I am far happier and more flattered by this proof of friendliness on their part, than if I had in fact given the most splendid concert in the ordinary way.

As for you personally I ask your permission to repeat the assurance of my lively gratitude for the trouble you took at the rehearsals of my unfortunate opera; you may be sure that if I suffered much at experiencing such a set back in your presence, the good relations which my momentary connection with Covent Garden have established between us are an ample reward.

London   *8 July*, 1853.

In later years this polite letter stood Michael Costa in good stead. He was able to produce it as a certificate of character, to rebut Berlioz' reflections upon him in the Memoirs.

My dear Sainton,
I am leaving next Saturday and I have so many things to do tomorrow that it will be impossible to avail myself of your kind invitation. So please excuse me. I have just written to Mr. Costa to beg him to convey my thanks to the artists of the Covent Garden orchestra for their courteous offer to take part in the performance at the concert which cannot take place. I am also writing to Beale to thank the members of the Committee of which you are one for the generous and charming idea which they have had to publish an English edition of my "Faust." It is impossible to imagine anything at the same time more artistic or in better taste.

My dear Mr. Smythson,
The concert for which the ladies and gentlemen of the chorus had so generously offered their services cannot take place. I am none the less profoundly touched by the evidence of sympathy which the artists have given on this occasion. Kindly thank them on my behalf and assure them that I am happier and prouder of this proof of friendship than if I had given the most splendid concert in the ordinary way.

Allow me also to say how grateful I am for the trouble you took in preparing the chorus for " Benvenuto Cellini."

Berlioz told Davison that Smythson was *the best chorus master* he had ever met.

On the day of his departure *The Musical World* published a letter from him (in an English translation) addressed to the Editor.

> *My dear* ——,
> *The concert cannot take place. The gentlemen of the Committee, organised to get it up, have conceived the delicate, charming, and generous idea of devoting the sum realised by the subscription opened for the concert to the acquisition of the score of my " Faust," which will be published, with English text, under the superintendence of Beale, and other members of the Committee. It would be impossible to be more cordial and artist-like at the same time; and I rejoice at the result of the performance at Covent Garden, since it has been the cause of a demonstration so sympathetic, intelligent, and worthily expressed. Give all the publicity in your power to this manifestation; you will render justice to your compatriots, and, at the same time, confer a very great pleasure on*
> *Yours etc.,*
> *HECTOR BERLIOZ.*

He told his sister that the proposal was to buy the English rights, retain a hundred pounds for the cost of engraving and printing, and let him have a hundred guineas for his manuscript. Next April he was asking Chorley: " How about our *Faust* ? Take care that I am sent the *final proof* of the English edition for revision before it is printed." What happened afterwards is obscure. It may be that the publication in English of the *Childhood of Christ*, which Beale was then urging him to complete, was substituted.

This year had seen a great gathering of distinguished foreign celebrities in London. Lindpaintner and Spohr, Berlioz' successors at the New Philharmonic, were engaged to lend weight and dignity to these concerts. The rumour that he was to be ousted in favour of " old Spohr " had come true. Ferdinand Hiller the pianist, who was playing at the Musical Union and heard the performance of *Benvenuto Cellini* at Covent Garden, was a great source of comfort to Berlioz during his stay. Although, in their student days in Paris, his introduction of Berlioz to Camille Moke had resulted in Hiller being robbed of that fickle lady's affections, they had remained very good friends. Others in London at the time were Vieuxtemps, Bazzini and Molique the violinists, and Barret the oboe player. All these eminent musicians, as will be seen in the illustration, were invited by John Ella to attend the meetings, and in some cases to take part in the concerts, of the Musical Union. Ella's notes to his programme had contained a eulogistic review of the newly-published *les Soirées de l'orchestre*.

During his stay in London Berlioz found time to write an account of a London Season. His picture could be recognised up to the end of the last century.

But after the French Season, " the London Season! the London Season! " is the cry of all the Italian, French, Belgian, German, Bohemian, Hungarian, Swedish and English singers; virtuosi of all nations repeat it with enthusiasm as they set foot on the steamboat, just as Aeneas' soldiers when they boarded their vessels repeated: Italiam! Italiam! In no country in the world is so much music consumed in a season as in London. Thanks to this immense consumption, all artists of geniune talent, after a few months spent in getting known, are sure to find work there. Once they have become known and been taken up, they are expected to come back every year; it is assumed they will re-appear just like the pigeons in Northern America. And never, up to the end of their lives, are they known to deceive the expectations of the English public, that model of fidelity, which is always ready to welcome, applaud and admire them, " without noting the irreparable ravages of years." One must have seen the rush, the turmoil of the musical life of favourite artists in London, to get a fair idea of it.

More curious still is the life of the professors who have been established in England for years past, such as Mr. Davison, his admirable pupil Miss Goddard, Messrs. Macfarren, Ella, Benedict, Osborne, Frank Mori, Sainton, Piatti. They are always running about, playing, conducting, either at a public concert, or at a private musical soirée, and they scarcely have time to greet their friends through the window of their cab as they cross the Strand or Piccadilly.

Chapter Sixteen

THE following year (1854) Berlioz was not asked to come to England. Paralysed and speechless, Henriette Smithson, Mme. Berlioz, gradually sank, and died on Friday, March 3:—

Dear Sister,

Henriette died on Friday last, March 4. Louis came and spent four days with us, he started back to Calais the preceding Wednesday. Happily she saw him again. I myself had just left her a few hours before her death, and I came in ten minutes after she had breathed her last without suffering or the least movement.

The last rites were yesterday.

I had to prepare everything myself, go to the Town Hall, the cemetery . . . I am suffering horribly to-day.

Her state was frightful, the paralysis was complicated by erysipelas, she only breathed with great difficulty. She had become a mass of shapeless flesh . . . and beside her was the radiant portrait which I had given her last year, where you can see her as she was, with her large eyes full of inspiration. Nothing more, my friends came to my help, a large number of literary people and artists with Baron Taylor at their head conducted her to Montmartre Cemetery close to her sad abode.

And the dazzling sunshine, the panorama of the plain of St. Denys . . .

I was unable to follow the procession, I remained in the garden.

I had suffered too much the night before, going to find the Pastor M. Haussmann who lives in Faubourg St. Germain; by one of those cruel chances as often happens, the carriage in which I was had to pass in front of the Odéon Theatre where I saw her for the first time 27 years ago, when she had at her feet the élite of the Intellect of Paris, that is to say of the world . . . The Odéon where I suffered so much . . .

We could neither live together nor leave each other and we realised the horrible problem during the last ten years. We have caused each other so much suffering. I have just come from the cemetery again, I am quite alone; she rests on the slope of the hill her face turned towards the north, towards England where she never wished to return.

I wrote to poor Louis yesterday. I am going to write to him again.

What a horrible thing life is! . . . Everything comes back to me at the same time, sweet and bitter memories! Her great qualities, her cruel selfishness, her injustice, but her genius and her misfortunes . . . Horrible, frightful! I cannot cry out. She made me understand Shakespeare and great dramatic art, she suffered poverty with me, she never hesitated when we had to risk our bare necessities for a musical enterprise . . . Then contradicting this courage, she was always opposed to my leaving Paris. She would not let me travel, if I had not used extreme means I should still be almost unknown to-day in Europe . . . And her groundless jealousy which ended in being the cause of all that has changed my life. My dear sister, I should very much like to see you but it is impossible . . . And in a month's time I am going to start again for Germany; I am engaged at Dresden.

The Intendant of the King of Saxony wrote to me yesterday that I am expected. I have no taste for anything, I don't care for music or anything else . . . I have kept her hair. I am here alone in the big drawing room next to her empty room. The garden is beginning to break into leaf. Oh! to forget! to forget! who will deprive me of memory? . . . Who will efface the many pages of the book of my soul . . . We live so long! . . . And then there is Louis who is so big, he is no longer like the dear child whom I saw running about in the garden. His portrait in daguerreotype is here taken when he was twelve years of age. I seem to have lost that child, the big one I kissed again six days ago does not console me for the loss of the other one.

Don't be astonished at the odd notion, I could cite many others of the same kind. O fatal faculty for remembering the past; so that is why I have succeeded in such a cruel way in provoking similar impressions with some of my works! . . .

And yet everybody says that one should congratulate oneself on having seen the end of her pain; it was a terrible existence. I am only too thankful for the care the three women took of her.

Good-bye dear sister, I congratulate you on having been able to save Mathilde. I kiss you, be careful what you write to me. Your letter may be able to help me to hold out or break me down still more. Good-bye.

Happily there is Time which goes on always and kills everything, sorrows like the rest.

Montmartre, Monday March 6, 1854.

Brooding on his loss and on the harsh fate that had attended their lives, in broken accents he told the story again in his Memoirs, with a moving appeal to Shakespeare, who alone could understand and pity them—" Father! Father! Where are you ? "

He wrote a letter the same day to his son Louis, on board the despatch-boat the *Corsican*, at Calais, and again some days later.

My dear boy,   *Paris, Thursday March 23, 1854.*

Your letter was an unexpected pleasure; now you have 70 francs a month, and, if you know how to manage and give up your way of using money, you can certainly save a part of it. Write me, if you think you can sooner or later redeem your watch which, I am afraid, you pawned at Havre at the time you were making a fool of yourself. It was given you by my father . . . If you cannot get it back, I will buy you another with the money which I have of yours . . . I think you have seen the charming things J. Janin said about your poor mother in his article of last Monday, and the delicacy with which he referred to my work on " Romeo and Juliet " when citing the words of the funeral march: " Jetez des fleurs.' Yesterday's " Siècle " also contained a few words: many other papers which you don't know have spoken of our cruel loss . . . God grant that my German tour will bring me in something! . . .

Good-bye, dearest child; my affection for you seems to have doubled since the loss we have both suffered.

The *Funeral March of Juliet* reveals an individual aspect of Berlioz' genius. Inspired by Shakespeare's " *With flowers thy bridal bed I strew*," he penned a movement whose simple pathos and tender beauty vibrate in the memory. The theme of the March, in fugal form, is pursued in poignant accents by the

1 *Romeo and Juliet*, a work so rarely heard in its entirety, was given with real insight for its countless beauties by Albert Wolff in the Queen's Hall in December 1936.

orchestra, the voices pointing a phrase on a single note in octaves, then in the major key the voices carry on the threnody, till it fades away as to the dying sound of a bell. The hearer is held spell-bound.

Berlioz left Paris on his German tour, and Louis wrote that he was sailing for the Baltic. Before starting he was transferred from the *Corsican* to the *Phlegethon*, a man-of-war. Berlioz wrote to him from Dresden.

Dresden, April 14, 1854.

My dearest Louis,

I have your letter and am answering it at once. Your news is good and bad. So you are obliged to go to the Baltic; but what are you going to do there? Seeing that you tell me you will not be in the fray I don't follow. Anyhow, I hope that, outside the theatre of war, you will be able to make yourself useful and deserve the respect of your new Commander . . . Buy a cheap watch, but it must be a good one . . . Good-bye, dear child; always write me as often as you can, especially when you have left France. Don't miss any opportunity of letting me have news of you and telling me exactly where I am to address my letters.

England and France had just declared war on Russia, and naval squadrons, under Vice-Admiral Parseval-Deschênes and Vice-Admiral Sir Charles Napier, were promptly dispatched to the Baltic. They maintained a strict blockade of the Russian ports, captured and sank merchantmen, and destroyed a large amount of naval stores. There was a gallant cutting-out expedition under Captain Hall, which penetrated seven miles up a creek, and towed out a valuable prize under heavy fire. When the French Expeditionary Force arrived in August, a landing was effected on the Aland Islands, and after a brief bombardment, the French batteries being directed by General Niel, the fortress of Bomarsund capitulated with all the Russian forces.[1]

[1] It is of interest to read the captious comments on this *side show* to be found in our history books, including the authoritative *Cambridge Modern History*. The *Annual Register* of 1854 knew better:

[1]—" It must be remembered that it (the combined fleet) kept on the shores of the Baltic and in the neighbourhood of Petersburgh, many thousands of the Czar's best troops, which might otherwise have been sent to the Crimea: that it neutralised the Russian Navy, which it kept shut up behind the batteries of Cronstadt and Sweaborg, not daring to trust itself out of reach of the protecting batteries; and also that the Russian merchant flag was swept from its own seas, while our own commerce was carried on in perfect security, as though in times of profound peace."

Berlioz was consumed with anxiety as to the fate of his boy, who had gone:

Far into the North, and battle, and seas of death.

Overworked and ill, he went to Saint-Valèry to rest, but within a few days he was back in Paris, the sooner to hear the news about Bomarsund. A letter arrived telling him that his son was safe and sound.

Berlioz took up his Memoirs once more, wrote what was intended to be the final chapter, and dated it: " Paris, 18 October, 1854."

The next day he married Marie Recio.

Not long after Louis returned to France, and found a letter from his father awaiting him at Cherbourg.

Paris, October 26, 1854.

I was very sad this morning, my dear Louis. I dreamed last night that we were together at la Côte and that we were both walking in the little garden. Not knowing where you are, I was painfully affected by the dream. Your note, which the porter handed me as I came out, made my mind easy . . . I have to tell you a piece of news which will probably not astonish you, I had already told my sister and my uncle beforehand on my last visit to la Côte. I have married again. You will understand this connection had lasted so long, that it was impossible to break it off. I could not live alone, nor could I abandon the person who had lived with me for fourteen years. My uncle, on his last visit to Paris, was himself of that opinion, and was the first to speak of it. All my friends think the same . . . My position is now more correct, it was the proper thing to do. I believe if you still retain some painful memories and not over-kind feelings towards Mlle. Recio, you will keep them carefully hidden for love of me.

The marriage took place very quietly, there was neither fuss or concealment. If you write me on the subject, write nothing which I cannot shew my wife, as I am very anxious that there should be nothing to cast a shadow on my home; I can trust you to do the right thing. I have seen Admiral Cécile who has received your letter. He told me that you cannot enter the Navy until after the expiration of a three years' cruise on a man-of-war; but that you had the right to do so if you wished after that period; that then you would

*be admitted as a master-at-arms or second navigating officer. I am
taken up with all the worries of preparing for a concert at which
my new work " The Childhood of Christ" is to be heard for the
first time . . .*

Louis wrote a " kind and sensible " letter in reply, and came
to Paris to say good-bye to his father before leaving for the
Crimea.

The Childhood of Christ was a real success and won applause
from all quarters, even the most recaltritant. The composer was
quite ready to admit that the brevity of the work, " only lasting
in all for an hour and a half, including intervals," was a not
unimportant factor. " It is not very boring, as you see, in
comparison with the holy bores, that bore you for four hours
on end." Two further performances followed, and Berlioz took
heart of grace.

He was in touch once more with the New Philharmonic
Society in London. They had reconsidered the whole position
and with a view to stimulating interest in their Society afresh
decided to engage him for two of the next season's concerts. No
sooner was the arrangement concluded than an offer came from
the directors of the old Philharmonic Society to conduct their
whole series of eight concerts, to which they took the precaution
of adding the condition that he should not conduct any of the
Concerts of the New Philharmonic Society, while requesting his
answer as speedily as possible. Berlioz was reluctantly compelled
to decline the invitation, and Richard Wagner was engaged
in his place.

In the predicament in which he now found himself, Berlioz
turned to Davison.

Paris, December 23, 1854.
19 Rue de Boursault.

Dear Davison,
*. . . I must let you know what has happened to me; the day before
yesterday I had a letter from Sainton offering me an engagement to
conduct the eight concerts of the Philharmonic Society. Now unfortunately a fortnight ago I was engaged by Wylde on very low
terms for two concerts of the New Philharmonic Society in March.
I have written to Wylde to get him to release me, if he does not
consent, I shall have to keep my word, and I shall lose a splendid*

*opportunity of showing myself off in London. It is a real disaster
for me. What has happened? Why has Costa given up conducting
their concerts? I am in complete ignorance* . . .

Costa's sudden resignation of the conductorship of the old
Philharmonic concerts had come as a great surprise to the musical
world. It was variously attributed to certain points of disagree-
ment with the directors of that institution, and the need of
leisure to compose a work for the Birmingham Festival. Anyway,
his oratorio *Eli* was the happy outcome. Rossini's comment
when he saw the music soon became common knowledge:
" That good fellow Costa has sent me the score of his oratorio,
and a Stilton cheese. The cheese was excellent."
In a letter to Wylde, Berlioz said:

> *I appeal to you not as a concert manager, but as an artist. A
> number of very advantageous proposals have been made me for next
> season, to which, by reason of yours, it will be impossible to answer
> in the affirmative. I cannot break my word which I have given you;
> but consider the immense harm you are going to do my career, by
> compelling me to refuse what is offered me. If you will be good
> confrère enough to release me I shall be deeply grateful to you;
> moreover it will be easy to replace me for the two concerts. Awaiting
> your prompt reply, which I hope will be favourable.*
>
> 19, *Rue de Boursault, Paris.*   *December 26,* 1854.

The appeal was made in vain. Writing to George Hogarth,
Secretary of the Philharmonic Society, Berlioz says:

> *Paris, January,* 1855.
> My dear Mr. Hogarth,
> *I wrote you an official letter four days ago in which I begged
> you kindly to convey the expression of my deep regret to the Committee
> of the Philharmonic Society. I found it impossible to get released
> by the New Philharmonic, and I must keep my word.*
> Gratefully yours,
> H. BERLIOZ.

It has long been an article of faith with Wagnerians that no
offer of an engagement was ever made to Berlioz by the Philharmonic Society, a notion that seemed to them in the nature
of *lèse-majesté* to The Master. The publication of this letter may
perhaps put an end to their delusion.

In a letter to Liszt, Berlioz expressed the hope that it might be possible to postpone his English engagement to a later month. This was eventually done.

To Humbert Ferrand he wrote:

January 2, 1855.

My dearest friend,

Your poem is admirable, splendid, magnificent (as the English say); it affected me the more as my son is in the Crimea . . . Poor boy! He was present at the taking of Bomarsund and only passed through here to join the Black Sea fleet . . . At first I was afraid it was a satire in the manner of Hugo's " Châtiments "! . . Hugo, furious at not being made Emperor! Nil aliud!

But you very soon put me at my ease; I am an out-and-out imperialist; I shall never forget that our Emperor rescued us from the vile stupid republic! All civilised beings should remember that. He has the misfortune to be a barbarian in art matters; but what of that! He is a barbarian who has saved society—after all, Nero was an artist . . .

I am engaged for three concerts in London to perform " Romeo " and " Harold." I don't know which way to turn, But I want to see you; you must make an appointment.

In his remarks on the Emperor, Berlioz, who was no politician, merely reflected the attitude of most Frenchmen, who had accepted the *fait accompli*. Of course he could not understand Victor Hugo's vigorous opposition to the régime.

After the *coup d'État* Victor Hugo, proscribed by the new Government, had found a haven of refuge in the Channel Isles, whence he issued *Châtiments*, his message to the world of scathing invective against the usurper. The work appealed to many in England. Swinburne hotly, and Browning, discreetly, expressed their contempt for Napoleon III. But Queen Victoria and Palmerston, the debonair, viewed the situation somewhat differently. It only needed a state visit by the Emperor to cement the alliance between the two countries, now fighting in a common cause. The crowd gave him and the Empress Eugénie a friendly reception, in April 1855, as they passed through London on their way to Windsor: and Queen Victoria noted " the great fascination of the quiet, frank manner of the Emperor," and the " uncommon " beauty of the Empress.

Chapter Seventeen

THE next year (1855) saw him on his travels once more. *The Childhood of Christ* was heard at Hanover and again at Weimar, where Berlioz spent a fortnight, reaping a succession of triumphs at his concerts. Several big works of his were given to enthusiastic houses. As he had Berlioz there to conduct the orchestra, Liszt played his E flat Concerto for the first time with immense éclat.

After a visit to Gotha, and three concerts at Brussels, he was back again in Paris ready to press on the preparations for the long deferred first performance of his *Te Deum*.[1] Composed six years previously, he had been deeply disappointed that it was not included in the music on the occasion of the Emperor's wedding. Now at last, with the help of friends, the first performance of it was to take place at the church of Saint Eustache, on the day before the opening of the Paris Exhibition. Henry Smart, the brilliant English organist, had been invited by Berlioz to come over to play the important organ part, but unhappily he was detained in London. His boy Louis was ever in his thoughts.

Dear Louis,   *Paris, April 27, 1855.*

Just a few lines in a hurry. I will do what you wish, beginning next week. The Admiral came to see me the day before yesterday, I was not in; I am going to look him up.

I was very ill the day before yesterday; I thought I should not have the strength to go on to the end of my rehearsals. To-day I am a little better. Yesterday we had the first orchestral rehearsal with the six hundred children at Saint-Eustache. To-day I am rehearsing the whole of my two hundred professional chorus. It will

---

[1] Sir Thomas Beecham alone has in recent years in London given us masterful performances of the work in all its grandeur. It is noteworthy that the delicate beauty of the pathetic *Dignare* especially appeals to him.

be all right. It is colossal! The devil take me, there is a finale which is greater than the " Tuba mirum " of my Requiem.

What a pity that you can't hear it!

Good-bye; be sensible, don't waste the small amount of money you have.

For the Exhibition he had had to agree to act as juryman of musical instruments, a task he could not refuse after his London experience in a similar capacity. His duties kept him busily engaged. When at last he could get away he hurried over to London, and arrived only just in time for the limited number of rehearsals which were to precede the first concert.

The day before starting, in a letter to Liszt, he wrote:

I shall see Wagner when I get to London; he is said to be in a very bad temper. I will tell you what I think is the truth about his position in England.

(Paris), June 2, 1855.

My dear Morel,

Excuse me not having answered you yet. You know Paris life and still I doubt if you've any idea of the life I have been leading for a month past. At last I am a little freer, now there are only proofs to correct from morning to night, errands to the engravers and printers etc., etc. . . . I am publishing the " Te Deum " myself in conjunction with Jemmy Brandus . . . Thank you a thousand times for your affectionate concern about Louis. He had to let the " Fleurus " leave without him, and at the moment he is convalescent in the hospital of Saint-Mandrier at Toulon. You ask me to tell you about the " Te Deum "; it is difficult to do so. I will only say this, the effect of the work upon me was tremendous and it was the same with my performers. In general they were wonderfully struck by the boundless grandeur of its plan and style and you can well believe that the " Tibi omnes " and the " Judex," in two different styles, are Babylonian, Ninivitic pieces, which will be seen to have a still more powerful effect when heard in a hall smaller and less sonorous than the church of Saint-Eustache.

I am leaving on Friday for London where I am engaged to conduct the last two concerts of the New Philharmonic Society. Wagner, who is conducting in London for the old Philharmonic Society (a post I was obliged to refuse as I was already engaged by the other Society), has collapsed under the attacks of the entire English Press. But he does not mind, it is said, as he is sure he will be master of the musical world fifty years hence.

Verdi is also at grips with all the Opera people. He made an awful scene yesterday at the dress rehearsal. The poor fellow has my sympathy; I can see myself in his place. Verdi is an artist of real worth and a man of honour. Rossini has arrived; he is talking rot on the boulevard every night. He looks like an old satyr in retirement.

Berlioz and Marie Recio, now Mme. Berlioz, arrived in London on Friday June 8, and took lodgings at 13 Margaret Street, at Miss Mary Panniers' the dressmaker. Rehearsals were called for the following Monday and Tuesday.

As now appears, difficulties started at once.

13 Margaret Street.

My dear Davison,

    I arrived on Friday evening, and I have not yet had a minute to visit you. To-day I shall again be at it all day with our final rehearsal, and on coming in, like a drowned rat, I shall probably have just enough strength left to go to bed. Till tomorrow! Here is my hand. These last few days I have been fighting to achieve the impossible, but I am happy to say I have got out of it by suppressing the whole of the first part of " Romeo and Juliet," it would have split your ears. To-day we shall perhaps be obliged to suppress the Scherzo on account of two or three wind instruments (a horn especially). Good-bye, a man can but do his best, no one is perfect, we live and learn, and other suitable saws.

Tuesday morning.

The date of the first concert had been changed, with the result that some of the principal members of the orchestra were prevented by other engagements from taking part.

PROGRAMME OF CONCERT, JUNE 13, 1855.

PART I.

Overture	The Templar	*Henry Leslie*
Symphony in G Minor		*Mozart*
Air	" Sorgete e in si bel giorno " (Maometto II) M. Gassier.	*Rossini*
Air	" Gli angui " (Zauberflöte) Mme. Gassier.	*Mozart*
Concerto pianoforte in E Flat	Mme. Oury	*Beethoven*

PART II.

Selection from Symphony	Romeo and Juliet	*Berlioz*
Aria	L'Addio Miss Corelli	*Mozart*
Valse	Mme. Gassier.	*Venzano*
Overture	The Magic Flute	*Mozart*

Conductor:

M. HECTOR BERLIOZ.

Thursday evening, (June) 14, (1855).

My dear Fiorentino,[1]

Yesterday my first concert of the New Philharmonic Society took place at Exeter Hall. I only gave three pieces from " Romeo and Juliet " in the middle of an immense programme (an English programme). I had a deafening reception and in spite of a lot of mistakes in the performance the effect of my pieces was altogether stupendous. The public was literally carried away by the instrumental

[1] Parisian musical critic.

scene of the " Fête " at Capulet's, and for the first time in the Symphony's existence it was encored with frantic calls and terrific applause. It must be said also that it has never been rendered as a whole with such dash. The immense orchestra with its 44 violins (etc.) seemed intoxicated with enthusiasm. " The Morning Herald," written by someone quite unknown to me, notes that the piece was encored " with the most vociferate enthusiasm."

" The Morning Post," written by one of my warmest supporters, promises an article which he has not as yet had time to write, and declares that never up to the present have I obtained a similar success in England. Davison was unable to get his article printed last night, and I was not able to catch sight of him. Only I know that he showed the warmest interest when in the Hall. So, all goes well. The next time we shall give " Harold " with viola solo by Ernst. They persist in asking me for " The Childhood of Christ " but I haven't got the singers, and the English translation is not finished.

Good-bye, a thousand greetings, and a thousand thanks for the permission you gave me to let you know (you alone) the result of my début in London this season . . .

Several columns of *The Times* that morning were occupied by long despatches and other news from the Crimea; it was therefore inevitable that Davison's critique on the concert could not be printed. It duly appeared two days later in *The Musical World*.

Apropos of Henry Leslie's overture Berlioz says: " Mr. Leslie met me one day on the pavement in Regent Street. He came up and said: ' I am delighted to meet you, Mr. Berlioz, I wanted to call upon you to find out why I can understand absolutely nothing about your music '." That is how his overture came to be included in the programme.

Berlioz had the proofs of the Paris edition of *The Childhood of Christ* on his hands, and got Édouard Silas to help him with them. Next year when Cramer Beale & Co. published an English version of *The Childhood of Christ*, with the title of *The Holy Family*, Silas again undertook the correction of the proofs. Berlioz thought highly of Édouard Silas' skill as a musician, and was much attracted by his witty outlook on things. Silas' luck in a Paris lottery, soon after Berlioz' return there, provoked a charming letter of congratulation[1]:

---

[1] Still unpublished.

My dear Silas,

Excuse my having been so slow in sending you your fortune; I was so tired out by the jury at the Exhibition and the thousands of musical instruments we had to listen to, I forgot the lottery.

Anyhow at last you are in possession of your millions. Make good use of them and don't be too proud with such poor devils as myself, but like the wise man in good " La Fontaine ":

> *Go learn from those who in vain splendour live*
> *That fortune sells all that she seems to give*[1]

You ought to found a home for poor musicians, poor poets, poor scholars, poor heroes, the deserving poor of all sorts who did not think of going in for the St. Roch lottery and have lost in the lottery of life. It would be set to your credit in the next world and would mean a more comfortable armchair in Paradise.

If you happen to pass the shop in Regent Street, and Beale has got back from his tour in the Provinces, try and find out what they are doing about the printing of my little score of " The Childhood of Christ," of which Chorley should have finished the translation.

September 20, 1855.

Berlioz' stay in 1855 lasted a month. A letter to his sister described the busy time he was having, and even spoke of the possibility of his settling in England.

London, June 22, 1855.
No. 13 Margaret Street, (Portland Place).

Dear Sister,

I have been here for ten or twelve days without having been able to find a moment to write to you. I hoped to get news of you and Louis; I am beginning to worry at seeing nothing come. Tell me, why this long silence? I shall be here till July 7 because of a third concert which I have been asked to conduct on the 6th at Covent Garden Theatre. I started with a glorious success at the concert of the New Philharmonic Society. The huge Exeter Hall bubbled over. They encored the piece of the " Fête " from " Romeo and Juliet," for the first time in the symphony's existence.

[1] *Lisez au front de ceux qu'un vain luxe environne,*
Que la fortune vend ce qu'on croit qu'elle donne
Berlioz was quoting the poem *Philémon et Baucis.*

Very probably, to judge by my increased influence here, the different proposals made to me, the friends I make here every day, I shall finish by settling in London where I am establishing my position little by little.

We are literally overwhelmed with invitations, Marie and I. We have not dined at home a single day this week; and on Sunday we are going to spend the day in the country with an English family who know scarcely any French. To keep up the conversation for so long will put my knowledge of the English language to a severe test.

Everyone in general, however, is very sad especially after the last news from Sebastopol. The lists of dead placarded in the streets, the levies of men and money announced in France, do not tend to calm one's mind. I am really tormented at having no word from Louis or from you. So do write without delay, I beg you.

Lately I spent part of the day at the Crystal Palace at Sydenham; it is one of the wonders of the world. I thought of Aladdin's palace, the Gardens of Semiramis . . . It is a dream.

Where is Uncle Marmion? If I knew I should write him when I find time.

My wife, who is very well at times, and at other times very dejected, sends you a thousand greetings and thanks you for asking after her health. We came here with a Frenchman, the father of an infant prodigy (little Ritter, fourteen years of age), who accompanied us merely to let his son hear " Romeo and Juliet." They are leaving tomorrow.

The Times that morning announced that an unsuccessful attack had been made by the English troops on the Redan and by the French on the Malakoff Tower, with heavy casualties.

Some of the choir had shown their resentment at the suppression of the choral part of the symphony by hissing Berlioz at the concert, a demonstration which had been drowned by a tumult of applause from the audience. Two letters appeared in *The Musical World* one from a member of the choir complaining that they had not been allowed to sing, the other from a professional, not engaged for the concert, expressing his indignation at the slight offered to the distinguished visitor. Berlioz' letter in reply was inserted in *The Musical World* of June 30th.

To the Editor of " The Musical World,"
                                London, June 26, 1855.

Sir,

A member of the choir of the New Philharmonic Society asks me for an explanation on the subject of the suppression of the choral parts of my Symphony (" Romeo and Juliet ") at the Concert which I conducted at Exeter Hall on the 13th of this month. The reasons which compelled me to do so were clear and imperative.

The small chorus of the Prologue, for fourteen voices only, had been studied in the French language, M. and Mme. Gassier having been to my great astonishment engaged for the solos of that part of my symphony, which it was impossible for them to sing in English. And, at the last moment, M. Gassier, a baritone, declared that he could not sing a tenor part, and that Mme. Gassier (a high soprano) could not sing a contralto part; that to me is pretty obvious. So we had to make a fresh start with the English text, and these extremely difficult choruses, the words of which should be pronounced very distinctly, and without accompaniment, could not be properly learned in so short a time.

As for the Capulets' song, about which the gentlemen of the choir had taken a lot of trouble, they knew it well. But on hearing that it was now usual to perform choral works publicly without the singers having had a single rehearsal with the orchestra, I became extremely nervous. The more so as a few of these gentlemen having only come to the last rehearsal and having twice in succession missed their cue after the re-entry of the orchestra, it was clear that those who were to sing at the concert, without having ever heard the orchestra (that is to say the greater number) would for a certainty miss their cue. Could I expose them to such an annoying proceeding? Could I expose the (New) Philharmonic Society to such a serious disaster? And could I expose myself to seeing one of the principal pieces of my work compromised in making the attempt?

Could an artist or anybody with the smallest knowledge of musical matters give me the answer? As far as I am concerned I do not think that such experiments ought to be made publicly.

Berlioz relates how once after a performance of the *Romeo and Juliet* Symphony at Vienna " A little man with a witty look on his face," came up to him, it was the day after one of his concerts, and the following colloquy took place: " Sir," said he brightly, " You are French, I am Irish, so there is no question of patriotism in my appreciation, and (seizing my left hand) will you allow me to clasp the hand that wrote the *Romeo* Symphony. You understand Shakespeare! "—" In that case, sir," I replied, " you are wrong about the hand; I always write with this one."

The Irishman smiled, took my right hand which I held out to him, shook it very cordially, and went away saying: " Oh, the French! the French! They must make fun of everything and everybody, even of their admirers."

Chapter Eighteen

THIS Season was memorable in the musical history of London. While Berlioz was at the New Philharmonic, Wagner was at the Old. He had been engaged to conduct the whole of their series of eight concerts, and had excited a good deal of interest among musicians, and hostility on the part of the press.

The two men had become acquainted in Paris many years before, and had met again at Dresden, when Berlioz scored one of the triumphs of his German tour. Wagner, then newly appointed to his post at the Opera, had been a great help to him at rehearsals, and Berlioz in his writings had spoken in appreciative terms of the younger man's works; he had heard the *Flying Dutchman* and part of *Rienzi* while in Dresden. Artists, he thought, on hearing of the appointment, might well have greeted the King of Saxony in similar fashion to Jean Bart addressing Louis XIV, when he dubbed that fearless sea-wolf[1] commodore: " Sire, you have done well! "

A long interval then elapsed, and Liszt, who in the meantime had produced *Lohengrin* and *Benvenuto Cellini* at Weimar, thinking that Berlioz felt offended at what Wagner had said about him in his writings, noticeably in *Opera and Drama*, tackled Berlioz on the subject. Berlioz at once replied:

Paris, July, 1853.

. . . I quite agree with you that Wagner and I might easily hit it off together, if only he would grease the wheels a bit. As for the few lines you mention, I have never read them, and don't feel the slightest resentment on their account; I have so often had a shot at others that I am not in the least surprised at being peppered in my turn . . .

Shortly afterwards, Liszt invited Wagner to accompany him to

---

[1] " Jack Tar", as given in a recent translation, is surely a weak rendering of the " Loup de Mer."

Paris, and was met by the remark " the idea of Paris begins almost to worry me; I am afraid of Berlioz, I shall be at a loss with my bad French." The two did, however, meet there in October of that year. On the 10th of the month, after dining *en famille* with Liszt, his three children and Princess Sayn-Wittgenstein, Wagner was engaged in reading the text of *Götterdämmerung* to an admiring circle, when Berlioz entered the room. Wagner in *Mein Leben* commends the courteous manner in which Berlioz behaved in an awkward situation. He was at once invited to a farewell luncheon at Berlioz' house; Berlioz and Marie Recio were just starting off again on a tour in Germany. Liszt played some of *Benvenuto Cellini* to Wagner, who remarks that Berlioz joined in, singing " in his own dry way."

These casual meetings had not resulted in their becoming friends, and there seems to have been some feeling on Wagner's part that Berlioz did not like him. They met in London this year on far more cordial terms. When Berlioz arrived, Wagner's visit was drawing to a close; he had only two more concerts to conduct. In a letter to Liszt, Berlioz explains how he was prevented from being at the Philharmonic Concert, when Wagner " at the command of Prince Albert conducted his *Tannhäuser* Overture "; this was on June 11. On June 13 Wagner was at the New Philharmonic Concert, and in a letter, dated June 15, to his wife Mme. Minna Wagner (he was writing to her twice a week), he gives his impressions of it, and also mentions a visit Berlioz had paid him the day before.

June 14 may therefore be taken to have been the date of their first meeting in London. At all events, the generally accepted theory that they met for the first time at Sainton's at dinner must be rejected. Wagner himself says that the dinner took place a few days after the New Philharmonic Concert.

They may have seen each other again at the houses of their mutual friends before the final meeting on the eve of Wagner's departure from London.

In his letter to his wife Wagner says:

> . . . *Berlioz came to see me yesterday; he is struggling for his daily bread and is really in a pretty bad way; in France he simply can't earn a sou, and he has to try and eke out a miserable livelihood by giving concerts in England and Germany (which, I know, bring*

*him in very little). He has been invited here by the New Philharmonic
to give two concerts. He has already got the right side of the Press
here, though in his case too they began by cutting him up frightfully.
Besides his " Romeo and Juliet " Symphony, he conducted a Mozart
Symphony, which he let them rattle off so horribly that it nearly
did for me. But that's quite English; that is how they like it,
and Berlioz, who is now only out for money, knows what he has
got to do. Besides there's no " Depth " in him anyhow* . . .

In contrast to this characteristic effusion on Wagner's part,
Franz Liszt received an account from Berlioz:

> 13 *Margaret Street, Cavendish Square, London.*
> *June* 25, 1855.

Dearest friend,

*Up to now I have not had two minutes to write you, such has
been the turmoil of London this year. To-day being Sunday they
have left me more to myself and I am making the most of it. We
talked a lot about you latterly with Wagner, and you can imagine
in what an affectionate way for, on my honour. I think he loves
you as much as I do myself.*

*No doubt he will tell you all about his stay in London and all
that he has had to put up with in the way of hostility and prejudice.
I like his enthusiasm and real goodness of heart, and I admit that
I am carried away by his violent outbursts. It seems that fate is
against my hearing his last compositions! The day when at the
command of Prince Albert, he conducted his " Tannhäuser "
overture at Hanover Square Rooms I was compelled to attend a
horrible rehearsal of the chorus for the New Philharmonic Concert
which I had to conduct two days later. It was a question of the
choruses in the first four parts of " Romeo " ; and it was so perfectly
awful that I had, in spite of the opinion of Dr. Wylde who thought
it had all been well sung, to cut short the horrors by suppressing
the singing part altogether. In spite of the absence, literally speaking,
of a few of the orchestra, the two first pieces of " Romeo " went
very well. The " Fête " was actually done with such spirit that, for
the first time in the Symphony's existence, it was encored amid the
loud cheers of all the huge audience at Exeter Hall. There were a
good many slips in the Scherzo* . . .

I am staying in London for a few days more, on account of a

Concert which I have been asked to conduct at Covent Garden after our last Philharmonic.

Wagner finishes with those at Hanover Square tomorrow, Monday, and he will be in a hurry to get away the next day. We are to dine together before the Concert. There is something peculiarly attractive about him, and if we both have our rough edges, at least they dove-tail into each other. Explain this to Cornelius.[1]

Wagner said that you were starting for Hungary; so write me three or four lines to London where I shall be till July 7, or to Paris.

I have had a good many odd proposals made to me here, I will tell you all about it later. They do not seem to me to be acceptable.

Meyerbeer has just arrived; his " Star " is rising at Covent Garden but it is rising rather slowly. It seems that his recitatives irritate the singers horribly. The day before yesterday Papa Lablache was actually in a state of fury and despair on the subject.

Good-bye, they are coming to fetch me to go to Champion Hill, where I have promised to spend part of the day.

Monday Morning. I am back from my rural excursion. That is, I came back last night. Klindworth was there, he played a delightfully sad piece of yours; then we sang, he, the two daughters of the house, a young German painter, and I, some five-part songs of Purcell which these ladies seem to know like their Bible; Klindworth and I were far less charmed. The others lapped it up like consecrated milk. Anyhow, there is musical feeling at the bottom of these English natures, but it is a conservative feeling, above all religious, and the reverse of impassioned. Wagner did for himself in the eyes of the London public by appearing to set small store by Mendelssohn. And Mendelssohn, for a good many people, is Handel and a half!!!

. . . On the other hand, if I had not the same defect in regard to other masters whom I abominate with the violence of a " 120 " gun, I should say that Wagner is wrong in not considering the puritan Mendelssohn as a richly endowed personality. When a master is a master and when that master has honoured and respected art always and everywhere, one must honour and respect him too, whatever be the divergence between the line you follow and the line that he has followed. Wagner might turn the tables on me if he knew whom I execrate so cordially, but I shall take care not to tell him. When I hear or when I read certain pieces by this big master, I am content to clench my teeth

---

[1] Peter Cornelius, the German composer, translated the libretto of *Benvenuto Cellini* and the words of the *Nuits d'Été*.

tight, until I have got back home, and when I am alone, I deflate, hurling curses at him the while.

No one is perfect.

Good-bye, lay all my imperfections at the feet of the Princess who will, I hope, honour them with a pitying glance.

P.S. Do send me your article on " Harold."

Meyerbeer's opera *l'Étoile du Nord* (" his star ") was produced shortly afterwards at Covent Garden.

Berlioz' hosts at Champion Hill, Camberwell, at that time more countrified than now, were Mr. and Mrs. Alfred Benecke. They used to entertain musicians a great deal; Richard Wagner had been there a few Sundays before. Mrs. Alfred Benecke, related by marriage to Mendelssohn, was a pupil of W. Ganz, the writer's father.

Many people have been puzzled about the identity of the " big master," and some grotesque suggestions have been made. The context shows that the reference is to Handel. In the letter he wrote to Theodore Ritter a few days later, Berlioz mentions having read Handel's *Samson* with unpleasant results.

Princess Sayn-Wittgenstein was at this time acting as Liszt's *châtelaine* at Weimar. A year later, on her particular insistence, Berlioz reluctantly undertook the composition of his opera *The Trojans*. " If you recoil before the troubles the work may and must cause you, if you are weak enough not to brave everything for Dido and Cassandra, never again appear at my house, I won't see you." Throughout the progress of the work Berlioz confided his innermost thoughts to her in a series of letters.

The same evening (the Monday) Berlioz went with his wife to the Concert at the Hanover Square Rooms. They came back afterwards with Wagner, who was staying at No. 22 Portland Terrace, Regent's Park (close to the Zoo), " to drink punch."

Richard Wagner wrote to Franz Liszt, to tell him all about it.

Zurich, July 5, 1855.

Dearest Franz,

. . . I bring back from London one real gain, a cordial and profound friendship I have conceived for Berlioz, which he reciprocates. I was at a concert of the " New Philharmonic " conducted by him, and I must admit I was scarcely edified by his way of performing Mozart's Symphony in G. Minor; the execution of his " Romeo

and Juliet " Symphony, which was very inadequate filled me with pity for him. But a few days afterwards we were alone at dinner at Sainton's; he was very lively, and I have made so much progress in French since I have been in London that I was able to have a rapid discussion with him on all questions relating to art, philosophy and life, during the five hours we were together.

This meeting filled me with deep sympathy for my new friend; he appeared to me in quite a different light to what he did formerly; each suddenly recognised in the other a companion in misfortune, and it seemed to me I was luckier than Berlioz.—After my last concert he came to see me with my other few London friends; his wife accompanied him; we remained together till three in the morning and embraced when we parted.—I told him too that you wanted to come and see me in September, and I asked him to give you a rendez-vous at my place; what seemed particularly to trouble him was the question of money. But certainly he would love to come. Let him know exactly when you are coming . . .

RICHARD WAGNER

The tête-a-tête between Berlioz and Wagner took place at 8 Hinde Street, Manchester Square, where Prospère Sainton, the distinguished violinist, was living. A native of Toulouse he was of a fiery but amiable temperament, and was much liked by all the artists. He married Miss Dolby, the contralto singer. His son was the delightful artist in silver-point, and his grandson is Philip Sainton, one of our leading viola players.

In *Mein Leben* Wagner gives an account of the conversation he had with Berlioz at Sainton's, and how he tried to expound his own idea of the secret of *Artistic Conception*:—" I tried to indicate the action of external experiences, which hold us captive in their own way, on the inner consciousness, how we escape from their influence purely by the development of our most intimate creative powers and that they are in no way called forth by such impressions but merely roused from their deep slumber, so that artistic creations are not in the smallest degree the outcome of external experiences, but on the contrary a liberation from them. Berlioz smiled with condescending appreciation and said: ' nous appelons cela digérer '." Wagner says he was amazed at his " prompt comprehension " of his " painstaking communications," and adds that Berlioz came to his farewell supper, " but soon left excusing himself on the plea of indisposition. The friends who remained behind made no secret of their belief that Berlioz was annoyed at the very enthusiastic farewell the Public had just given me."

This amiable suggestion scarcely accords with Wagner's letter to Liszt, where he says that Berlioz and his wife stayed at his place till three in the morning.

A few days later, Wagner says he was pleased to receive a charming letter from Berlioz enclosing a copy of *les Soirées de l'orchestre*. The book " in spite of much that is grotesque in the author's taste, which amazed me here as in his musical compositions, entertained me immensely."

On receiving Wagner's letter of July 5, Liszt at once replied: " By the way I am also delighted to hear of your friendly relations with Berlioz. Of all present-day composers I regard him as the one whom you can meet on the simplest frankest and most interesting terms. Take him all in all he is an honest, splendid and tremendous fellow. At the same time as your letter I had one from him in which he tells me among other things—" . . . Liszt then repeats the earlier passages about Wagner from Berlioz' letter of June 25.

In the following September, Wagner wrote to Liszt: " Your article about the *Harold* Symphony was very fine and filled me with fresh enthusiasm. Tomorrow I am writing to Berlioz, he is to send me his full scores; he will never get to know me properly; he is prevented by his ignorance of German; he will always have a wrong impression of me. So I will use my advantage honestly and try in this way to bring him nearer to me."

Wagner sent an invitation as he had promised to do, and Berlioz replied in a characteristic letter.

Paris, September 10, 1855.

My dear Wagner,

Your letter gave me great pleasure. You rightly deplore my ignorance of the German language, and what you tell me as to the impossibility in the circumstances of my appreciating your works is only what I have often felt myself. Language nearly always looses its freshness in the process of translation, however apt the translation may be. There are accents in true music which need their special word, there are words which need their accent. To separate one from the other or give them approximate values is like a puppy sucking a nanny-goat and vice versa. But there you are! I am infernally bad

*at languages; a few words of English and Italian—and that is
about all I know . . .*

*Well you are at work on your " Niebelungen " and melting the
glaciers in the process !. . . It must be splendid writing in the
presence of the grandeurs of nature! . . . That is another pleasure
which is denied me! Beautiful landscapes, high peaks, the sea in
its grander moods absorb rather than stimulate me. My feelings get
the better of my powers of expression. I can only draw the moon
when I see it reflected at the bottom of a well.*

*I should like to be able to send you the scores which you are kind
enough to ask for; unhappily my publishers long since stopped
giving me any. But there are two or even three, the " Te Deum,"
" The Childhood of Christ " and " Lelio " (lyrical monodrama)
which are to appear in a few weeks' time, and these, at any rate,
I shall be able to send you.*

*I have got your " Lohengrin "; if you would let me have
" Tannhäuser," I should be delighted. The meeting you suggest
would be a real treat; but I dare not think of it. I have to travel, it
is true, but not for my health. Paris has nothing for me but Dead
Sea fruit.*

*It is all the same; if we lived another hundred years, I believe
we might get the better of many men and things. Old Demiurge up
above must laugh heartily into his old beard, at the invariable
success of the old trick he is playing us . . . But I won't speak ill
of him, he is one of your friends, and I know you will stick up for
him. I am an impious fellow but I am full of respect for the pious.*[1]
Pardon this frightful pun with which I end while pressing your hand.

HECTOR BERLIOZ.

*P.S.   I should love to send you on the many coloured ideas which
have come whirring through my brain, but I haven't time.
Write me down an ass, till further orders.*

Shortly after, Richard Wagner sent an interesting communica-
tion to Franz Liszt.

October 3, 1855.

Dearest Franz,

*. . . Berlioz recently answered a letter of mine in which amongst
other things I had asked him to make me a present of his collected
scores, if he could get them for nothing (gratis); that he cannot do*

---

[1] This is a play on words. In French " pies " means " pious " and also " magpies."

now as his former publishers will not let him have any more free copies. I admit that it would now be of great interest to me to make a careful study of the full score of his Symphonies. Have you got them, and will you lend them to me; or would you by any chance like to make a present of them? I should be very grateful; but I should like to have them soon . . .

RICHARD WAGNER.

These letters show that Wagner, at the time he was writing about Berlioz' works, had not seen them in full score. This, however, in no way hampered him.

It does not come within the scope of the present book to deal with their relations a few years later. Certain observations, however, may be permissible. When in January 1860 Wagner conducted some of his music in Paris, Berlioz discussed it at length in the *Journal des Débats*, later reprinting what he had said in *A travers chants*, as his considered opinion. Then came the sensational performances of *Tannhäuser* at the Paris Opera in March 1861, when Berlioz, having attended several of the rehearsals, decided to ask his colleague d'Ortigue to take his place as critic. He has actually been blamed for doing so. And, when, after his death, his private correspondence was published, Wagnerians were incensed at the sacrilegious affront to their idol it disclosed. But, since Berlioz' own opinion of the opera is alone of importance, it is as well to quote what he said about *Tannhäuser*, when he heard it in quieter conditions, at Weimar. To Morel, on April 7, 1863, he wrote:

Yesterday I saw a performance of " Tannhäuser." Mme. Milde is the idealised personification of Elizabeth. I thought her admirable and adorable in her maidenly beauty. There are some very fine things especially in the last act, it is profoundly sad but great in character; why need it? etc., etc., it would be too much to say.

Chapter Nineteen

DURING the concluding week of Berlioz' stay in London he conducted concerts at Exeter Hall and Covent Garden. A letter, addressed by Mme. Marie Berlioz Recio to Mme. Duchêne de Vère, is preserved in the library of the Paris Conservatoire.

London (Monday) July 2, 1855.

My dear Madame,

. . . You must have been astonished to have seen nothing about Hector in " The Times." Davison wrote an article which was crowded out by political news; it was inserted in " The Musical World." In the same paper there has been an exchange of letters between members of the chorus and Hector's reply on the subject of " Romeo and Juliet " (performed at the last concert), but we shall tell you all about it next week. Hector is also conducting at Mrs. Anderson's concert on July 6 at Covent Garden, Mme. Viardot will sing " la Captive," the rest of it is the usual big show. We are very pleased in every respect with our stay here. We are overwhelmed with invitations of all sorts.

The performance of " The Childhood of Christ " is fixed for next February. Last week we went to the Crystal Palace and I am still lost in admiration at it! Hector will tell you about the proposal which has been made him to be director of the music of that institution and your husband will be able to advise him on the subject.

My poor Hector has come in from his first rehearsal for the next concert worn out and literally wet through. He has asked me to greet you most sincerely. " Harold " is to be given at Wednesday's concert the viola solo played by Ernst.

MARIE BERLIOZ.

This simple letter has been closely scrutinized with a view to discovering some allusion to Wagner, and ideas that clearly never crossed Mme. Berlioz' mind have been read into it. It is therefore worth while to re-state the facts. Berlioz' first New Philharmonic Concert was on June 13; Davison was present and wrote a critique in the usual way. The next morning *The Times* printed several columns of Crimean despatches and there was no room for Davison's article. It was printed in *The Musical World* on June 16. Mme. Berlioz states this in perfectly clear language. Wagner left London ten days later.

The Musical World of June 30 came out with an instalment of Wagner's *Opera and Drama* criticizing Berlioz' music; the translation of the whole work had been appearing regularly for some weeks past. The same issue contained Berlioz' letter on the subject of the chorus in *Romeo and Juliet*. Mme. Berlioz also refers to this number of the paper.

By a strange misapprehension of the facts " Davison's article " has actually been identified with the extract from *Opera and Drama*, and this letter of Mme. Berlioz has been quoted as proving that the Wagner extract was kept out of *The Times*, save the mark, " par la politique "*!* Mme. Berlioz had met Wagner at his own house the night before he left London. If she had any cause of complaint against him, it was perfectly easy to say so in her letter to her friend. She does not allude to Wagner in any way.

Next day Berlioz wrote his last letter from London. Théodore Ritter, to whom this letter is addressed, was the pianist and infant prodigy, aged fourteen at the time, who had come over from Paris with his father, played the antique cymbals in *Romeo and Juliet* at the first New Philharmonic Concert, and left London again a few days later. Young Ritter was engaged in writing the pianoforte transcription of the Symphony.

London, Tuesday morning (July 3) 1855.

My dear Théodore,

(I detest nick-names, sobriquets, pet names, that is why I don't say: my dear Tintin.) Your letter gave me great pleasure, and if I am rather late in answering it is because, since you left, I have had a very bad time, plenty of visits, dinners and piano trios,

correspondence in " The Musical World " with members of the amateur chorus as I would not let them sing in " Romeo and Juliet," luncheon at Beale's, piano rehearsals at Glover's, riots in Regent's Park, a hundred arrests, workmen wanting to rescue their comrades, several hurt, my wife coming back in a fright, head-ache, reading Handel's " Samson," recrudescence of head-ache, yesterday an awful rehearsal at Exeter Hall, Glover's Cantata, style very piquant but difficult, I sweated till the gutters in the Strand overflowed, and the Finale of " Harold " and a fearsome concerto by Henselt performed by M. Klindworth in a free style so that I was all on wires, for an hour on end, and Cooper, our first violin, who unable to contain himself any longer exclaimed: " Sempre tempo rubato! " and the cornets who couldn't come because of the military troupe in " l'Étoile du Nord " which kept them at Covent Garden . . . You can't avoid " l'Étoile du Nord," Soirée at Glover's where Meyerbeer was to come, excuses from the great man—horrible gripes, quotation from Heine's book, " le Marquis de la diarrée " (or " de la dyharr e ") or some other spelling, (I know well enough that it is diarrhée!!!) then at last Meyerbeer turning up when everybody had finished saying how sorry they were he couldn't come, congratulations on the end of his gripes, wanderings in the London streets by moon-light, I go and rejoin my wife at Ernst's, Mme. Ernst asks me if I like Molière, ye Gods!! and in a jiffy, well I will recite or declaim something of his: A scene from the " Misanthrope," after which the chessmen are brought up and Ernst sits down to the table with M. Louis Blanc and there they are crouching over these stupid combinations till three in the morning, Ella's Matinée where the said Ella presents to " his public " Meyerbeer between two Bishops, Wagner's departure, after honest Mr. Hogarth had presented him in his turn to M. Meyerbeer, asking the two Lions if they knew each other, Wagner's joy at leaving London, renewal of critics fury against him after the last concert at Hanover Square, he conducts, of course, just as Klindworth plays the piano, in a free style, but he attracts one very much by his ideas and conversation, we go and drink punch at his place after the concert, he swears eternal friendship, he kisses me most affectionately, saying he used to be full of prejudice against me, he weeps, he prances, he is no sooner gone, than " The Musical World " publishes the passage in his book in which he pulls me to pieces in the most diverting and witty fashion, frantic joy of Davison when translating same for my benefit, " All the World's a stage," Shakespeare and Cervantes have said so, Ella gives me a present of a splendid book, the complete works of the said Shakespeare, " Poet," as they took the precaution to inform the visitors to the Crystal Palace.

W. SHAKESPEARE,

Poet! (very good of you to let me know)
and I shake you all by the hand, and I sign myself (as the Germans say) your very devoted

H. BERLIOZ, *non-stop man of letters*
. . . . *God bless you and Farewell* (.)

To add interest to Richard Wagner's appearance in London—he was here for over three months—*The Musical World* decided to give its readers an opportunity of studying his ideas as expressed in *Opera and Drama*. The translation had been appearing week by week for some time past. It was a mere chance that the passage containing Wagner's attack on Berlioz' music happened to be included in the instalment printed five days after they parted. There appears therefore to be no reason for suggesting a deliberate slight on Wagner's part, or a practical joke by the Editor. Anyhow Berlioz saw the humour of it. There is nothing in the tone of this facetious epistle to suggest that Berlioz took the circumstance in bad part. That it killed a nascent friendship between him and Wagner, as has been suggested, is equally unfounded. Berlioz' sending him a copy of *les Soirées de l'orchestre* and three of his scores certainly belies any such suggestion.

In speaking of " riots " he is referring to demonstrations of protest by the working classes against a Sunday Trading Bill introduced into the House by Lord Robert Grosvenor, M.P. They came to Hyde Park in huge numbers " to see how the aristocrats kept the Sabbath." Fashionable folk taking the air in their carriages were stopped, and, amid cries of " Go to Church," horses were removed from the shafts and they were left stranded. The police made a baton charge. Had Berlioz known the cause of these demonstrations, he might have been more sympathetic.

His friend Heine was lying prostrate in Paris, on his " mattress grave."

Though he is half dead, his mind is as active as ever. He looks as if he was at the window of his tomb, having a final look at the world which he has quitted, and laughing at it. One of the last visits I paid him, when he heard my name announced, he greeted me from his bed with this sad and delightful epigram: " What, Berlioz, so you haven't forgotten me! Odd, as usual!"

Louis Blanc, writer on Socialism and originator of the idea of National Workshops, had fled from Paris at the time of the *coup d'État*, and was living in London.

The story of *l'Étoile du Nord* deals with early scenes in the life of Peter the Great and his Catherine. Brass bands are introduced on the stage to grace the military parades.

Meyerbeer was the guest at one of the matinées of the Musical Union. The director, John Ella, conducted him to a seat of honour in the most aristocratic corner of the room, close to himself, and between " London " and " Canterbury." As soon as he was recognised, the whole audience stood up and gave him an enthusiastic reception.

Wagner in *Mein Leben* says that when he went to see Mr. Hogarth,[1] to bid him good-bye, Meyerbeer came in. It then flashed across his mind that whereas he had only met Mr. Hogarth as Secretary of the Philharmonic Society, he was also critic of *The Illustrated London News*, and that Meyerbeer had sought him out in the latter capacity. Wagner says Meyerbeer was paralysed at the sight of him, and they didn't exchange a word. Mr. Hogarth, who felt sure they must know each other, was very much surprised that two such great composers should act in so strange a fashion. He had not read Wagner's *Judaism in Music*.

Mr. Hogarth, it will be remembered, was Charles Dicken's father-in-law.

PROGRAMME OF CONCERT, JULY 4, 1855.
PART I.

March	Athalie	*Mendelssohn*
Cavatina	from Brides of Venice *Julius Benedict*	
	Mlle. Falconi.	
Concerto for pianoforte	Herr. Klindworth	*Henselt*
Cantata	Tam O'Shanter *W. Howard Glover*	
Symphony in C Minor		
(Opus II)		*Mendelssohn*
Aria	Resta, O Cara	*Mozart*
	Mme. Amadei	
Overture	Fidelio	*Beethoven*

[1] The German text erroneously prints the name as " Howard."

PART II.

Symphony	Harold in Italy	*H. Berlioz*
	Viola Solo: M. Ernst.	
Scena	from le Prophète-Fides	*Meyerbeer*
	Mlle. Falconi.	
Cavatina	Ah! Quell giorno	*Rossini*
	Mme. Amadei.	
Overture	Abellino	*Praeger*[1]

Conductor: M. HECTOR BERLIOZ.

The *Harold* Symphony was magnificently played. The character of Harold, represented by a Viola solo, was undertaken by Ernst, as great a master on the viola as on the violin, who gave every passage with an expression so poetical that the design of Berlioz was clearly rendered.

Howard Glover was called on after his cantata *Tam O'Shanter*, which was much liked by the audience. The execution of the work was irreproachable, and it was said that Berlioz took even more pains than he would, in all probability, have accorded to one of his own compositions. Howard Glover had visited Paris the Christmas before, and heard the first performance of *The Childhood of Christ*. Berlioz gave him a copy of the score.

William Ganz, my father, again a member of the orchestra, noted in his diary: "July 4, 1855. Last New Philharmonic Concert . . . Meyerbeer was there: he sat right in front, he is a small thin man, with an interesting face, and attracted a good deal of attention."

On his return to Paris, Berlioz wrote to Auguste Morel:

Paris, July 21, 1855.

. . . I had a brilliant excursion to London, where I am getting more and more into the swim. I shall go back there this winter, after a tour I am arranging in Bohemia and Austria, if we are not at war with the Austrians by then. At the moment I am doing nothing

---

[1] Ferdinand Praeger. The account contained in his book of a meeting between Berlioz and Wagner unfortunately does not tally with contemporary documents which have since come to light.

but correcting proofs from morning till night. They are publishing three works together, " The Childhood of Christ," " Lelio " and the " Te Deum."

Thank you for having found me some subscribers for the last work; it will be published very shortly.

While in London I was given a commission for a small work entitled: " The Conductor's Art," which is to be added to the revised augmented English edition of my treatise on instrumentation. This will keep me busy all next month . . . Since my return from London I have seen and heard nothing, so I have nothing to tell you . . . Meyerbeer ought to be pleased with his " Étoile " at Covent Garden; they threw bouquets at him like a prima donna. And Gouin[1] was not there! Bennet and his son (Ritter) had followed me to London. After hearing the Adagio of " Romeo and Juliet " played by our big orchestra at Exeter Hall, Bennet, the father, is beginning to think that the piano cannot approach it in power and expressiveness, a thing he did not believe before . . .

His son is a nice boy; I think he will soon be a great artist. He replaced you in the " Queen Mab," playing the little cymbals in B.

The *Te Deum* was dedicated to Prince Albert, and the names of all the crowned heads of Europe were included in the subscription list.

The English edition of Berlioz' great work, the *Treatise on Modern Instrumentation and Orchestration*, with the supplement on *The Conductor's Art*, was published a year later by J. Alfred Novello of Dean Street, Soho. For the English rights Berlioz was paid £40 (1,000 francs).

Berlioz' last appearnce in London was on the afternoon of July 6, when (by permission of the New Philharmonic Society) he conducted the orchestra at Mrs. Anderson's Annual Grand Morning Concert at Covent Garden. The concert was under the Immediate Patronage of Her Majesty the Queen. Queen Victoria, when a girl, had received pianoforte instruction from Mrs. Anderson, and later chose her as teacher for the young Princes and Princesses. Her husband was Master of the Queen's Music. Every star in the operatic firmament was there in full blaze. After the *Euryanthe* Overture, there followed a succession of Italian arias, relieved by the inclusion of the exquisite Quintet

---

[1] Meyerbeer's factotum.

from Mozart's *Cosi fan tutte*, sung by—just think of it—Grisi, Bosio, Mario, Tamburini and Lablache. Berlioz' music, however, found a place. Mme. Nantier-Didiée sang Ascanio's air from *Benvenuto Cellini* with rare archness, and Mme. Viardot Garcia imparted infinite pathos and expression to *la Captive*. Mrs. Anderson showed her skill as a pianist in Beethoven's Choral Fantasia, and Ernst electrified the house with his *Carnaval de Venise*. In the second part Berlioz had the felicity of directing an admirable rendering of " the old satyr's " *Stabat Mater*.

The next day he left England, never to return.

In the autumn, however, negotiations were on foot for securing the presence of Berlioz in London during the coming Spring Season. Frederick Beale proposed to make arrangements for two concerts at St. Martin's Hall in Long Acre, at which both *The Childhood of Christ* and the *Te Deum* were to be heard, with John Hullah's choir and Henry Smart at the organ. But Jenny Lind arrived, and the whole scheme was abandoned. Berlioz confided to Sainton: " I shall not come to London this year. Beale has just written me that our chances of success are nil, as the *Lind fever* makes any musical enterprise impossible." The " Swedish Nightingale," after a long absence from this country, was engaged in a triumphal progress throughout Great Britain.

Almost complete silence than falls on the London scene. When a rumour reached him that the newly-formed *Musical Society of London* thought of trying the *Symphonie Fantastique*, Berlioz, through G. A. Osborne, urged them to desist. They contented themselves with the *King Lear* overture, Alfred Mellon conducting. The old Philharmonic Society, while it refrained from performing his works, decided however, in 1859, to make Berlioz an Honorary Member, a distinction he was " very happy and very proud " to accept. Then for many years his name very rarely appears in a London programme. Indeed, it was not until the seventies, when France decided to repair the neglect of her greatest composer during his lifetime by a posthumous apotheosis, that rumours of the trend of affairs reached musical circles in England and our conductors, led by Hallé, Ganz and Manns, vied with one another in doing him honour.

The vitality of Berlioz' genius, his originality, his rare distinction and the wide range of his appeal have become clearer to each succeeding generation. To-day we have unequalled opportunities of hearing his works performed under the best conditions, and brilliant interpretations by Sir Thomas Beecham, Sir Hamilton Harty,[1] Albert Wolff and Felix Weingartner enable us to realise the enthusiasm which Berlioz himself aroused in our public in the middle of last century.

[1] Harty died in 1941; Weingartner in 1942.

Postscript

Two unpublished letters of Henriette Smithson, Mme. Berlioz, afford a glimpse into her character. They show her to have been a woman of refinement, and a delicate sense of humour, tinged with Irish melancholy.

The first is addressed to Adèle Berlioz, Hector's favourite sister, who stood out against the whole of his family in their opposition to his marriage. It was written two months after the wedding-day. Berlioz' French translation which accompanied the letter has been printed. The other letter was written six years later, when she and Berlioz were still living together.

Mme. Henriette Berlioz-Smithson to Mlle. Adèle Berlioz.

Dear Madam,

The affectionate course you have pursued towards your brother is the proof of an amiable and good heart, it has made a deep impression on us both—and the greatest pleasure that could result from our future efforts, should they be successful, would be to prove to you how truly grateful we feel for your kindness; at present I can only offer my heartfelt acknowledgments.

I am sure your kindness is as sincere as my gratitude for we can neither of us be actuated by any interested motive. True friendship is so rare in this World that you could offer to me nothing so valuable, according to my mode of thinking, and I accept it and hope I may live to repay it in every way.

Yours most sincerely,

H. BERLIOZ SMITHSON.

Thursday, 26th Dec., 1833.
Rue Neuve St. Marc, No. 1,
    Paris.

Mme. Henriette Berlioz-Smithson to Mme. Adèle Suat.
                                    July 28, 1839.

At last my dear Adèle I have resolved to take up my pen to try and express my heartfelt pleasure on hearing that you and my brother-in-law have arrived safe and sound in your peaceful retreat— You tell me that you hope to have found a friend the more in me, yes, my dear Adèle I have a sincere friendship for you and I believe you have perceived that I can neither flatter nor pay compliments. Hector would like to correct my letter but no—it is incapable of correction so let it go as it is, it will make you laugh—so much the better—

I hope you and your dear Husband will be happy until I can write the French language well, then it will be for eternity.

                                God Bless both of you.
                                    H. BERLIOZ.

Hector has been very ill and I, at this moment I am rather unwell with inflammation caused by tooth-ache. I have been to see your portrait with Louis and M. Duffeuillent. Louis examined several pictures which we told him were your portrait; he shook his head and said " no "; but on letting him look quite alone, he discovered the real one under a chair and clapping his hands called out: " Here she is! Here she is!!" I could not help shedding a few tears when I saw him; because God alone knows if we shall meet one another again in this World—but you will always have my best wishes for you and yours.

                                God bless you.

Mlle. Adèle Berlioz had married Marc Suat in April of that year. Louis was nearly five years of age.

Writers have so often shown inability to do Henriette Smithson justice, that it is right to draw attention to what Berlioz said of her, as she lay on her death-bed. " She suffered poverty with me, she never hesitated when we had to risk our bare necessities for a musical enterprise." After all, this only confirms an earlier letter where Berlioz relates how, when he was panic-stricken at the thought that the expenses of an orchestral concert might not be met, his wife had more confidence than he, and urged him to persevere. Those who—heaven knows why—reproach her with not appreciating his music, should remember his admission that she was rather proud of having foretold the success of the *Romeo and Juliet* symphony.

The estrangement, which began with his association with Marie Recio in the autumn of 1841 and his taking her with him on his foreign tours, should not make one forget the happier times they undoubtedly had previously known, ample proof of which is to be found in published letters.

HECTOR BERLIOZ IN 1865

Many years ago my friend Benoit Hollander, the violinist and composer, whom I knew as an ardent admirer of Berlioz' genius, told me the story of his meeting with the great man:

" I met Berlioz in 1865. A boy of twelve, I had come to Paris to study the violin with M. Massart, the great virtuoso. At the end of one of my lessons, M. and Mme. Massart asked me to stay to dinner. Hector Berlioz and M. Taudou were expected. As he entered the room he looked a striking figure. I can see him now, very aristocratic, like an old émigré. Of medium height, his body was very emaciated. Thin-lipped, with a Roman nose, his long hair was white. It had been a reddish blonde colour and he had the white skin of that type.[1] If he had had his hair short he would have resembled a Roman Emperor. He wore a black satin tie well up the collar. His trousers were a white and black check. They told him who I was. He was very kind and gentle in his manner. I remember as he sat there he made me sit on a foot-stool and began plaiting my hair (I wore it long) at the back of my head, and talking about Shakespeare. Of course I did not know what it was all about. When he left, he put on a light grey overcoat with a fawn collar. This much impressed me and later on when I had the money I had one made of the same colours. His best portrait is the one where he is seated, with the theme of the *Fantastique* written below, and the date (1865). I played the viola solo in the *Harold* Symphony for your father, William Ganz, when he conducted it at one of his orchestral concerts at St. James' Hall. He was a great Berlioz enthusiast."

[1] " une épaisse chevelure blonde souverainement ébouriffée "—Alberic Second, *Les Petits Mystères de l'Opéra*. 1844. p. 284.

In December 1873, hearing that Dr. Henry Wylde intended to give up the New Philharmonic Concerts, my father, William Ganz, proposed that they should continue them on their joint responsibility, while sharing the duties of conductor. To this Wylde agreed. Five years later he retired from the enterprise, and my father signalized the change by reviving the works of Hector Berlioz, which he had learned to know under the composer's bâton. *Harold in Italy* was given at the first concert, Charles Hallé and G. A. Osborne attending the rehearsals (three were held). Next year he repeated it, with Hollander playing the viola solo, having in the meantime re-named the concerts Ganz's Orchestral Concerts.

On April 30 1881, my father had the proud distinction of conducting the first performance in London of the *Symphonie Fantastique*. He had large bells, of the essential deep notes C and G, specially cast for the *Nuit du Sabbat*, and engaged four harpists for the *Ball* scene. It was his opinion that the effect intended by Berlioz could not be obtained with less than four harps. He also observed the repeats in the first movement and in the *Marche au Supplice*, as indicated by the composer. These repeats have since been usually disregarded, thus upsetting the balance of the work as conceived by Berlioz. Of course he also had four bassoons, as is customary in French orchestras, two cornets, an ophicleide and an E flat tuba. The idea of observing a composer's indications in the layout of the orchestral forces was still an innovation for London. Further, he conducted the *Romeo and Juliet* Symphony (the first four movements as given by Berlioz), and two more performances of the *Fantastique*.

Berlioz' music made a vivid impression upon the mind of a small boy who was taken to these concerts. The present book is the outcome.

A.W.G.

Index

CONCERTS IN LONDON :

CRITIQUES OF LONDON CONCERTS:

LETTERS QUOTED IN THE TEXT: